LEADERSHIP IN EDUCATION

Edited by
Mark Brundrett, Neil Burton and Robert Smith

SAGE Publications

London • Thousand Oaks • New Dehli

Editorial material and preface
© Mark Brundrett, Neil Burton and Robert Smith 2003

Chapter   1 © Clive Dimmock 2003
Chapter   2 © Peter Gronn 2003
Chapter   3 © Marianne Coleman 2003
Chapter   4 © Peter Ribbins 2003
Chapter   5 © Ray Bolam 2003
Chapter   6 © Peter Newton 2003
Chapter   7 © Kenneth Leithwood 2003
Chapter   8 © Helen M. Gunter 2003
Chapter   9 © Clive Harber and Lynn Davies 2003
Chapter 10 © Mark Brundrett and Neil Burton 2003
Chapter 11 © Graham Peeke 2003
Chapter 12 © David Watson 2003

First published 2003

SAGE Publications Ltd
6 Bonhill Street
London EC2A 4PU

SAGE Publications Inc
2455 Teller Road
Thousand Oaks, California 91320

SAGE Publications India Pvt Ltd
B-42, Panchsheel Enclave
Post Box 4109
New Delhi 110 017

Library of Congress Control Number: 2002093387

A catalogue record for this book is available from the
British Library

ISBN 0 7619 4047 2
ISBN 0 7619 4048 0 (pbk)

Typeset by Anneset, Weston-super-Mare
Printed in Great Britain by Cromwell Press, Trowbridge

CONTENTS

FIGURE AND TABLES

SERIES EDITOR'S FOREWORD

The relationship between high-quality leadership and educational outcomes is well documented. Despite the editors' cautious remarks in the preface to this volume, generations of research on school effectiveness shows that excellent leadership is one of the main factors in high-performing schools (Beare, Caldwell and Millikan, 1989; Creemers, 1996, Reynolds, 1991; Sammons, Hillman and Mortimore, 1995). This connection is fully acknowledged by England's National College for School Leadership (NCSL):

> The evidence on school effectiveness and improvement during the last 15 years has consistently shown the pivotal role of effective leadership in securing high-quality provision and high standards ... effective leadership is a key to both continuous improvement and major system transformation. (NCSL, 2001, p. 5)

The early years of the twenty-first century have seen a lively debate about the relative significance of leadership and management for education. I have generally taken the view that 'management' is the broader term within which 'leadership' can be subsumed. However, there is little doubt that leadership is in the ascendancy, not least in England where the National College is ostensibly for leadership and not management. Leadership is generally associated with the concept of 'vision', a mental picture of a preferred future for the organisation. It is essential to have this sense of direction for schools and colleges but it is just as important for institutions to be managed effectively, if only to ensure that the vision is translated into practice.

It is now widely accepted that educational leaders and managers need specific preparation if they are to be successful in leading schools and colleges. The development of effective leaders requires a range of strategies, including high-quality courses and tuition, mentoring by experienced and successful principals, and opportunities to practise management at appropriate stages in professional careers. It also needs the support of literature which presents the major issues in clear, intelligible language while drawing on the best of theory and research. The aim of this series, and of this volume, is to develop a body of literature with the following characteristics:

- Directly relevant to school and college management.
- Prepared by authors with national and international reputations.
- An analytical approach based on empirical evidence but couched in intelligible language.
- Integrating the best of theory, research and practice.

Leadership in Education is the tenth and final volume in the series, which was launched in 1997. This book provides a thorough discussion of concepts of leadership and considers how leaders and leadership may be developed. It provides a valuable section on the neglected topic of teacher leadership and concludes by examining leadership in practice in schools, further education and higher education. The editors have attracted many of the best known authors on these topics and the chapters in this book provide a most valuable introduction to leadership in education.

Educational Management: Research and Practice has been a most successful series that has attracted capable authors, sold many thousands of copies and been influential in reporting the state of the field of educational management and leadership. As the series comes to an end, I should like to thank all editors and authors for their scholarship and skill. I believe that this volume is a fitting way to conclude the series.

Tony Bush
The University of Reading
September 2002

REFERENCES

Beare, H., Caldwell, B. and Millikan, R. (1989) *Creating an Excellent School*, London: Routledge.

Creemers, B. (1996) 'The school effectiveness knowledge base', in D. Reynolds, R. Bollen, B. Creemers, D. Hopkins, L. Stoll and N Lagerweij (eds), *Making Good Schools: Linking School Effectiveness and School Improvement*, London: Routledge.

National College for School Leadership (NCSL) (2001) *First Corporate Plan: Launch Year 2001–2002*, Nottingham: National College for School Leadership, www.ncsl.gov.uk

Reynolds, D. (1991) 'School effectiveness in secondary schools: research and its policy implications', in S. Riddell and S. Brown (eds), *School Effectiveness and its Messages for School Improvement*, Edinburgh: The Scottish Office, HMSO.

Sammons, P., Hillman, J. and Mortimore, P. (1995) *Key Characteristics of Effective Schools: A Review of School Effectiveness Research*, London: Office for Standards in Education and Institute of Education, University of London.

PREFACE

Over the period of a generation, leading educational researchers have attempted to discover the factors that can enhance school effectiveness and, for many, the term 'leadership' has become centrally synonymous with school effectiveness (Teddlie and Reynolds, 2000, p. 141). Within the ubiquity of these laudatory attitudes one can forget that leadership is a complex and contestable construct, and it is important to be aware that there are actually comparatively few studies that find direct linkage between leadership and learning outcomes (Bell and Bolam, 2003). For this reason this text contains especially commissioned chapters based on recent research and attempts to offer a broad perspective, in both its theoretical base and its scope, which seeks to investigate leadership in all sectors from primary to higher education. The editors offer a number of positional commitments which include: to ensure an international perspective where possible; to seek interconnections between research, theory and practice; and to provide a number of conceptual perspectives on leadership rather than an overreliance on a 'best fit' or one 'hegemonic' model of leadership. In relation to the last commitment a number of key themes are interwoven into the text which exist in counterpoint to one another. These themes include: the efficacy of centralised versus distributed notions of leadership; the contrast between competency and academic models of leadership development; and the contradistinction between functionalist and democratic models of leadership. In this sense the text addresses some of the ambiguities first identified by Bush et al. (1999).

The text completes the highly successful series *Educational Management: Research and Practice* which provides a source of reference for those engaged in educational management. It is conceived in four sections that move from conceptualisation through leadership development, teachers as leaders, to leadership in practice, thus embedding the interconnection between theory and praxis. The 'geography' of the text is thus intended to offer a high degree of structural integrity through an examination of both theoretical and practical issues, while enabling a strong appeal to the different 'audiences' that are being addressed. These audiences include practitioners, those undertaking higher degree programmes, researchers in the field of educational management, policy-makers and educational administrators.

Section A of the text focuses on 'conceptualising leadership'. Clive Dimmock has, for instance, argued consistently for an innovative restructuring of school leadership in order to enhance school-based management (see, for instance, Dimmock, 1993; Dimmock and O'Donoghue, 1996; O'Donoghue and Dimmock, 1997). In this initial chapter of the text Dimmock provides an overview of cross-cultural research into the nature of leadership and leaders which develops the perspectives first outlined in his recent text on leading future schools (Dimmock, 2000). Peter Gronn has proposed a reconceptualisation of leadership (Gronn, 2000a). Many current conceptualisations construct leadership in the form of 'dualisms'; these are to be rejected in favour of the claim that the leadership of organisations is most appropriately understood as a distributed, rather than a focused, phenomenon. To this end he has examined the attributes, dimensions and applications of distributed leadership, and proposed a revised approach to action in organisations based on recent developments in activity theory (Gronn, 2000b). In Chapter 2 Gronn reaffirms his view that the concept of leadership, as it is conventionally understood, is problematic since it is based on a prevailing leader-centric, 'elixir orthodoxy'. The increasingly influential work of Coleman has examined the number and distribution of female school leaders (see, for instance, Coleman, 1996; 2001). In Chapter 3 she explains and extends her work on notions of 'masculine' versus 'feminine' leadership qualities and considers key issues that affect the work of female school leaders such as career constraints and overt and covert discrimination within the workplace.

Section B focuses on developing leaders and leadership within which area Peter Ribbins has proposed a 'natural history' approach (see Pascal and Ribbins, 1998; Rayner and Ribbins, 1998). In Chapter 4 Ribbins provides an examination of the life histories of headteachers and offers a typology for describing and categorising the main stages of leadership development. Focusing on the humanistic and instrumentalist aspects of the headteacher knowledge base, this chapter offers a means of examining leadership development, making specific comments upon the work of the National College for School Leadership in the UK.

The development of 'national programmes' for school leadership in the 1990s has posed a series of opportunities and dilemmas for those engaged in university education (Bolam, 1997). The national programmes, based on an adapted competency framework, contrast with the academic qualifications provided by institutions of higher education and offer the challenge of designing a suitable qualifications framework which reconciles these inherent tensions. Moreover the issue of 'political control' creates the danger of an increasing 'bureaucratisation' of national qualifications. In Chapter 5 Ray Bolam offers a critique of school leadership training programmes as they have emerged internationally in recent years.

The National College for School Leadership was established in 2000 in order to 'provide a single national focus for leadership development and research' (DfEE, 1999). The college is still in its formative stages but is attempting to build a national network of school leaders across the country. As the institution develops it is envisaged that it will take formal control of the 'national programmes' of school leadership training and development such as the National Professional Qualification for Headship (NPQH), Headteachers' Leadership and Management Programme (HEADLAMP) and Leadership Programme for Serving Headteachers (LPSH). Peter Newton is a former member of the senior management team of the college and offers one of the first detailed expositions of its role. In Chapter 6 Newton explains that calls for the establishment of a systematic framework for the training and development of school leaders in the UK actually stretch back over many years. The National College for School Leadership was given government imprimatur in 1999 and moved into its permanent home in 2002. Newton outlines the dynamic and wide-ranging plans for the organisation.

Section C examines 'teachers as leaders' and commences with a chapter by Kenneth Leithwood who has, with his colleagues at the Ontario Institute for Studies in Education, conducted a series of six major studies into teacher leadership. Three of these were 'grounded' in design and relied on qualitative data to describe the nature of informal teacher leadership in elementary and secondary schools (Leithwood, Jantzi and Steinbach, 1999). The three remaining studies inquired about the effects of teacher leadership on selected aspects of school organisation, as well as on students (Leithwood and Jantzi, 1999). Chapter 7 summarises the evidence and implications from the six studies to answer three key questions: what is 'teacher leadership'? How much does it contribute to school effectiveness? And how can it be developed?

In a contrasting perspective Helen Gunter provides a critique of the functionalist and effectiveness approaches to leadership. An argument is then presented in favour of teachers and pupils as educational, rather than organisational, leaders. The positional framework for the chapter begins with the importance of the relationship between teachers and pupils and argues against the leader–follower dichotomy. The leadership role of teachers at the learning interface with students is explored, particularly in relation to the management of individual or independent learners. In Chapter 8 Gunter questions the location of leadership within schools, drawing strongly on the educational leadership context found within the English state system of education. The divergent pressures of teacher professionalism and the accountability of schools to the state, particularly in terms of the educational objectives that are required to be met, form the basis of wider conceptual analysis of the nature of school leadership.

Clive Harber and Lynn Davies have conducted extensive research on education in Africa and have both described and analysed the ways in which schools operate in developing countries (see, for instance, Harber and Davies, 1997) arguing that, in such situations, the basic economic climate, which creates widely distributed small schools, dictates that teachers must act as leaders. They have offered arguments for an increased 'democratisation' of education previously articulated by Harber (1997) in contraposition to what they perceive to be the current dominant leadership constructs. In Chapter 9 Harber and Davis explore the moral basis on which educational leadership is based and question, at a foundation level, the extent to which leadership can exist as a politically and morally pure field where external objectives are set. Current conceptions are challenged by reference to a wide rage of educational contexts, stretching the concept of 'effective leadership' to its limits.

The final section, Section D, examines 'perspectives on leadership in practice' and is grounded in the fact that recent governmental initiatives, both in the UK and in many international contexts, have focused on notions of excellence defined in terms of achievable targets. This notion of effectiveness can be viewed as both a challenge and burden for educational leaders in that it clearly delineates goals for achievement but is also susceptible to the critique that it offers a debased and instrumental depiction of education. In Chapter 10 Mark Brundrett and Neil Burton examine the leadership of high-performing schools based on their work with those institutions involved in the Beacon Schools scheme (Burton and Brundrett, 2000; Brundrett and Burton, 2001), an initiative that has turned into one of the central planks of government policy for the sharing of best practice among schools in England.

Since incorporation in 1993, managers of further education colleges have faced a series of challenges including creating strategic plans despite highly constrained strategic choices. Indeed, managers of further education colleges are accused, at one and the same time, of failing to manage processes in a sufficiently businesslike way and of being too business-driven in their approaches (Lumby, 1999). These tensions have led to concerns about the potential lack of coherence and mission in provision (Kennedy, 1997). In Chapter 11 Graham Peeke explores these apparently contradictory strains on leaders in the sector. Similarly universities have periodically 'reinvented' themselves to meet new social, professional and epistemological challenges and have revealed themselves to be simultaneously capable of insulation from and resistance to market-driven changes in practice (Watson, 2000). In Chapter 12 David Watson argues that, from an international perspective, external pressures on universities have converged but that the leadership roles charged with meeting them have stubbornly maintained their national characteristics. Nonetheless, Watson suggests that, measured by its outcomes, the management and leadership of UK higher education has been outstandingly successful in several areas during two decades of intense turbulence. Watson goes on to reflect on how top leadership within universities may be different from both the other educational cases covered in this volume and from the commercial and industrial models that are so frequently alluded to. Reassuringly, he concludes by affirming that academic and institutional leadership is about values and setting the balance between continuity and change.

As noted earlier in this preface, the empirical evidence for the impact of leadership on learning outcomes may not be as incontrovertible as some would wish to portray. Equally the conception of what we mean by leadership may not be the simple, monolithic and unidimensional construct that is often portrayed in the simpler 'manuals' which seem to offer magic potions that will transform organisations through the application of certain heroic but superficial characteristics that, it is often suggested, represent good 'leadership'. Nonetheless those who work in educational and other organisations seem to know when they are well led and are often eager to express their indebtedness to colleagues who offer leadership, wherever they may be situated in the organisational structure. It is hoped that this text will provide a stimulating and challenging contribution to the debate on leadership which will challenge many prevailing orthodoxies but will also reaffirm the importance of high-quality leadership and leadership training development.

Mark Brundrett, Neil Burton
and Robert Smith

REFERENCES

Bell, L. and Bolam, R. (2003) *EPPI Study of Relationship between Leadership and School Outcomes* (forthcoming).

Bolam, R. (1997) 'Management development for headteachers', *Educational Management and Administration*, **25**(3), 265–83.

Brundrett, M. and Burton, N. (2001) 'Sharing success: the development of the first Beacon Schools in England', *International Studies in Educational Administration*, **29**(1), 19–28.

Burton, N. and Brundrett, M. (2000) 'The first year of Beacon School status: maintaining excellence and sharing success', *School Leadership and Management*, **20**(4), 489–98.

Bush, T., Bell, L., Bolam, R., Glatter, R. and Ribbins, P. (1999) *Educational Management: Redefining Theory, Policy and Practice*, London: Paul Chapman Publishing.

Coleman, M. (1996) 'The management style of female headteachers', *Educational Management and Administration*, **24**(2), 163–74.

Coleman, M. (2001) 'Female secondary headteachers in England and Wales', *School Leadership and Management*, **21**(1), 75–100.

Department for Education and Employment (DfEE) (1999) *National College for School Leadership: A Prospectus*, London: DfEE.

Dimmock, C. (ed.) (1993) *School-Based Management and School Effectiveness*, London: Routledge.

Dimmock, C. (2000) *Designing and Leading the Future School: A Cross-Cultural Perpective*, London: Falmer Press.

Dimmock, C. and O'Donoghue, T.A. (1996) *Innovative Principals and Restructuring*, London: Routledge.

Gronn, P. (2000a) *The Making of Educational Leaders*, London: Cassell.

Gronn, P. (2000b) 'Distributed properties: a new architecture for leadership', *Educational Management and Administration*, **28**(3), 317–38.

Harber, C. (1997) *Education, Democracy and Political Development*, Brighton: Sussex Academic Press.

Harber, C. and Davies, L. (1997) *School Management and Effectiveness in Developing Countries*, London: Continuum.

Kennedy, H. (1997) *Learning Works: Widening Participation in Further Education*, Coventry: FEFC.

Leithwood, K. and Jantzi, D. (1999) 'Transformational leadership: 'How principals can help reform school cultures', *School Effectiveness and Improvement*, **1**(4), 249–80.

Leithwood, K., Jantzi, D. and Steinbach, R. (1999) *Changing Leadership for Changing Times*, Buckingham: Open University Press.

Lumby, J. (1999) 'Strategic Planning in Further Education', *Educational Management and Administration*, **27**(1), 71–83.

O'Donoghue, T. and Dimmock, C. (1997) *School Restructuring*, London: Kogan Page.

Pascal, C. and Ribbins, P. (1998) *Understanding Heads and Headship in Primary Education*, London: Cassell.

Rayner, S. and Ribbins, P. (1998) *Headteachers and Leadership in Special Education*, London: Cassell.

Teddlie, C. and Reynolds, D. (2000) *The International Handbook of School Effectiveness Research*, London: Falmer Press.

Watson, D. (2000) *Managing Strategy*, Buckingham: Open University Press.

NOTES ON CONTRIBUTORS

Ray Bolam is Professor of Educational Management at the University of Cardiff and a visiting Professor of Educational Management at the University of Leicester.

Mark Brundrett is Academic Director for Master's Degree programmes at the Centre for Educational Leadership and Management at the University of Leicester.

Neil Burton was formerly Strand Leader for the campus-based MBA in Educational Management at the Educational Management Development Unit of the University of Leicester. Dr Burton now teaches in the Secondary Sector.

Marianne Coleman was formerly the Deputy Director of the Educational Management Development Unit (the predecessor to CELM) at the University of Leicester where she held special responsibility for research and publications. Dr Coleman is now Senior Lecturer in Educational Management at the Institute of Education in London.

Lynn Davies is Professor of International Education and Director of the Centre for International Education at the University of Birmingham.

Clive Dimmock was formerly Associate Professor of Education at the University of Western Australia in Perth. He is now Director of the Centre for Educational Leadership and Management and Professor of Educational Management at the University of Leicester.

Peter Gronn is Professor of Education at Monash University, Victoria. He edits the influential journal, *Leading and Managing*.

Helen M. Gunter is Reader in Educational Leadership and Management in the School of Education at the University of Birmingham.

Clive Harber was formerly Dean of Education at the University of Natal, Durban; he is currently Reader in International Educational Management at the University of Birmingham.

Kenneth Leithwood is Professor of Education within the Centre for Leadership Development, Ontario Institute for Studies in Education, University of Toronto.

Peter Newton was formerly Director of Courses at the National College for School Leadership, which is in Nottingham.

Graham Peeke is a member of the senior management team at the Learning and Skills Development Agency.

Peter Ribbins is Professor of Educational Management at the University of Birmingham and was formerly Dean of the Faculty of Education and Continuing Studies. He is a former editor of the leading journal, *Educational Management and Administration.*

Robert Smith is Programme Leader for the MSc in Educational Leadership and takes special responsibility for international students undertaking the MBA in Educational Management at the Centre for Educational Leadership and Management, University of Leicester.

Professor Sir David Watson is Director of the University of Brighton. He was a member of the National Committee of Inquiry into Higher Education (the Dearing Committee) and is a leading member of 'Universities UK'.

ABBREVIATIONS

AST	advanced skills teachers
BELMAS	British Educational Leadership, Management and Administration Society
CEO	chief executive officer
CLD	Centre for Leadership Development
CoVE	Centre for Vocational Excellence
DES	Department of Education and Science
DfEE	Department for Education and Employment
DfES	Department for Education and Skills
EPPI	Evidence for Policy and Practice
FE	further education
FEDA	Further Education Development Agency
FEFC	Further Education Funding Council
FENTO	Further Education National Training Organisation
HEADLAMP	Headteachers' Leadership and Management Programme
HE	higher education
HEFCE	Higher Education Funding Council for England
HEI	Higher Education Institution
HESDA	Higher Education Staff Development Agency
ICT	information and communication technology
LEA	Local Education Authority
LLSC	Local Learning and Skills Council
LMS	Local Management of Schools
LPSH	Leadership Programme for Serving Headteachers
LRC	Learner Representative Council
LSC	Learning and Skills Council
LSDA	Learning and Skills Development Agency
NCSL	National College for School Leadership
NFER	National Foundation for Educational Research
NPQH	National Professional Qualification for Headship
OECD	Organisation for Economic Co-operation and Development
OFSTED	Office for Standards in Education
PC	personal computer

PHIP	Professional Headship Induction Programme
RDA	Regional Development Agency
RQA	Raising Quality and Achievement
SCRELM	Standing Conference for Research in Educational Leadership and Management
SCOP	Standing Committee of Principals
SMT	Senior Management Team
TTA	Teacher Training Agency
UAE	United Arab Emirates
UCET	Universities' Council for the Education and Training of Teachers
UUK	Universities United Kingdom
VET	vocational and educational training

Section A: Conceptualising Leadership

LEADERSHIP IN LEARNING-CENTRED SCHOOLS: CULTURAL CONTEXT, FUNCTIONS AND QUALITIES

Clive Dimmock

INTRODUCTION

A renewed drive to develop and improve school leadership is currently under way, and has been so for some time in many countries. Initiatives aimed at improving school leadership have taken place in previous decades, especially in the USA and the UK. What is novel about the current drive is its more global and international nature on the one hand, and the broader approach being taken to the concept of leadership, on the other.

In relation to the globalising and internationalising of leadership development, governments as far apart as the Australian states, Hong Kong, China, Singapore, the UK and the USA are not only promoting models of principal development for similar purposes, namely school improvement, but are also encouraging reciprocal visitations and exchanges between principals. In regard to the broadening of the concept of leadership development, at least three new aspects warrant consideration. The first concerns the stronger conception than hitherto, being given to the connectivity between leadership and other key processes, activities and goals of schools, such as learning and teaching (Dimmock, 2000). The second relates to the recognition being given to leadership as a distributed phenomenon in schools and its emergence at teacher and middle management levels, alongside more traditional conceptions centring on senior management and the principalship. The third distinguishes senior or principal leadership in terms of phases, identifying at least three – aspiring, newly appointed/induction and experienced.

The first years of the new millennium have continued the trends of the previous century in being characterised by turbulence in educational policy-making. Continuous and evolving change, it seems, is endemic to policy and practice on an international scale. Leadership lies at the centre of such change in education, both as a key component of educational organisations in its own right and as a catalyst for the successful reorganisation of other activities. Studies have consistently revealed the centrality of leadership to school improvement and quality schools (Hallinger and Heck, 1997). For some time, governments, and others, have accepted and embedded this realisation in their policy-making.

That leadership has assumed such high importance in the minds and values of policy-makers, as well as researchers and practitioners, creates a problem in two respects. First, if leadership is so important, it behoves clarification as to what are its key qualities. Secondly, what kind of philosophical and values base underpins such qualities to provide their justification?

This chapter addresses both of these questions. It presents a set of leadership functions and a set of qualities seen as appropriate for contemporary school leaders in diverse cultural contexts, and a justification for them. Accordingly, the chapter is structured into four parts. The first outlines the complex context in which leadership is exercised and highlights some perennial problems confronting its development. The second presents a rationale and justification for the view of leadership endorsed. The third outlines a set of contemporary leader functions appropriate for successful schools, both present and future. The fourth and final part refers to these functions to generate a set of leadership qualities which, it is argued, form part of a framework for conceptualising leadership, and for planning its future growth and development.

A broad canvas of leadership is thus covered. Implicit is the realisation that current turbulent policy-making environments, with changes advocated to most aspects of schools and schooling – curriculum, learning, teaching, assessment, standards and accountability – place a premium on coherent and synergistic approaches to leadership. Such a view endorses the connectivity between leadership and other school activities, such as learning and teaching, it being no longer sufficient to see leadership as a discrete entity. Moreover, leadership should relate to the wider issue of the type of schools and educational organisations society needs. That being the case, leadership reflects the prevailing social and cultural condition. Hence, different societies may well have culturally different expectations of their schools and thus of leadership, despite powerful global forces towards convergence.

EDUCATIONAL LEADERSHIP: CONTEMPORARY CONTEXT AND PERENNIAL ISSUES

Some of the more clearly distinguishable trends in leadership thinking and practice have already been alluded to in the introduction to this chapter. They, along with other important developments in the field, justify further discussion in this section. Some are perennial issues revisited; others, however, are markedly new. These developments are structured into five aspects: global and cultural issues; leadership connectivity; leadership as a distributed concept; leadership phases; and training and preparation for leadership.

Leadership Betwixt Global and Cultural Forces

Powerful global and international trends in education policy are creating leadership contexts that are increasingly alike. School-based management, outcomes-oriented curricula, market forces and competition, a need to forge united school communities and a focus on standards and accountability are commonplace environments within which school leaders are expected to function.

A consequence of globalisation is the emergence of generic or ubiquitous expectations of leaders. For example, there is now a cross-cultural expectation that leaders be more proactive in leading and managing school resources to secure improved performance of staff and students. While they are increasingly held accountable for their schools' performance, they are also urged to consider their schools in relation to the outside world. This externalising includes almost everything, from local to international and global levels, taking in the school community, the local and business community, the national society and citizenship, and even the broader international and global issues of world environmental, political and economic concerns.

Global and international trends are also discernible in other aspects of leadership. Many education systems are joining the USA in expecting a professionally accredited cadre of school leaders. It is intended that initiatives such as this will create a true profession of the principalship. England, for example, plans for all new headteachers to have, or be taking, the National Professional Qualification for Headship (NPQH) by 2004. Hong Kong is planning the same for its new principals.

That powerful forces are at work to internationalise and globalise the principalship, is beyond dispute (Dimmock and Walker, 2000). They include the Internet, jet travel, and international media and publishing. Opportunities abound for principals, academics and policy-makers to travel abroad to conferences, to undertake international consultancies, and to gain leadership training through study visits and projects conducted overseas. Part of the professional development of Hong Kong principals, for example, includes study visits to Beijing and Shanghai to study practices in mainland China. The National College for School Leadership in England sponsors programmes of study visits by overseas principals to disseminate international best practice. There are countless examples of this type.

Despite all this, the indomitable fact is that leadership is culture-bound to an extent that cannot or should not, be ignored (Dimmock and Walker, 2000). Yet, it has been largely ignored in education. For some years, the present author has argued that concepts, theories, research findings, policies and practices conceived in the Anglo-American world may not apply, or may need adaptation, in other societies (Dimmock, 1998; Dimmock and Walker, 1998a; 1998b). For example, we know that the distribution of power and influence varies cross-culturally, so that in some societies, such as the USA and the UK, power tends to be more evenly distributed, whereas in others, such as Asia, it is more concentrated. In addition, some societies tend to be more individualistic, such as the USA and the UK, while others are more collectivist, as in Asia. There are other cultural differences, too, but consideration of these two alone has important implications for leadership. The Chinese principal, for example, experiences a much greater respect and deference for her/his authority than her/his 'western' counterpart. Equally, she/he is less inclined to 'confront' difficult interpersonal conflicts for fear of 'losing face' and disturbing apparent harmonious relations, than is the English or American principal. More weight is given to conformity and to hierarchy and seniority in Chinese schools than is the case in British or American schools. Leadership styles and expectations thus differ cross-culturally (Walker and Dimmock, 1999a; 1999b).

Globalising and internationalising forces are tending to lead to convergence of educational policies and practices, including leadership. However, while some aspects of culture are susceptible to change, other more deep-seated cultural characteristics, forged over centuries, remain stubbornly in place. The resultant tension helps explain many of the world's present problems. They are no less applicable to leadership. The implications for educational leadership are profound. They are likely to affect how leaders are prepared and trained, what emphasis leadership is given in particular societies, what are the societal expectations of leaders, and so on. Few ubiquitous solutions to leadership issues can be assumed. Differences in societal values and thus in leadership practices and expectations, abound. It is abundantly clear that more research is needed on how societal cultural impacts on leadership.

Leadership connectivity

In earlier work (Dimmock, 2000), the present author described at some length the idea of leadership as a connected concept. He argued that it was a failure to see it in such terms that partly allowed Weick's (1976) conception of schools as 'loosely-coupled' organisations to continue to survive. It also helps explain why so many system and school restructuring initiatives fail to penetrate beyond the principal's door into classrooms.

Essentially, in the context of school improvement and student learning, it is important to understand the links between all elements that comprise the school and schooling, including leadership, and to do so in a backward-mapping way (Dimmock, 2000). This entails identifying, and then relating, student learning outcomes derived from the curriculum, learning processes, teaching methods, use of computer technology, organisational structures, human and financial resource management, and culture building. All of these are linked to each other and to leadership.

Thinking connectedly is important strategically in securing school improvement and in micro-managing the daily work of schools (Dimmock, 2000). Leaders who think connectedly are more likely to foresee the consequences of their actions. A decision to change curriculum content, for example, might well relay on to imply new ways of learning, which in turn indicate new ways of teaching, the need for professional development, different organisational structures and patterns of resource allocation, and the building of a new culture. Any or all of these are possible consequences and spread effects of an initial idea for change. Developing the skills of connected thinking will hopefully become a central part of the study and practice of leadership in future, since it is an integral part of strategic and micro-leadership.

Leadership as a distributed concept

It used to be the case that leadership was thought of wholly in terms of the headteacher or principal. This is not so nowadays, with the prevailing view that leadership is a permeable process that is widely distributed throughout the school. Indeed, many talk about it as an empowering process enabling others in the school to exercise leadership. Behind such notions is the rationale that a high-performing organisation can only be achieved if all of its sections and departments are 'full-on', and that any slack or underperformance is eradicated. Leadership as a distributed rather than monopolistic concept is more likely to achieve this, it is contended, through its capacity to apply pressure and motivation more successfully throughout the organisation.

Leadership as a distributed concept is increasingly being incorporated into professional development initiatives. For example, the National College for School Leadership (NCSL) in England, has developed a programme called Leading from the Middle, specifically aimed at middle managers such as department heads and year co-ordinators. Furthermore, a growing number of scholars in the field are propagating ideas and practices based on the notion of teacher leadership. Still others conceive of student leadership. Behind all this is a view of leadership as an influence process rather than a set of tasks associated with a particular position. In reality, leadership is both. It is an influence process, and that is what makes it generic across levels of an organisation. However, incumbents of different positions also need to apply the influence processes to particular spheres of responsibility, and those are often, and likely to be, different. The interconnection between leadership as a process and a set of tasks connected to position is likely to be of interest to those charged with designing leadership courses. They will need to consider how the content of such programmes will differ between teacher, middle manager and senior leadership.

Phases of leadership

Scholars in the field of educational leadership have given relatively scant attention to developing theories of career progression in the profession. This is particularly the case for empirically supported theories. Recent interest has focused on identifying leadership stages and a number of schema have resulted. These originate, however, more from a conceptual than an empirical base. Consequently, this aspect of leadership remains a 'hot topic' for future empirical research. As the following paragraphs reveal, there is as yet no universally agreed, unequivocal consensus on a stage theory of leadership.

Many of the conceptual schema proposed recognise stages or phases of leadership, and have been conjured by policy-makers and professional developers seeking to improve the training and preparation of school leaders. In Hong Kong, for example, the government has based its policy of needs assessment and school leader professional development on a three-stage structure of aspiring, newly appointed and experienced principals (Education Department, Hong Kong, 2002). There are problems of terminology with this taxonomy. For example, the term 'aspiring' is condescending, especially when many such candidates already occupy senior leadership positions. Likewise, some 'newly appointed' principals may have already been principals, but in other schools.

In England, the NCSL has published a five-stage model of career leadership as follows (NCSL, 2001). The first stage is recognised as 'emergent leadership', which is meant to apply to teachers who begin to take on management and leadership responsibilities and perhaps aspire to become headteachers. There is some equivocation here, because subject or specialist teachers are distinguished from emergent leaders and are regarded as 'middle' leaders. Clearly, the membership of both groups will overlap, even if the purpose of their tasks is ostensibly different. A second stage of 'established leadership' comprises assistant and deputy heads, who are experienced leaders, but who do not intend to pursue headship. A third stage is recognised as 'entry to headship' and this stage combines the professional preparation for headship with the induction of new heads, a process seen as continuous and seamless. A fourth stage of 'advanced leadership' applies to mature leaders who are looking to refresh and update and widen their experience. Finally, a fifth stage, known as 'consultant leaders', are those who are sufficiently able and experienced to act in the capacity of trainer, mentor or inspector and to put something back into the profession.

This is not the place to critically review the above stages. Suffice to say that it is not an easy task to conjure a stage theory or framework. However, the NCSL stages raise many issues. For example, while the sequence is indisputable, dependent as it is on the length of time people are in leadership, how valid is it to equate experience and expertise with maturity or length of service? How useful is the terminology with labels such as 'advanced' and 'consultant'? Does it imply that leaders who are not in the 'consultant' stage are not sufficiently mature or expert to advise, mentor or inspect? Is it not possible for a leader to occupy stage 4 and 5 at the same time?

Leader preparation and training

In the UK, as in many other education systems, leadership training has attracted a large share of the professional development budget during the late 1990s and early part of the twenty-first century. However, while such initiatives have generally been greeted favourably, they have resurrected some perennial conundrums. Brundrett's (2001) account comparing the development of leadership preparation programmes in England and the USA ably demonstrates this. For our purposes, these issues can be grouped as follows: central versus dispersed; academic/liberal versus practical/instrumental; and business versus education orientation. It is worth briefly elaborating on each.

- *Centralist versus dispersed*: this issue centres on the extent to which central government rather than local agencies, and higher education, should control the agenda for leadership training. Brundrett (2001), for example, when comparing the relatively long history of leadership preparation in the USA with that of England, notes that America has a tradition of federal and state governments as well as higher education all working closely together. He argues that despite long periods of harsh controversy and conflict, the American leadership agenda has benefited from 'a sophisticated academic critique', while by contrast, in England, 'central governmental organisations have interjected national programmes . . . which present the dangers of arrogating training' (ibid., p. 229).

  The point at issue is that a number of sectors have vested interests in leadership training – national and state governments, universities and higher education, industry and business – each of which is competing for influence. And this excludes the voice of the profession

itself, which is often drowned out. Nonetheless, Brundrett claims that
in the move to licensure in the USA, the place of higher education has
been preserved. This remains to be settled in England, where strong
central government initiatives in the mid and late 1990s have seen the
introduction of the National Professional Qualification for Headship
(NPQH), the Headteachers' Leadership and Management Programme
(HEADLAMP) and the Leadership Programme for Serving Headteachers
(LPSH). The place of universities in this framework and the
relationship between NPQH and masters' degrees in educational
leadership and management remain somewhat ambivalent (Bush,
1998).

A recent development in the central versus local tension in England
is the move to establish a number of regional affiliated centres to the
National College through which the national programmes will be run.
The affiliated centres will likely be conglomerates of local education
authorities, independent agents, and institutions of higher education.

- *Academic/liberal versus practical/instrumental*: the argument here
  revolves around the general aim and approach taken to training and
  development, namely, whether it should be academic and liberal or
  practical and instrumental in nature. Some advocate a knowledge for
  understanding approach, implying a more liberal academic orientation,
  whereas others espouse a knowledge for action approach, grounded in
  the practical and instrumental. This dispute surfaced in England in the
  1980s when courses spawned under the aegis of the National
  Development Centre, with little or no central control from the
  government, were often attacked for their limited instrumental aims
  and content. A more recent criticism has focused on the compilation
  of daunting lists of standards and competences used in the assessment
  of leaders, and the consequent elevation of expectations well beyond
  the capabilities of most.

- *Education versus industry/business orientation*: a similar tension to the
  academic/practical dichotomy has characterised leadership preparation
  and development, namely, whether it should be exclusively
  educational in its orientation, or whether it would benefit from
  influence and values associated with the world of business and
  industry. Those favouring the exclusivity of education appeal to the
  fundamental differences in aims, values and cultures between the two
  sectors, while those supporting the inclusion of business stress the
  generic nature of leadership and management, believing that
  educational leadership would benefit from such broadening. The
  debate surfaced in England in the 1980s, when individuals and
  organisations representing industrial leadership played a prominent
  role in headteacher training. It has lingered on since with debates about

the relevance of industrial content to educational leadership courses and, more recently, with the notion of business mentors for headteachers as part of the LPSH programme.

It is against these complex issues and trends that the landscape of leader functions and qualities continues to be mapped. The following sections present a framework of leader functions and qualities, which is preceded by a justification.

IDENTIFYING AND JUSTIFYING LEADER FUNCTIONS AND QUALITIES

Contemporary thinking about leadership espouses the importance of leaders developing a values base on which to build their strategies, priorities and styles. Attempts to explicate the type of leadership appropriate for contemporary schools need to provide an underpinning rationale, philosophy or justification. The perspective adopted by this author views leadership as a highly connected phenomenon (to other processes and activities) and one which is largely derived from them. Accordingly, in advocating a perspective of leadership, there is need to look at its purposes, aims and ends. As Covey (1990) aptly reminds us, it is wise to start with the end in mind. It follows that since the purposes and aims may change with time, so may the preferred versions of leadership.

To what purposes and aims is leadership geared? There can be no more important answer to this than the connection it enjoys to the organisation – the school or college – being led. Thus, in espousing a view on the nature of leadership, it is necessary to envision the type of school we, that is, society, wants. Murphy (1992) recognised this important tenet more than a decade ago. Thus, the problematic issue of what should be the nature of leadership can be addressed through the following questions: how do we want our future schools to look? What is expected of our future schools? What kind of education do we want schools to provide? What values, knowledge and skills do we expect students to acquire? In short, what kind of graduate(s) do we advocate for our schools?

Answers to these questions provide some powerful insights into the type of leadership required of our schools. Hence the claim that leadership is a connected and derived concept, being dependent on the bigger and more crucial issue of what is meant by successful, quality schools for the present and for the future and what type of leadership is necessary to their materialisation. The importance of values, and their influence on leadership, is central to this approach, since values undergird our visions of future schools and schooling. It is to these visions and their associated leader functions that the following section turns.

LEADER FUNCTIONS IN
LEARNING-FOCUSED SCHOOLS

A number of the key characteristics of future schools are predictable. They will be increasingly self-managed, with responsibility for their own planning, but within system frameworks. Pressure to make them accountable for their performance and standards will likely intensify. Performance will be largely judged, as at present, by student scores on examinations and tests. Concerns for equity will continue, manifesting in such initiatives as more individualised curricula. Greater effort will be given to raising the learning performances of the underprivileged, of minority groups and of the disabled. Increased store will be placed on improving teachers and teaching. Greater emphasis on the use of computer technology in the classroom, for purposes of enhancing both learning and teaching, will reflect past failures in this respect. As the multicultural nature of societies continues to generate problems, more prominence will be placed on the school as a microcosm of multiculturalism, as a possible palliative for addressing the multicultural problems of the wider society.

This brief and partial picture distils into schools as learning-focused organisations. Whether it be an emphasis on individualised learning, computer-driven learning, improving examination scores, or acquiring more tolerant and enlightened attitudes towards diverse cultures, the generic and underlying theme is learning. Academic, social, ethical, ethnic, liberal; cognitive, affective or psychomotor – they all reduce to the school as an effective learning environment. The issue can be posed in two questions: How can schools cope with such challenges? How can they become better learning-focused organisations?

An earlier study of the future-orientated, learning-centred school (Dimmock, 2000) presented a description of how schools, if appropriately designed, might address both of the above questions. The study systematically profiled key elements of curricula, teaching, learning, use of computer technology, organisational structures, evaluation and appraisal, personnel and resources, and leadership, in order to arrive at a redesigned notion of what a truly learning-centred school looked like. The same process – backward mapping – not only portrayed leadership as a peremptory part of attaining and maintaining such schools, but generated a perspective of the functions of leaders in such schools derived from the key elements of design. It is to these functions that the discussion now turns.

Building on earlier analyses (Dimmock, 1995a; 1995b; 2000), a conception of leadership is derived that emphasises ten components, each of which dovetails and overlaps. Leadership of the learning-centred school, it is argued, emphasises:

1   a strategic capacity based on a holistic conceptualisation of

organisational change and innovation towards a vision of the learning-centred school;

2 goal orientation in regard to student learning outcomes;

3 a focus on teaching and learning;

4 practice based on research evidence of 'what works' and 'informed practice' in respect of teaching and learning, school effectiveness and school improvement;

5 commitment to embedding computer technology;

6 building of supportive organisational structures that promote effective teaching and learning and decision-making;

7 creation of an organisational culture that values learning for all and a positive, collaborative climate of human relations;

8 allocation of human, financial and physical resources that supports learning for all, coupled with a performance monitoring and reviewing process that provides feedback and positive reinforcement;

9 ability to model desired behaviours and values;

10 capacity to mould multicultural schools into harmonious communities which benefit and learn from diversity.

Each of these roles is now briefly discussed.

It is fitting to start with the importance of vision, the ability to think holistically and conceptually, and the capacity to develop strategy and to oversee change. These are multiple functions which enjoy a close interrelationship. A vision provides the leader with a sense of purpose, aim and direction, which can then be shared with others and used as a basis for prioritising and decision-making. Vision is realised through strategies geared to change, a process requiring an ability to conceptualise and to see the school as a whole, as well as the interconnections between the parts. Implicit in all of this is a group of leadership functions variously defined as visionary, strategic and transformational (Leithwood and Jantzi, 1990).

Learning-centred schools prompt a major shift in the mind-set of leaders away from business matters to the centrality of students and learning. They become goal-oriented in respect of improving student learning outcomes, interpreting their work roles and judging their performance in terms of the contribution they make to enhancing learning (Levine and Lezotte, 1990). Above all, they hold students' welfare uppermost in their values, believing that they are in school primarily to serve the interests of all students.

Leading the learning-centred school demands a close knowledge of learning, teaching and curriculum (Leithwood and Steinbach, 1993), or what is traditionally termed the instructional core. Equipped with knowledge and expertise of the core instructional processes, teachers can be led in a truly professional way (Duke, 1987). Possession of such technical knowledge enables leaders to relate to teachers and students on classroom-level issues as well as provide whole-school perspectives on curricular and pedagogical issues.

Leaders promote practices in their schools that are based on evidence-informed, research-validated approaches. They also respect and value intuition and experience. As learners themselves, leaders demonstrate that they value the importance of research findings as guides to informed practice and future innovation. They encourage teachers to be cognisant of research on effective teaching and learning by obtaining and disseminating relevant literature and by resourcing and arranging staff development to keep staff informed (Duke, 1987). In addition, they familiarise themselves with research on principal effectiveness, school effectiveness and school improvement, and seek appropriate opportunities to apply important findings. In regard to research, they demonstrate through their own behaviour the value they place on reading, understanding, reflecting, conceptualising and transforming ideas into practice.

A key feature of contemporary leadership is a commitment to computer technology as an integral and embedded part of learning and teaching, and of school decision-making. Leaders need to be conversant with the capabilities and potentialities of technology. They aim to achieve the twin goals of access for all, and integration across the whole curriculum. Computer technology is central to the delivery of the curriculum programme and the attainment of student outcomes in the learning-centred school. Its intrusiveness into the classroom means that traditional notions of teaching and learning have to be reconfigured. Leaders have a responsibility to ensure the visions, goals and policies concerning technology are adopted and implemented across all faculties.

If leadership is focused on core processes of learning and teaching, it has also to be concerned with the organisational structures that enable the processes. The configuration of structures should support, not hinder, the delivery of a quality curriculum to all students. In traditional schools, structures such as standard lesson times, inflexible standardised curricula, regimented timetables and school routines have come to govern decisions about core technology. Leaders may thus need to dismantle existing dysfunctional structures. This calls for an understanding of alternative structures and their likely impact on, and ability to allow flexibility in furthering, the cause of promoting learning (Murphy et al., 1985).

Concern for culture is acknowledged as one of the key roles leaders play. Tight coupling and synergy is achieved when all parts of a school share common values, goals and practices. A strong, tightly knit organisational culture helps dismantle the barriers and internal divisions which often characterise schools (Wilson and Firestone, 1987). New configurations of teaching and learning are dependent on building a culture that supports learning for all and values productive human relations. Effective school leaders recognise the multiple and mutually reinforcing strategies available to them in building supportive learning and collegial cultures. These range from more explicit forms of verbal communication with all groups in the school community, to modelling and demonstrating through their own behaviours, as well as more subtle uses of symbols, ceremonies and rituals. High but realistic learning expectations are conveyed, rewards, recognition and resources for learning are provided and learning time protected (Smith and Piele, 1989).

Effective leadership of human resources is likely to be supportive of improved levels of learning productivity in schools. Such leadership motivates effective teaching and learning, enthusing people to capitalise on the virtues of working collaboratively. Leaders provide teachers with the opportunity to develop collaboratively and individually as reflective practitioners. Human resources are used to maximum effect, securing synergy of effort through collaboration (Moore Johnson, 1990; Rosenholtz, 1989). Good leaders connect school-based management with school improvement and core technology. Thus, financial management is conceived more in terms of how it can influence resource allocation to enhance the core technology and student outcomes than for its intrinsic importance (Duke, 1987). Resource levels are carefully considered in relation to student need and learning outcomes (Knight, 1993). Schools perform well when leaders recognise the need for agreement on goals, when resources are allocated to support goal achievement and when all parts of the school work consistently and collaboratively towards the same ends. Purposeful professional development is accorded a key role in resource allocation.

Effective leaders monitor and review performance at whole-school and sub-school levels (Cuttance, 1993). They realise the importance of monitoring and reviewing as prerequisites for providing feedback and positive reinforcement, both of which are consistently found among the factors contributing highly to learning (Fraser et al., 1987). In their capacity as leaders, they give abundant feedback and positive reinforcement to teachers and students, and at the same time build the culture for these behaviours to permeate all levels and members of the school community.

In the learning-centred school, leaders deliberately and consciously demonstrate in their own professional work the core values and behaviours they wish to promulgate in others. They model the behaviours and values they advocate for teachers and students (Dimmock, 1995a; 1995b). With the leader as role model, desirable values and practices are deliberately replicated at different levels. In advocating a school focus on student learning, effective principals and teachers approach their own professional work with a learning orientation (Barth, 1990).

Finally, due recognition should be given to leadership capacity to mould multicultural school communities into harmonious learning environments. Most of the aforementioned functions are involved in this, especially the building of learning cultures, the modelling of certain behaviours and the focus on the learning of all. Increasingly in future, leadership will involve a cultural sensitivity and appreciation such that the cultural diversity of school communities is seen as a rich resource to be tapped rather than a problem to be concealed. Leaders will need to ensure that their schools engage cultural diversity through the curriculum, in teaching and learning, and in the social, spiritual and aesthetic life of the school.

For most leaders, the above functions present not only a formidable challenge, but a requirement to undergo training and to develop knowledge and skills in new directions. Hence the task of mapping contemporary leadership involves more than identifying a set of functions. Account also needs to be taken of the qualities needed to fulfil the functions. Accordingly, these are the focus of the next section.

LEADER QUALITIES

In earlier work on school leadership, Walker and Dimmock (2000), in concert with an assembled panel of experienced principals, professional developers, policy-makers and academics identified four interrelated components of what they termed 'key qualities' for leadership. These were values, knowledge, skills and attributes. All four, it was argued, needed to be meaningful and professionally relevant. The 'expert' panel was then charged with identifying particular core values, professional knowledge, skills and attributes deemed to be central to contemporary school leaders. The results of their deliberations are given below. While these are not claimed to be exclusive, they provide a useful framework for conceptualising essential leader qualities. A key question is the extent to which the values, knowledge, skills and attributes are thought to be generic and cross-cultural, given the tensions discussed in the earlier part of this chapter. The panel assumed that they were mostly generic, since they are responses to the needs for school improvement more than particularities of culture. They thought, however, that cultural difference would be more likely to affect *how* all four components were expressed and exercised.

EDUCATIONAL VALUES

Essential to leaders is the development of a coherent set of educational values on which to base leadership for school improvement. These values serve as fundamental principles on which to develop and design their schools and to provide consistency across all aspects of their leadership. Eight pivotal values were identified:

- *Learning-centred*: a belief in the primacy of learning as the focus of all that happens in the school.

- *Innovation*: a belief in experimentation with new ideas and with change as a means of school improvement.
- *Lifelong learning*: a belief that a major goal of the school is to develop among its community a view of learning as a continuous and ongoing process.
- *Education-for-all*: a conviction that all students have a right to a relevant and meaningful education.
- *Service-orientation*: a belief that the school be flexible and responsive in meeting the diverse needs of its community.
- *Empowerment*: a commitment to the meaningful involvement and participation of school community members in the life of the school.
- *Equity and fairness*: a belief that the rights of all in the school community are duly recognised and that individuals be treated with justice and integrity.
- *Whole-person development*: a commitment to producing students with a well-rounded, balanced education.

It is a substantial challenge for the present preparation and development of educational leaders to fully embrace these values. Yet to do so is axiomatic if leaders are to be successful school innovators and improvers.

Professional knowledge

Leadership for school improvement and student achievement depends on a clearly conceptualised and shared body of knowledge which, together with a set of educational values, guides and informs professional practice. This body of knowledge relates to the roles identified earlier, or, expressed in a different way, to each of the following:

- strategic direction and policy environment
- teaching, learning and curriculum
- leader and teacher growth and development
- staff and resource management
- quality assurance and accountability
- external communication and connection.

The challenge is to ensure that leaders possess a balanced and comprehensive knowledge across the six domains. In practice, leaders tend to possess strengths and weaknesses in some only, according to their preferred areas of focus. There may be a substantial lack of knowledge in other domains, with an overreliance on experience and intuition. Hence the recent attention in the UK given to evidence-informed practice and research-based knowledge of 'what works'.

Skills

Leadership skills are grounded in educational values and professional knowledge. The skills of leadership for school and student improvement are exercised in relation to the leader functions identified earlier. Skills may be grouped into the following three categories:

- *Personal*: these relate to how leaders manage their own behaviours and thoughts in their professional lives.
- *Communicative and influence*: these relate to how leaders interact at an interpersonal level with colleagues and other members of the community, and how they mobilise colleagues and other school community members towards sustained commitment to school improvement.
- *Organisational and technical*: these skills concern the tasks and techniques that are associated with running the whole school and securing school improvement.

The key skills essential to running good schools and colleges are personal and interpersonal on the one side, and technical and task-oriented on the other. It is the achievement of high levels of both, and a balance between the two, that distinguishes effective leaders.

Attributes

Educational values, professional knowledge, and skills are integral parts of leadership qualities. However, they are not sufficient. There is a fourth element, namely personal attributes, that leaders bring to the role. In the context of school-based management and school improvement, certain attributes, in particular, seem to assume prime importance. The expert panel selected the following:

- *Adaptability* and *responsiveness* in school decision-making and in managing people while retaining *commitment* to core values, such as student needs and learning outcomes.
- *Courage* of conviction with regard to their values, principles and actions and *resilience* in times of adversity and opposition.
- *Self-confidence* in their abilities and actions, while maintaining *modesty* in their interactions and dealings with others in and outside their school communities.
- *Tough-mindedness* in regard to the best interests of staff and students while showing *benevolence* and *respect* in all their interactions.
- *Collaboration* as team *members* coupled with *individual resourcefulness* and *decisiveness*.

- *Integrity* in their dealings with others combined with *political astuteness*.

The noteworthy feature of these attributes – as conceived by the expert panel and highlighted in italics – is their arrangement in pairs. With the exception of the second attribute, which combines two similar qualities, namely, courage and resilience, they are subtle combinations of opposites, constituting checks and balances that provide the range of responses demanded of leaders in complex situations. They permit leaders the range and flexibility to make appropriate responses to given situations. For example, leaders are expected to display self-confidence while at the same time remaining modest. They are expected to be collaborative while maintaining individual resourcefulness. They are expected to act with integrity and honesty, yet be politically astute. They need to be tough-minded, yet benevolent and respectful. While displaying courage, resilience and commitment, they need adaptability and responsiveness.

These attributes, along with leader values, professional knowledge and skills provide a framework for understanding the complexities of leader qualities. As always in dynamic, interactive situations, it is the mix and combination of all elements that determines the efficacy and effectiveness of the leader.

It may well be that these four elements of leader qualities are relevant and applicable to different societal cultures. In other words, in addressing the same policy agenda of school improvement, they are generic and thus applicable to leaders in many cultural settings. However, *how* particular values, knowledge, skills and attributes are displayed and exercised, and what combinations of them are considered appropriate, are likely to be culturally sensitive.

CONCLUSIONS

This chapter has painted a broad canvas of the landscape of educational leadership. It has argued that the importance of leadership to school improvement is no longer in doubt. Policy-makers, academics, administrators and practitioners have come to accept its centrality to the process of reform and improvement. Consequently, this places high responsibility on those groups to provide answers to such questions as, what constitutes leadership? How should leaders be prepared and trained? What is the relationship to teaching, learning and other organisational elements? How, at its most effective, does leadership connect with them to exert positive influence for student and school improvement? While a chapter such as this cannot possibly do justice to all these, it has begun to address them conceptually.

There is much to be done to improve the knowledge base. There are relatively few empirical studies detailing how leadership connects to influence teaching and learning. Many scholars and practitioners have criticised the quality of professional preparation and training for educational leaders. Improvements are being made in this respect, but there is still some way to go. Perhaps one of the most telling points is that as the roles and functions of leaders have generally extended with the increasing turbulence in educational policy-making, the methods of studying leaders have generally failed to keep pace (Dimmock and O'Donoghue, 1997). There is a need for more innovative methodological approaches, such as life history, to enrich contemporary research on educational leadership and leaders.

Equally, in response to the ethnocentric, largely Anglo-American bias of much of the literature on school leadership, there is an urgent need for more culturally sensitive and cross-cultural studies: 'One size does not fit all.' We need culturally based theories of leadership that are generated from, and inform, practice in different parts of the world, such as China, Africa, India, Russia and South America.

Within societies, we need to realise that leaders of multicultural schools are asked to make decisions about complex cultural matters for which they have little training or expertise. Inadequate preparation and knowledge of intercultural relations may result in an incomplete understanding of the values and interests of those entrusted to their care (Corson, 1998). Schools can easily become islands of alienation in the very communities they are meant to serve. In all of these ways, much remains to be done in the theory, research, and practice of leadership and the development of school leaders.

REFERENCES

Barth, R.S. (1990) *Improving Schools from Within: Teachers, Parents and Principals can Make the Difference*, San Francisco: Jossey-Bass.

Brundrett, M. (2001) 'The development of school leadership preparation programmes in England and the USA', *Educational Management and Administration*, **29**(2), 229–45.

Bush, T. (1998) 'The National Professional Qualification for Headship: the key to effective school leadership?', *School Leadership and Management*, **18**(3), 321–33.

Corson, D. (1998) *Changing Education for Diversity*, Buckingham. Open University Press.

Covey, S. (1990) *The 7 Habits of Highly Effective People*, New York: Simon & Schuster.

Cuttance, P. (1993) 'School development and review in an Australian state education system', in C. Dimmock (ed.), *School-Based Management and School Effectiveness*, London: Routledge, (pp. 142–64). .

Dimmock, C. (1995a) 'Restructuring for school effectiveness: leading, organising and teaching for effective learning', *Educational Management and Administration*, **23**(1), 1–13.

Dimmock, C. (1995b) 'Reconceptualising restructuring for school effectiveness and school improvement', *International Journal of Educational Reform*, **4**(3), 285–300.

Dimmock, C. (1998) 'Restructuring Hong Kong's schools: the applicability of Western theories, policies and practices to an Asian culture', *Educational Management and Administration*, **26**(4), 363–77.

Dimmock, C. (2000) *Designing the Learning-Centred School: A Cross-Cultural Perspective*, London: Falmer Press.

Dimmock, C. and O'Donoghue T. (1997) 'The edited topical life history approach: a new methodology to inform the study of school leadership', *Leading and Managing*, **3**(1), 48–70.

Dimmock, C. and Walker, A. (1998a) 'Towards comparative educational administration: Building the case for a cross-cultural, school-based approach', *Journal of Educational Administration*, **36**(4), 379–401.

Dimmock, C. and Walker, A. (1998b) 'Comparative educational administration: developing a cross-cultural comparative framework', *Educational Administration Quarterly*, **34**(4), 558–95.

Dimmock, C. and Walker, A. (2000) 'Globalization and societal culture: re-defining schooling and school leadership in the 21st century', *Compare*, **30**(3), 303–12.

Duke, D.L. (1987) *School Leadership and Instructional Improvement*, New York: Random House.

Education Department, Hong Kong (2002) *Continuing Professional Development for School Excellence*, Hong Kong: Education Department.

Fraser, B.J., Walberg, H.J., Welch, W.W. and Hattie, J.A. (1987) 'Syntheses of educational productivity research', *International Journal of Educational Research*, **11**(2), 147–247.

Hallinger, P. and Heck, R. (1997) 'Exploring the principal's contribution to school effectiveness', *School Effectiveness and School Improvement*, **8**(4), 1–35.

Knight, B. (1993) 'Delegated financial management and school effectiveness', in C. Dimmock (ed.), *School-Based Management and School Effectiveness*, London: Routledge, (pp. 114–41).

Leithwood, K. and Jantzi, D. (1990) 'Transformational leadership: how principals can help reform school cultures', *School Effectiveness and School Improvement*, **1**(4), 249–80.

Leithwood, K. and Steinbach, R. (1993) 'The consequences for school improvement of differences in principals' problem-solving processes', in C. Dimmock (ed.), *School-Based Management and School Effectiveness*, London: Routledge, (pp. 41–64).

Levine, D.U. and Lezotte, L.W. (1990) *Unusually Effective Schools: A Review and Analysis of Research and Practice*, Madison, WI: National Centre for Effective Schools Research and Development.

Moore Johnson, S. (1990) *Teachers at Work: Achieving Success in our Schools*, New York: Basic Books.

Murphy, J. (1992) *The Landscape of Leader Preparation: Reframing the Education of School Administrators*, Newbury Park, CA: Corwin Press.

Murphy, J., Weil, M., Hallinger, P. and Mitman, A. (1985) 'School effectiveness: a conceptual framework', *The Educational Forum*, **49**(3), 361–74.

National College for School leadership (NCSL) (2001) *Leadership Development Framework*, Nottingham: NCSL.

Rosenholtz, S. (1989) *Teachers' Workplace: The Social Organisation of Schools*,

New York: Longman.

Smith, S.C. and Piele, P.K. (eds). (1989) *School Leadership: Handbook for Excellence* 2nd edn, Eugene, OR: ERIC Clearinghouse on Educational Management.

Walker, A. and Dimmock, C. (1999a) 'Exploring principals' dilemmas in Hong Kong: increasing cross-cultural understanding of school leadership', *International Journal of Educational Reform*, **8**(1), 15–24.

Walker, A. and Dimmock, C. (1999b) 'A cross-cultural approach to the study of educational leadership: an emerging framework', *Journal of School Leadership*, **9**(4), 321–48.

Walker, A. and Dimmock, C. (2000) *Key Qualities of Newly Appointed Principals in Hong Kong,* Hong Kong: Hong Kong Centre for the Development of Educational Leadership, The Chinese University of Hong Kong.

Weick, K.E. (1976) 'Educational organizations as loosely-coupled systems', *Administrative Science Quarterly*, **21**, 1–19.

Wilson, B.L. and Firestone, W.A. (1987) 'The principal and instruction: combining bureaucratic and cultural linkages', *Educational Leadership*, **45**(1), 18–23.

FURTHER READING

Dimmock, C. (2000) *Designing the Learning-Centred School: A Cross-Cultural Perspective*, London: Falmer Press.

Dimmock, C. (2002). 'Cross-cultural differences in the understanding and conduct of research', in M. Coleman and A. Briggs (eds), *Researching in Educational Management and Leadership*, London: Paul Chapman Publishing.

Dimmock, C. (in press). 'Effective schooling in the Asia-Pacific region', in J. Keeves and R. Watanabe (eds), *The Handbook on Educational Research in the Asia-Pacific Region*, Dordrecht: Kluwer Academic.

Dimmock, C. and Walker, A. (2002). 'School leadership in context: societal and organisational cultures'. In T. Bush and L. Bell (eds), *Educational Management, Principles and Practice*, London: Paul Chapman Publishing.

Dimmock, C. and Walker, A. (in press). 'Connecting school leadership with teaching, learning and parenting in diverse cultural contexts: Western and Asian perspectives', in K. Leithwood and P. Hallinger (eds), *Second International Handbook of Educational Leadership and Administration*, Dordrecht: Kluwer Academic

Walker, A. and Dimmock, C. (eds) (2002). *Educational Administration and Leadership: The Cultural Context*, New York: Routledge Falmer.

Walker, A. and Dimmock, C. (in press). 'Moving school leadership beyond its narrow boundaries: developing a cross-cultural approach', in K. Leithwood and P. Hallinger (eds), *Second International Handbook of Educational Leadership and Administration*, Dordrecht: Kluwer Academic.

2

LEADERSHIP'S PLACE IN A COMMUNITY OF PRACTICE

Peter Gronn

INTRODUCTION

In this chapter, I hope to show that the idea of leadership, at least as it is conventionally understood, is in trouble. The reasoning behind this claim is that the construct 'leadership', and the closely associated and well-rehearsed constructs 'leader', 'follower' and 'followership' have ceased to provide adequate ways of representing the work activities of organisations. Typically, leadership commentators commit three grievous errors when they undertake organisational analyses. First, they tend to take for granted the presence of leadership in the work practices of various educational contexts. That is, the existence of leadership is assumed to be incontestable, and the only matters in dispute concern its texture, specifically the amount and the quality of leadership. Second, commentators also tend to assume that leadership will be manifest in a stylised, bifurcated relationship between two abstract categories of persons: i.e., a leader (although sometimes leaders) and her or his followers, into either of which categories an organisation's entire membership may be grouped. Sometimes, the membership composition of these categories may change – so that followers may occasionally display leadership and leaders become followers on some issues – but the commitment to the leader–follower binary is pretty much immutable. Third, and finally, leadership theorists also assume that among the various ingredients which might be invoked to account for organisational outcomes and achievements, leadership is more significant than any other factor. But why might this be? Why, for example, should leadership be paramount and not something else? And why, more importantly, is it that leadership finds its way into the explanatory equation in the first place?

These three assumptions underpin a view of leadership as a kind of organisational elixir. That is, similar to the way in which, for an alchemist, an elixir was a preparation for transforming metal into gold or, from the point of view of those who quested after the magic formula for immortality, a substance for the prolonging of life, for many people leadership has become the prescription for the cure of organisational ills. How often, for example, does one hear the bleating of critics of the government of the day that, 'The Prime Minister has to provide some leadership on this issue!' In this example, the shorthand symbol 'leadership' is intended to signal a number of things, such as the prime minister is not doing her or his job properly in the view of critics, or that the opponents of a government do not like the policies to which it is committed. The pervasiveness of this elixir view of leadership may be taken as evidence of the kind of mental maps which commentators typically bring to, and utilise for the construction of, leadership discourse. That is, 'leader', 'follower' and the like are abstract cognitive categories which observers impose on reality, procrustean-like, to account for what they believe they see or what they prefer to see. To construe the accomplishment of those actions which form part of organisational practice in terms of a leader–follower binary, however, is not merely to engage in a game of pinning labels on organisational members, but also to impose a crude cause and effect model on social reality. Thus, in the elixir view, causal agency is typically assumed to be the property of an individual, with the causal effects of the individual manifest in the changed behavioural responses of follower agents.

In the present discussion I shall let pass the question of whether 'leader' and 'follower' have really ever been helpful constructs. Instead, I shall argue that, whatever their previous utility, they have long since passed their use by date. Part of my reasoning will be that leadership, per the agency of leaders, is incorrectly positioned at the front or input end of the explanatory template normally used to account for the flow of action. That is, with very few exceptions, leaders are conventionally constructed as agents or triggers of initiation. A more helpful alternative starting point for understanding the place of leadership, I want to suggest, might be to begin the analysis and explanation at the opposite rear or back end. That is, a different approach would be to focus on the outcomes of workplace practices to be accounted for and then to comb back through the universe of explanatory possibilities, of which leadership may (or may not) turn out to be just one. This strategy is similar to what Kerr and Jermier (1978) originally proposed with their idea of substitutes for leadership, although, as they have more recently acknowledged (Jermier and Kerr, 1997), their proposal met with mostly muted enthusiasm from their fellow commentators. From the perspective of action outcomes, two alternative questions about the work of organisations which are likely to provide a much more accurate understanding of the place of leadership alongside other potential causal explanations are: for any period of time under review or consideration, what is the totality of the work that is to be performed by an organisation? Within that time frame, what does it take as part of an organisation's totality of work practices, to accomplish that body of work?

As a helpful means of answering these questions, I consider the merits of conceptualising workplaces in educational and non-educational settings as communities of practice. The idea of a 'community of practice' is a recent phenomenon. The recency of a concept or construct, of course, brings with it its own inherent difficulties. For one thing, the straightforward substitution of an existing set of well-rehearsed categories for framing reality with another which might be presumed to be superior leaves the latter open, potentially, to accusations of trendiness. Such a difficulty highlights the need for a carefully argued exposition outlining both the possibilities and potential pitfalls inherent in the preferred alternative. With this consideration in mind, the purpose of this chapter is to discuss the recent endorsement of the idea of a community of practice, with a view to its substitution for the ailing leader–follower binary. The discussion begins with a short explanation for the strength and endurance of the prevailing elixir view of leadership. This is followed by a review of some of the main problems and shortcomings associated with elixir assumptions. Finally, the chapter examines the claims of proponents of communities of practice and the consequences of this idea for a dramatically revised and scaled down view of leadership practice.

BEFORE AND AFTER THE FLOOD

The *Shorter Oxford Dictionary* devotes almost an entire three-column page of definitions and etymological detail to 'lead' and its various derivatives: 'leader', 'leading', etc. To 'follow the leader', for example, is said to date from 1863 and 'to give a lead', as when the front rider in a hunt leaps a fence, originated in 1859. The point of these and the numerous other examples cited in the dictionary is that they illustrate perfectly Calder's (1977, p. 181) point that leadership is a lay, everyday knowledge term, rather than a scientific construct. Precisely when words such as leader, follower, leadership and followership became part of common usage is impossible to be certain about. On the other hand, the uptake of such terms within the scholarly community, which were veneered as 'science' (Calder, 1977), increased dramatically during the twentieth century. Indeed, the amount of scholarly attention accorded leadership has been extraordinary. As an illustration, one need look no further than the third edition of *Bass and Stogdill's Handbook of Leadership* (Bass, 1990). Surprisingly, however, despite the 7,500 or so studies reviewed in that 1,200-page tome, the focus on the leadership of organisations, in the sense of organisations as a whole, as opposed to the parts of organisations, has been of fairly recent origin. A significant proportion of traditional leadership research, for example, was concerned with small group processes in natural and experimental groups.

There can be no doubt that the study of leadership in a whole-of-organisation sense really boomed during the last two decades of the second millennium. On this point the evidence of Rost's (1993) exhaustive review is incontestable: a sample of 312 books, chapters and journal articles written in the 1980s, along with an estimated 200 textbook chapters he did not manage to read, probably 50 other chapters and articles he missed, with allowance made for another 300 popular magazine articles and 200 unpublished papers. This is an output reflecting a burgeoning of interest which is 'staggering by any standard' (Rost, 1993, p. 10). Yet, things were not always so, for immediately before these fat years there had been a thin period in the late 1970s, when a cacophony of voices of 'calamity', as Hunt (1999, p. 134) termed them, were heard, including those of Calder (1977) and Kerr and Jermier (1978). So what happened to change things? The short answer is that, for US commentators (who constitute the significant, perhaps overwhelming, proportion of scholars in the leadership field), the US economy was seen to be languishing in increasingly competitive global markets and the main culprit for this disaster was the vast army of US organisation managers. The demonisation of the twentieth-century manager, whose rise and rise had been so ably depicted by James Burnham (1962; first published in 1942) in *The Managerial Revolution*, began with William H. Whyte's (1963; first published in 1956) *The Organization Man*. In his rather spirited polemic, Whyte had launched a scathing attack on the human relations movement in industry which, at the time of his writing in the 1950s was at its apotheosis, as legitimating a numbing social ethic of groupism that was corrosive of the traditional work ethic of entrepreneurialism. The aspirations of typical 'organisation man' managers were not to be rapacious, hard-driving buccaneer capitalists, but to be a faithful, conforming and earnest bureaucrats who hankered after the good life.

It was two decades after the publication of Whyte's book that Zaleznik (1977) again took up this theme. He crafted it with a very carefully chosen title, 'Managers and leaders: are they different?', thereby introducing another highly influential binary which, to this day, has been pervasive and, with a handful of exceptions, virtually unquestioned throughout leadership circles. The most highly publicised instance of this leader–manager dichotomy was Bennis and Nanus's (1985, p. 21, original italicised) slick marketing gimmickry: 'Managers are people who do things right and leaders are people who do the right thing.' A similar leader–manager dichotomy lay at the heart of Bass's (1985) distinction between leaders who were deemed to be transformational rather than transactional. In the most recent version of Bass's (1998) approach to leadership, the behaviour traditionally associated with managerialism, which formed part of transactional leadership (e.g., rewarding employees in exchange for effort and output, rather than seeking to motivate them by appealing to norms of exceptionalism), has now been incorporated into a full-range spectrum of leadership possibilities (Bass, 1998). This overall process of demonising management was driven by the insistence that US firms had to change. The scope of the change deemed necessary was root and branch transformation, rather than incrementalism, which meant that, given their apparently inherently conservative instincts, most managers were discursively positioned as thoroughly inadequate agents of change. It was in this kind of economic context that leadership was discursively constructed as qualitatively different from, and superior to, management. Those of us working in education, witnessed a similar kind of transposition and borrowing of this corporate sector reasoning. Thus, as part of the reform movement which swept the school sector during the late-1980s and 1990s, the role of principals was subjected to a visionary, transformational role reconstruction paralleling that of corporate chief executive officers (CEOs).

SPENT CATEGORIES

The obverse process of demonisation is canonisation. The canonisation of change-oriented leadership over the last two decades has drawn extensively for its justification on the historically robust archetypes of greatness and heroism (Gronn, 1995; Yukl, 1999). In retrospect, one of the key pressures on company management in the 1980s to shrug off its stuffy conformity came from return-hungry shareholders and investors. Entrusting a company's market fortunes to a high-profile change agent quickly came to be thought of as the surest guarantee of securing 'value-added' profitability. If recent writings on leadership are any guide, then commentators' confidence in both this particular paradigm and in the distinctiveness of leadership as a construct may well be beginning to wane (e.g., Lakomski, 1999). After his long and extensive experience as a consultant, Nicholls (2002), for example, has recently called for the abandonment of leadership as a behavioural category and its substitution by management. Nicholls' disillusionment rests partly on his claim that describing some of what managers do as 'leadership' merely serves to confuse an understanding of their actions. Why try to arbitrate between two words (leadership and management) when one will do? If it is deemed necessary to focus attention on the significance and prominence of the deeds of some managers as somehow adding value, so the argument runs, then why not simply refer to this phenomenon as 'high profile' management?

Nicholls' arguments aside, the inherent weakness of such shorthand categories as 'leader' and 'follower' is that they rest on a number of highly questionable assumptions. Part of the appeal of the words themselves is that they have become a convenient means of simplifying complex reality. In this sense, they are no different from the well-known media typecasting of public figures and celebrities into 'good' vs 'bad' and 'hero' vs 'villain' categories. The problem with this particular binary, however, is that it is not always clear who is doing the leading and who the following, nor in relation to what it is that each group can be said to be leading or following. And what if the membership of the categories changes, as foreshadowed at the beginning of the chapter? Of what use are the two terms then, if their meaning can be blurred by the possibility that leaders can become followers and followers leaders? As an alternative mode of representation, why not simply refer to various colleagues who behave differently in relation to particular events and issues from time to time? The confusion created by this blurred, dualistic reductionism is compounded by the presumption that particular role incumbents are worthy of either one or the other attribution according to where they are positioned on a hierarchy of role relations. How often, for example, is the leader–follower distinction overlaid on a superior–subordinate binary (notwithstanding the above discussion of demonised managers), so that it becomes taken for granted that senior managerial role incumbents automatically do the leading while everyone else does the following? No doubt this pattern of usage accounts for the recent currency accorded the expectation that senior position-holders will, by definition, perform 'leadership roles'.

These difficulties could be multiplied. The point about them as illustrations, however, is that they are clumsy and crude ways of depicting the performance of organisational work. In short, they are an inadequate means of describing a division of labour because they presume the form that a division takes rather than being able to demonstrate its form. My point is similar to that made by Brown and Duguid (1991, p. 41) in relation to canonical and non-canonical ways of understanding work practices. Canonical (or prescriptive) ways of representing how work gets done rely on formal job descriptions, 'despite the fact that daily evidence points to the contrary'. Non-canonical practices, on the other hand, refer to the reality of work improvisation and what it takes to get a body of work done. The force of this distinction equates to the difference between what organisations espouse about themselves and what they actually do. Moreover, such a distinction matters in a whole host of ways. Careful analyses of workplace divisions of labour, for example, are important in yielding accurate understandings of job demands, job designs and job redesign, and in particular the articulation of work and workplace infrastructure (Star, 1999). A central concern of research into the division of labour will always be the simultaneous processes of work visibilisation and invisibilisation. That is, changing modes of work articulation will bring a variety of new occupational needs and roles to the surface, while at the same time suppressing or containing others by expanding the duties captured by existing categories (e.g., by 'add-ons'). Both positive and negative consequences ensue from either the surfacing or suppressing of work. A good example of the latter is what I have referred to elsewhere as 'designer-leadership' (Gronn, 2003) in which, as a result of the adoption of national standards-based designs for accrediting school leaders, growing accountability expectations of school principals and senior teachers to perform as 'super leaders', coupled with the reality of work intensification associated with their dramatically expanded roles, are fuelling a culture of disengagement from leadership among teachers.

WHAT IS A COMMUNITY OF PRACTICE?

'Community of practice' is one of a number of current vogue terms for designating lateral, semi-informal, quasi-autonomous work formations. Other popular formations include hot groups, networks, cells, project teams, self-managing and self-leading work teams. A common feature of each of these formations is their de-emphasis on hierarchy. Far from suggesting a jettisoning of control and co-ordination, however, this apparent 'hands-off' dimension reflects a renewed awareness of workplace interdependence and the way in which work is a conjoint, rather than an a merely aggregated, accomplishment. This emphasis is particularly evident in the writings of Wenger (1999, p. 45), a prominent advocate of the idea of a community of practice, when he notes that 'collective learning results in practices that reflect both the pursuit of our enterprises and attendant social relations' and that these practices are 'the property of a kind of community created over time by the sustained pursuit of a shared enterprise'.

This recent resurgence of awareness of lateral work formations is part of the growing significance attached to the theme of organisational intelligence. Implicit in Wenger's point about collective learning, for example, is a recognition of the inherently dispersed, tacit nature of much workplace knowledge (Orlikowski, 2002). There is also a parallel awareness among commentators of the significant potential for a loss of collective memory through the downsizing of middle managers (Grey, 1999), and a willingness to tolerate new synergies (Goold and Campbell, 1998) in the pursuit of enhanced competitive capabilities (Loasby, 1998). No doubt these developments have arisen partly as a response to some of the unintended consequences of workplace reform. The renewed emphasis on laterality also reflects how organisations are attempting to grapple with the problem of employee homelessness. That is, if the kinds of traditional workplace groupings associated with allegedly outmoded practices (e.g., bounded divisions, departments, branches, unions) have suddenly been de-legitimated after all of the recent restructuring and de-layering of organisations, the introduction of fluid processes and the flexibilisation

of work, then where is 'home'? This theme of home also lay at the heart
of Whyte's (1963) discussion in *The Organization Man* where he
highlighted the way in which the disciples of human relations in industry
sought to engineer a sense of 'belongingness' and 'togetherness' in a
workforce. From the perspective of 'home', there can be few more enduring
and powerful symbols of connectedness, membership and anchorage than
'community'. As a vehicle for integrating a workforce, imbuing it with a
sense of overriding common purpose, instilling in it a collective sense of
identity and providing it with a means of personal self-enhancement, the
idea of a community of practice has a strong discursive appeal among
managers and workplace reformers.

This potential has been acknowledged in a recent consultant's report to
the Australian National Training Authority which, while it recognises
some of the inherent limitations of communities of practice, nevertheless
promotes them as previously 'hidden [i.e., invisible] assets' in contributing
to 'the ongoing construction of a multi-dimensional national training
system', particularly within the vocational and educational training (VET)
sector (Mitchell, 2002, p. 97). This kind of endorsement tinged with
wariness is understandable, for there are problems with the notion of a
community of practice. One is that a community of practice does not have
an exclusive claim on the allegiance of its members. Most employees have
at least dual points of reference: they are members of both a community
(or communities) of practice as well as occupational communities.
Socialisation through recruitment and training into the norms, values,
skills and vocabularies of an occupational community (e.g., plumbing,
accountancy, teaching) is an equally important source of individual and
collective identification and membership (Van Maanen and Barley, 1984).
For employees, therefore, there exist potentially rival communities of
interest, a point which is sometimes lost on advocates of communities of
practice. In their discussion of the attainment of mastery through
apprenticeship in situated learning contexts, for example, Lave and
Wenger (1991, p. 95) seem to conflate these different senses of community
in their use of 'the enterprise' as the locale for apprentices' learning.
Another problem is that the unbounded fluidity of communities of
practice can prove both a strength and a weakness. What counts as a
community as opposed to a network configuration? It is claimed, for
example, that communities are emergent and self-organising, that their
members often self-select spontaneously, that community membership
fluctuates and invariably sprawls across formal organisational units (and
even entire organisations), and that in some cases the links between
community members may be entirely virtual (Mitchell, Wood and Young,
2001; Wenger and Snyder, 2000). Such attributes raise questions about the
strength of unity, shared history and identity between community
members, as well as questions about their entitive status, from the point
of view of communities of practice as units of analysis.

LEADING COMMUNITIES AND THE ACCOMPLISHMENT OF WORK

This recent recognition accorded the significance of non-canonical patterns of work, or the 'road conditions' rather than 'the map', as Brown and Duguid (1991, p. 41) term it, may amount to nothing more than a formalisation of previously hidden (or invisible) informal work practices. Recognition of the informal side of organisational life forms part of a long and venerable tradition in organisation theory extending as far back as Barnard (1982; first published in 1938, p. 115) who, while acknowledging them as 'indefinite and rather structureless', saw that without informal relations – contacts, habits of action, interactions, groupings etc. – there could be no formal organisation, no legitimation of authority and no effective system of communication.

Unlike Barnard, however, for whom the leadership of organisations was a purely executive function, institutionalised through an implicit hierarchical contract entailing assent of the lower ranks to their co-operative engagement (secured through an economy of incentives and inducements) with morally purposeful activities as determined by their superiors, the leadership of communities of practice is much more spontaneous, fleeting and evanescent. Here, the visibilisation of leadership in informal sets of relations comprises a diversity of emergent, fluctuating roles. In one of the few explicit statements about leadership by community of practice proponents, Wenger (2000, p. 231) suggests that:

> Communities of practice depend on internal leadership, and enabling leaders to play their role is a way to help the community develop. The role of 'community co-ordinator' who takes care of the day-to-day work is crucial, but a community needs multiple forms of leadership: thought leaders, networkers, people who document the practice, pioneers, etc. These forms of leadership may be concentrated on one or two members or widely distributed and will change over time.

This passage attempts to provide a non-reified view of leadership, in the sense that it disavows the kind of direction-setting influence normally associated with formally defined organisational roles (Rost, 1993, p. 79). While allowing for the possibility of leadership being focused on just one or two individuals, it is mainly a distributed view in that it also conceives of leadership as encompassing a diversity of forms of behaviour, numerous people and constantly changing requirements.

Clearly, the potential for reification when theorising communities of practices is a headache for their proponents. Yet, avoidance or minimisation of discursive rigidities and shorthand abstractions is one thing for, as communities of practice prove to be successful (i.e., as they achieve their self-proclaimed goals of mutual engagement, and sustained, productive and useful social learning), their members and their managers have to confront the issue of whether to capitalise on that improvised success. (After all, the whole idea of 'leveraging', as it has become known, takes for granted such an imperative in which improvisation, inventiveness and serendipity attain a more permanent official status by first being identified and then woven into the existing stock of overall capabilities in order to bolster market competitiveness.) Reification of practices through their institutionalisation opens up a whole terrain of issues associated with organisational design, work visibilisation and invisibilisation. An important dilemma with informal sets of working arrangements, as Star (1999, p. 386) notes in a study of nurses' work practices, is whether to live and let live or to reveal them. 'Leave the work tacit, and it fades into the wallpaper (in one respondent's words, "we are thrown in with the price of the room")', whereas 'make it explicit, and it will become a target for hospital cost accounting'. The irony is not lost on Wenger (1999, pp. 261–62), for example, who, in an attempt to resist the commodification of learning and its institutional solidification wrestles with what he sees as the trade-off between privileging particular forms of localised knowlegeability and their incorporation into organisational features, and a potential loss of engagement and imagination through formalisation.

Leaving to one side for the moment any caveats concerning the adequacy with which these theorists have addressed the tensions between organisational design and emergence, community of practice theory has some important implications for leadership. First, the focus of theorists on informal practices exposes the extent to which conventional dyadic leadership discourse, with its fixed leader–follower dichotomy, renders actual work practices invisible. One of the virtues of community of practice studies, unlike many leadership commentaries, is that (through detailed ethnographies of work) they are in tune with, and tracking changes in, the division of labour. Second, this brief review of work on communities of practice has been sufficient to highlight the reciprocal and negotiated character of the exchanges through which work colleagues accomplish their joint endeavours. This pattern stands in bold contrast to that body of leadership commentary which champions the deeds of high-profile, heroic figures in which the influence flows are either presumed to be one-way (i.e., from leader to follower) or are significantly undertheorised (Yukl, 1999, p. 287). On the other hand, while it allows for the possibility of distributed, as opposed to focused, leadership practice, community of practice research by no means exhausts the range of distributed leadership alternatives. It tends be restricted to what I have termed elsewhere (Gronn, 2002) multiple leadership behaviour, or the aggregated influence of plural individual leaders, as opposed to concertively performed actions in which couples and threesomes, for example, strive to achieve conjointly defined ends through intuitive working partnerships. Third, and finally, with its emphasis on collaborative learning, and knowledge generation and utilisation, community of practice research suggests that community members share co-equal work status as co-learners while performing a variety of changing informal roles. If so, then while this fluidity need not negate the periodic need for emergent and transient patterns of leadership, it does call into question the entire validity of followership. That is, if work communities facilitate the potential exercise of influence by all of their members, however briefly, then 'colleague' would appear to be a far more appropriate category for capturing this possibility than 'follower'.

CONCLUSION

In this chapter I have considered some recent developments in studies of communities of practice and their implications for current understandings of leadership. Methodologically, the main thrust of this area of academic endeavour has been to substitute understanding of 'community' for 'organisation' as the principal unit of analysis and, theoretically, to foreground the analysis of work practices as participatory learning systems. These strategies have positioned this work within the antecedent traditions of research into autonomous work group formations, informal organisation and workplace ethnographies. The epistemological significance of this broad line of inquiry has been its capacity to document changes in the division of labour, with the implication that emergent role relations in communities of practice render existing leadership constructs problematic.

The prevailing leader-centric, elixir orthodoxy of the field of leadership studies has been under challenge for some time. The reception accorded some of this new thinking has not always been one of unalloyed joy. In response to a number of recent attacks on leader-centrism, Shamir (1999, p. 51), for instance, has resisted alternative understandings such as distributed leadership, and the substitution of mutuality and reciprocity for 'leader' and 'follower', as discussed in this chapter and in recent theoretical revisions. 'Mutual and reciprocal influence processes,' Shamir suggests, 'do not necessarily imply symmetric processes.' For this reason, 'leadership' remains an appropriate way in which to characterise asymmetrical influence processes and situations in which individuals exercise preponderant or disproportionate levels of influence. Maybe so, but one obvious problem with this line of defence, apart from the various difficulties identified throughout the chapter, is that while it might help sustain a case for retaining the category of 'leadership', it does not provide a robust default argument for the residual construct of 'follower.' Another larger problem, of course, is that Shamir's argument begs the whole question of why it is, if leadership reduces to a form of influence, that commentators do not simply construct and represent workplace and organisational relations in terms of levels and patterns of influence, and leave matters at that. On the other hand, that is not just a problem for Shamir, but for the entire scholarly leadership community, and it is also the subject of another, future chapter.

REFERENCES

Barnard, C.I. (1982) *The Functions of the Executive*, Cambridge, MA: Harvard University Press.

Bass, B.M. (1985) *Leadership and Performance Beyond Expectations*, New York: Free Press.

Bass, B.M. (1990) *Bass and Stogdill's Handbook of Leadership: Theory, Research and Managerial Applications*, 3rd edn, New York: Free Press.

Bass, B.M. (1998) *Transformational Leadership: Industrial, Military, and Educational Impact*, Mahwah, NJ: Lawrence Erlbaum Associates.

Bennis, W. and Nanus, B. (1985) *Leaders*, New York: Harper and Row.

Brown, J.S. and Duguid, P. (1991) 'Organizational learning and communities-of-practice: toward a unified view of working, learning and innovation', *Organization Science*, **2**(1), 40–57.

Burnham, J. (1962) *The Managerial Revolution*, Harmondsworth: Penguin.

Calder, B.J. (1977) 'An attribution theory of leadership', in B.M. Staw and G.R. Salancik (eds), *New Directions in Organizational Behavior*, Chicago, IL: St. Clair, pp. 179–204.

Goold, M. and Campbell, A. (1998) 'Desperately seeking synergy', *Harvard Business Review*, **76**(5), 131–43.

Grey, C. (1999) ' "We are all managers now"; "we always were": On the development and demise of management', *Journal of Management Studies*, **36**(5), 561–85.

Gronn, P. (1995) 'Greatness re-visited: the current obsession with transformational leadership', *Leading & Managing*, **1**(1), 13–27.

Gronn, P. (2003) *The New Work of Educational Leaders: Changing Leadership Practice in an Era of School Reform*, London: Paul Chapman Publishing.

Hunt, J.G. (1999) 'Transformational/charismatic leadership's transformation of the field: an historical essay, *Leadership Quarterly*, **10**(2), 129–44.

Jermier, J. and Kerr, S. (1997) ' "Substitutes for leadership: their meaning and measurement": contextual recollections and current observations', *Leadership Quarterly*, **8**(1), 95–101.

Kerr, S. and Jermier, J. (1978) 'Substitutes for leadership: their meaning and measurement, *Organization and Human Performance*, **22**, 374–403.

Lakomski, G. (1999) 'Against leadership: a concept without a cause', in P.T. Begley and P.E. Leonard (eds), *The Values of Educational Administration*, London: Falmer Press, pp. 36–50.

Lave, J. and Wenger, E. (1991) *Situated Learning: Legitimate Peripheral Participation*, Cambridge: Cambridge University Press.

Loasby, B.J. (1998) 'The concept of capabilities', in N.J. Foss and B.J. Loasby (eds), *Economic Organization, Capabilities and Co-ordination: Essays in Honour of G.B. Richardson*, London: Routledge, pp. 163–82.

Mitchell, J. (2002) *The Potential for Communities of Practice to Underpin the*

National Training Framework, Melbourne: Australian National Training Authority.

Mitchell, J., Wood, S. and Young, S. (2001) *Communities of Practice: Reshaping Professional Practice and Improving Organisational Productivity in the Vocational Education and Training (VET) Sector: Resources for Practitioners*, Melbourne: Australian National Training Authority.

Nicholls, J. (2002) 'Escape the leadership jungle: try high-profile management', *Journal of General Management*, **27**(3), 14–35.

Orlikowski, W.J. (2002) 'Knowing in practice: enacting a collective capability in distributed organizing', *Organization Science*, **13**(3), 249–73.

Rost, J.C. (1993) *Leadership for the Twenty-first Century*, Westport, CT: Praeger.

Shamir, B. (1999) 'Leadership in boundaryless organizations: disposable or indispensable?', *European Journal of Work and Organizational Psychology*, **8**(1), pp. 49–71.

Star, S.L. (1999) 'The ethnography of infrastructure, *American Behavioral Scientist*, **43**(3), 377–91.

Van Maanen, J. and Barley, S. (1984) 'Occupational communities: culture and control in organizations', in B.M. Staw and L.L. Cummings (eds), *Research in Organizational Behavior*, vol. 6, Greenwich, CT: JAI Press, pp. 287–365.

Wenger, E. (1999) *Communities of Practice: Learning, Meaning, and Identity*, Cambridge: Cambridge University Press.

Wenger, E. (2000) 'Communities of practice and social learning systems', *Organization*, **7**(2), 225–46.

Wenger, E. and Snyder, W. (2000) 'Communities of practice: the organisational frontier', *Harvard Business Review*, **78**(1), 139–45.

Whyte, W. H. (1963) The Organization Man, Harmondsworth: Penguin.

Yukl, G. (1999) 'An evaluation of conceptual weaknesses in transformational and charismatic leadership theories', *Leadership Quarterly*, **10**(2), 285–305.

Zaleznik, A. (1977) 'Managers and leaders: are they different?', *Harvard Business Review*, **55**(3), 67–78.

FURTHER READING

Gronn, P. (1995) 'Greatness re-visited: the current obsession with transformational leadership', *Leading and Managing*, **1**(1), 13–27.

Gronn, P. (1999) *The Making of Educational Leaders*, London: Cassell.

Gronn, P. (2000) 'Distributed properties: a new architecture for leadership', *Educational Management and Administration*, **28**(3), 317–38.

Gronn, P. (2003) *The New Work of Educational Leaders: Changing Leadership Practice in an Era of School Reform*, London: Paul Chapman Publishing.

3

GENDER IN EDUCATIONAL LEADERSHIP

Marianne Coleman

INTRODUCTION

Most leadership positions in education and elsewhere are held by men. Although the proportion of women managers and leaders is gradually increasing (DfEE, 2000), there has been no radical change in England and Wales as a result of the equal opportunities legislation of the late twentieth century. In most countries, Western, developed and developing, men are more likely to be leaders in education and elsewhere (Coleman, 2002; Davies, 1998). Gender proportions are more balanced in a few countries where particular circumstances such as affirmative action apply or have applied, but the underlying gender–power relationships still tend to prevail. Blackmore (1994; 1999) claims that in Australia where affirmative action was tried, the increase in the number of women principals was accompanied by a change in the locus of power to a higher level of administration dominated by men, a situation she compares to that of Israel where the majority of secondary principals are women but where power has tended to shift out of the school towards the male-dominated ranks of senior local administrators (Goldring and Chen, 1994). Affirmative action policies to promote women are now being used in Africa, for example, in South Africa and Zimbabwe, but numbers of women in leadership in education remain very low (Kotecha, 1994). In countries where there is a tradition of domestic help, such as Singapore (Morriss, Coleman and Low, 1999), the proportion of women reaching management positions is relatively high. However, it is doubtful that traditional gender–power relations are breaking down. Even where help at home may be available and where there is wide provision of nurseries, as in China, women are seldom regarded as suitable for a leadership role (Coleman, Quiang and Li, 1998).

Outside education, the difficulties of women in breaking through the glass ceiling are well documented (for example, Davidson and Cooper,

1992). In the UK, a national management survey in 1998 indicated that only 3.6 per cent of all directors were women (Vinnicombe, 2000). Sinclair (1998) reports that around 10 per cent of director positions among the largest 500 companies in the USA are held by women but that this is only true for 2.7 per cent of the directors of the top 596 Australian companies. In respect of gender and leadership it would therefore appear that despite equal opportunities legislation and a general awareness of concepts such as the glass ceiling, the chances of women obtaining leadership positions continue to be considerably less than those of their male peers.

The disproportionate dominance of leadership positions by men provides the context for this chapter which considers gender in relation to leadership and management theory and practice, rather than specifically focusing on issues of equal opportunities. Leadership tends to be defined as a male characteristic (Schein, 1994) although current views on leadership in education and elsewhere (Kouzes and Posner, 1990; Leithwood, Jantzi and Steinbach, 1999) favour a style that is far removed from stereotypical masculine leadership and has more in common with styles that could be termed feminine. The stereotypical masculine style is relatively authoritarian and 'heroic', while the feminine equivalent is seen as nurturing and collaborative. This chapter considers the 'maleness' of leadership and reviews the feminine and masculine stereotypes in the context of current models of leadership. The question of whether men and women do tend to operate as leaders in distinctly different ways and the impact of gender on being an educational leader are also considered.

THE LEADER IS MALE

Leadership is a very 'gendered' concept. In a wide variety of cultural contexts, leadership continues to be identified with the male. Even though women occupy positions of leadership and responsibility, there is a tendency to assume that the 'rightful' leader is male. Schmuck (1996, p. 356) sums this up in relation to women superintendents and high school principals in the USA, who could be considered as 'insiders' since they have designated senior status, but remain 'outsiders' as women leaders. For example, on a mundane level, women headteachers report that they are commonly taken to be the secretary by parents visiting the school or that, if accompanied by their male deputy to a meeting, he is assumed to be the head and she the deputy (Coleman, 2002). These are commonplace misunderstandings which are brushed aside by the women who mentioned them, but they still have to be regularly overcome and are indicative of an underlying assumption that the leader is male and that women as leaders are 'outsiders'. Research undertaken by Schein (1973, 1994) has consistently shown that the qualities that are identified as those of a leader or manager are also the qualities that are quite independently assessed by both men and women as being those of men. Our unthinking identification of maleness with leadership has a counterpoint which is an equally unthinking reduction of women and 'women's work' to a lesser status: 'Even if sexism was eliminated and both sexes participated fully, the patriarchal nature of structures and value systems would still ensure that men and women were placed in unequal positions of power, and that female activity was defined as marginal and of lesser significance than male experience' (Usher, 1996, p. 124).

The identification of leadership with men is deeply ingrained in our understanding of society and the family (Sinclair, 1998) and this continues even though considerable changes have been taking place in terms of work participation. For example, 69 per cent of women of working age in the UK were working in paid employment in 1999 in comparison with 47 per cent in 1959 (ONS, 2001). However, there is still an automatic association of women with the domestic and private sphere and with roles associated with support and nurturing, and an association of men with work in the public sphere.

'FEMININE' AND 'MASCULINE' STYLES

There is an element of duality in many management and leadership theories. Two seminal models illustrate this: the first conceptualises the options open to managers in terms of decision-making, ranging from the authoritarian to the consultative (Tannenbaum and Schmidt, 1973); the second identifies the extent to which a manager or leader may be either task oriented or people oriented (Blake and Mouton, 1964). These two basic models can be related to the diametrically opposed ideal types of feminine and masculine leadership styles. The masculine stereotype is authoritarian and target oriented while the feminine stereotype is collaborative and people oriented.

One of the best known identifications of masculine and feminine characteristics is that of Bem (1974) whose juxtaposed lists illustrate the feminine and masculine stereotypes in some detail. A briefer but similar range of masculine and feminine qualities has been used by Gray (1993) in his work in the training of female and male headteachers. The qualities are presented as gender paradigms (Table 3.1), and have been used by him to open up discussion about gender and self-awareness among head-teachers as leaders.

Just as in the Tannenbaum and Schmidt and Blake and Mouton models there is room for a range of behaviours between the extremes, so a model identifying polar opposites of gender-related characteristics provides the potential for a range of behaviours incorporating elements of both masculine and feminine styles. Before discussing this further, current ideals of leadership in education and their relevance to the feminine and masculine stereotypes will be considered.

Table 3.1 Gender paradigms

The nurturing/feminine paradigm	The defensive/aggressive masculine paradigm
Caring	Highly regulated
Creative	Conformist
Intuitive	Normative
Aware of individual differences	Competitive
Non-competitive	Evaluative
Tolerant	Disciplined
Subjective	Objective
Informal	Formal

Source: (Gray (1993, p. 111)

CONCEPTUALISATIONS OF LEADERSHIP IN EDUCATION

One of the most influential conceptualisations of approaches to leadership is that of Leithwood, Jantzi and Steinbach (1999, pp. 8–20) who drew on a review of American and UK educational administration journals to identify six major categories of leadership models:

- instructional
- moral
- participative
- managerial
- contingent
- transformational.

The instructional style is one which focuses on student learning. Moral leadership encompasses the ideas that there are particular duties incumbent on those who have care for the young and that values should predominate in matters of leadership. In addition, moral leadership is often identified with the development of democracy. Participative leadership focuses on shared decision-making. Managerial leadership can be identified with managerialism and the rather 'cold' achievement of targets, while contingent leadership means that the leader adapts his or her style to the particular demands of their context. Of these styles, it is transformational leadership that Leithwood, Jantzi and Steinbach (1999. p. 21) identity as being the one most likely to: 'offer a comprehensive approach to leadership that will help those in, and served by, current and future schools respond productively to the significant challenges facing them'.

The concept of transformational leadership is sometimes defined as being diametrically opposed to transactional leadership (Burns, 1978).

Transactional leadership is a contractual relationship between the leader and followers, where 'the leader rewards or disciplines the follower depending on the adequacy of the follower's performance' (Bass and Avolio, 1994, p. 4). In contrast, transformational leadership, which, as a predominant style of leadership, can be used in combination with transactional leadership (Bass and Avolio, 1994), is thought to bring about superior results by the use of what is termed the four Is:

1 Idealised influence – the leader models behaviour and acts as a role model.
2 Inspirational motivation.
3 Intellectual stimulation.
4 Individualised consideration – the leader encourages the development of each person and acts as a coach or mentor.

In relation to the contrasting transformational and transactional styles it is also possible to identify that there is one that aligns more obviously with masculine and one with feminine stereotypes of leadership. The feminine paradigm of nurturing and individual consideration is clearly more allied to transformational leadership (Rosener, 1990), and the masculine paradigm of regulation and formality is more aligned to transactional leadership and to the managerial (Leithwood, Jantzi and Steinbach, 1999) or managerialist style (Collinson and Hearn, 2000).

There is a positive stereotype of women that identifies them as nurturing, caring and people orientated (Noddings, 1984). At a time when emotional intelligence is being recognised as an essential component of leadership and management (Goleman, 1996), women may be seen to have the advantage in terms of management style. The identification of transformational leadership as essentially based on relationships (Burns, 1978) would also seem to favour the style of women. In fact it is now possible to build a whole body of theory and evidence to establish a counter-claim about leadership; that women are actually more suited for leadership than men.

WOMEN MANAGE DIFFERENTLY

In an attempt to remedy the neglect of gender in leadership (Hall, 1997), much of the empirical work on women in educational leadership and management considers women separately from men, and documents what appear to be a number of dominant characteristics in the management and leadership style of women.

1 A collaborative style coupled with an empowering attitude and preference for teamwork (Adler, Laney and Packer, 1993; Blackmore, 1989; Coleman, 1996a; Hall, 1996; Jirasinghe and Lyons, 1996). This style would certainly equate to the participative model and elements of the

transformational model of Leithwood, Jantzi and Steinbach, (1999).

2   An emphasis on communications (Schick-Case, 1994; Shakeshaft, 1989). Again this could be seen to relate to both the transformational and participative models.

3   The importance of educational or instructional leadership (Coleman, 1996a; Grogan, 1996; Gross and Trask, 1976; Hill and Ragland, 1995; Shakeshaft, 1989). Empirical work indicates that women are strongly identified with this particular model identified by Leithwood, Jantzi and Steinbach, (1999).

Some of the trends are interrelated, for example a collaborative style of management may be linked to a particular attitude to power and the likelihood of having good communication skills. This interrelationship is exemplified by the research findings of Shakeshaft who claims that the effectiveness of women as leaders has much to do with their socialisation as women:

> I also believe that it is socialisation that accounts for women's greater ability to provide an environment that is empowering for teachers. Because women have been taught to pay attention to relationships, to be polite, to give technical and specific feedback, and to use power with rather than power over, they are more likely to use language that helps achieve these ends.

(Shakeshaft, 1989, p. 21)

As is evident from this quotation, research that has concentrated on the leadership style of women does tend towards the conclusion that women are better educational leaders than their male colleagues. The evidence seems to show that they are likely to have styles that are normatively considered superior: participative, instructional and transformational. Very little work has been done specifically on men as leaders, (Collinson and Hearn, 2000; Mac an Ghaill, 1994) but the main stereotype attached to them is of being managerial, a relatively negative concept in comparison with the leadership qualities more often associated with women leaders.

WOMEN DO NOT MANAGE DIFFERENTLY

Alongside the evidence that indicates differences between the ways that men and women manage, there are findings that seem to indicate there is no difference. There are a range of studies in general management that show: 'that few actual gender differences in personal factors and behaviour have been consistently and empirically confirmed' (Vinkenburg, Jansen and Koopman, 2000, p. 130). However, the authors do concede that this may be due to both men and women aspiring to the accepted 'prototype' of manager and that the evaluation of women as managers is biased by social expectations that mean that the identical behaviour of men and women managers may be judged differently. In education, research with 98 heads in the Netherlands, although showing some distinct gender differences, found that there was no difference in the decision-making styles of the female and male heads: 'women seemed to include others in decision-making processes as much as men and used relatively democratic styles' (Kruger, 1996, p. 453).

The findings of Jirasinghe and Lyons (1996) are that male and female headteachers may be more like each other in style than like managers outside education. In particular, both men and women headteachers may be fairly directive while also maintaining a consultative mode. My own research on the self-perceptions of men and women headteachers (Coleman, 2002) shows that most of both sexes believe that they are operating in consultative and people-oriented ways and that neither correspond to their gender stereotypes. When asked to describe their style in three adjectives there was little difference between the men and the women. Their wide choice of words was analysed into the five groupings indicated in Table 3.2.

Although there was little difference, the women tended to be more likely to choose words relating to people than the men, something that is in keeping with both existing stereotypes and empirical findings. However, in contrast the women were also more likely to choose words that can be defined as 'autocratic'. For example a woman head styled herself: 'bloody-minded, belligerent and aggressive'. The men were slightly more likely to choose words that are related to collaboration, efficiency and values. Collaboration is more often associated with women and feminine management styles, although efficiency would be identified with the managerial stance more closely associated with masculinity. However, the single most popular group of words indicating a style of management for both men and women was the one I termed collaborative. The potentially overlapping 'people-oriented' style of management was also strongly

Table 3.2 Styles of management identified by choice of adjectives

	Women		Men	
	No. of words	*% of total*	*No. of words*	*% of total*
Collaborative	458	38.5	401	40.0
People oriented	283	23.8	212	21.3
Autocratic/directive	177	14.9	119	11.9
Efficient	139	11.6	126	12.7
Values	132	11.1	138	13.9

Source: Coleman (2002)

indicated by the choice of adjectives that could be grouped within that theme. Judging from these two broad categories, there is a clear indication of a favoured style of management for both men and women, which is similar for both and which aligns more with the participative and possibly even the transformational styles of Leithwood, Jantzi and Steinbach, (1999).

This finding was corroborated elsewhere in the survey, since when choosing the ideal type adjectives of Gray (1993) quoted above, most of the male and female headteachers in my survey saw themselves as operating in a way that is more like the feminine stereotype. The styles most often chosen do not conform to the gender stereotypes and show very little difference between the self-concepts of the male and female headteachers (Tables 3.3 and 3.4). The actual qualities identified by more than 50 per cent of the men and the women are the same, with relatively small differences between the sexes. Even where the difference between women and men is in the region of 10 per cent, as with 'tolerant' identified by 68.7 per cent of the women and 79.6 per cent of the men, this seems to be tempered by another concept, e.g., 'aware of individual differences' which was identified by 86.0 per cent of the women and just slightly less of the men.

Research undertaken by Evetts with 10 female and 10 male heads led to the conclusion that leadership and management behaviour were not necessarily gender based:

> some of the male heads emphasised collegial relations and participatory forms of management in schools while some of the female heads were inclined towards hierarchy and authority in management.

Table 3.3 Qualities identified by 50 per cent or more of the women headteachers

		%
Aware of individual differences	(f)	86.0
Caring	(f)	79.4
Intuitive	(f)	76.2
Tolerant	(f)	68.7
Creative	(f)	63.0
Evaluative	(m)	61.1
Disciplined	(m)	60.4
Informal	(f)	59.4
Competitive	(m)	50.6
Objective	(m)	50.6

Note: (f) = feminine (m) = masculine
Source: Coleman (2002)

Table 3.4 Qualities identified by 50 per cent or more of the men headteachers

		%
Caring	(f)	84.2
Aware of individual differences	(f)	84.0
Tolerant	(f)	79.6
Evaluative	(m)	70.0
Intuitive	(f)	66.0
Objective	(m)	61.7
Informal	(f)	60.4
Competitive	(m)	57.3
Creative	(f)	54.1
Disciplined	(m)	51.0

Note: (f) = feminine (m) = masculine
Source: Coleman (2002)

> Significant differences in styles of leadership are not difficult to demonstrate in general ... although the clear linkage of style with gender is more problematic.
>
> (Evetts, 1994, p. 88)

However, Evetts does agree that: 'it is not difficult to show gender differences in the *experience* of headship' (ibid., p. 89 original italics). While a range of styles may be expected from both men and women, there is agreement that the perceptions of the ways in which men and women operate may be different and that the social experience of being a leader is different for men and women. In addition, self-reported findings such as those reported in Tables 3.3 and 3.4, are limited in their validity, and an alternative research approach, for example observation and in-depth interviews (see Hall, 1996) may reveal more grounded insights into the ways in which women and men actually manage and lead.

A RANGE OF STYLES

Models provide useful analytical tools, but it is not expected that individuals will fit any one model exactly. This applies to the six Leithwood models and also to the feminine and masculine stereotypes. It has already been shown in Tables 3.3 and 3.4 that self-reported characteristics of male and female headteachers indicate a range of feminine and masculine leadership characteristics for both. Use of the Bem scale showed that some individuals score high on both masculine and feminine characteristics leading them to be termed androgynous leaders:

The concept of psychological androgyny implies that it is possible for an individual to be both assertive and compassionate, both instrumental and expressive, both masculine and feminine, depending upon the situational appropriateness of these various modalities; and it further implies that an individual may even blend these complementary modalities in a single act, being able, for example, to fire an employee if the circumstances warrant it but with sensitivity for the human emotion that such an act inevitably produces.

(Bem, 1977, p. 196)

Those rated as androgynous, i.e., scoring higher on both masculine and feminine ratings, showed greater independence, ability to nurture and self-esteem than those who scored low on both. Ferrario reports that such 'androgynous' individuals: 'are able to respond more effectively than either masculine or feminine individuals to a wide variety of situations' (Ferrario, 1994, p. 116).

It would be unduly deterministic to hold to an idea that all men operate in a certain way and all women in another. Women and men cannot be regarded as two coherent groups that lead and manage in different ways:

As our understanding of gender issues has developed, we have moved from considering men and women as two great, opposed sexual blocks to realising that differences within each sex are much greater than those between the sexes and that a simple view that all men or all women fall into one category of behaviour is quite false.

(Gray, 1993, p. 107)

Gold (1996, p. 422) points out that profiles of management style linked to men and women are unhelpful, since they make no allowance: 'for any notion that some men manage sensitively and some women manage in a dominating and authoritarian fashion'. However, 'what is not disputable is that organizational and leadership theory neglects the significance of gender' (Blackmore, 1989, p. 104).

THE IMPACT OF GENDER ON THE PRACTICE OF LEADERSHIP IN EDUCATION

We can accept on a rational level that men and women are equally equipped to manage and lead. However, as indicated at the start of the chapter, stereotypes prevail throughout societies that link males with leadership and women with supportive and subordinate roles. Even a recognition that the more 'feminine' models of transformational and participative leadership are normatively best to meet the challenges for leaders in education does not mean that women are more readily seen as suitable leaders. One interpretation of the espousal of a more transformational model on the part of men is that they are recognising the benefits and popularity of the more feminine style and annexing it in order to maintain their pre-eminence as leaders. Another may be that education as an environment is one which predisposes its leaders, both male and female, towards a more democratic and participative style. Blackmore (1999, p. 207) claims that: 'Women's stated preferences for more democratic styles of management and collegiality are discursively produced practices arising from being located in a particular array of communities' (work, home, community) practices and discourses. Education is a community of practice located in a feminised and highly gender-segmented occupation centred around children . . .'.

Despite this context, there is an awareness on the part of women leaders in education of how being a woman impinges on their leadership (Blackmore, 1994; 1999; Coleman, 2002; Grogan, 1996; Hall, 1996; Restine, 1993). Drawing on my empirical work (Coleman, 2000; 2001; 2002) although the men and women headteachers surveyed saw themselves as operating almost entirely similar management styles, there is no doubt that being a woman and a headteacher is a very different experience from being a man and a headteacher. Generally, men have no cause to question their status, and are accepted in it, whereas a woman is likely to have to explain her position. The majority of women headteachers I surveyed and interviewed felt that they had to justify their existence as managers and leaders, both at the time of application for headship and while serving as heads. Two-thirds of the women reported experiencing some form of discrimination on the basis of their sex and the majority of them thought that they had to be better than a man to get the job (Coleman, 2001).

Since the dominant image of the leader and manager is of a male, women who take on the role of headteacher are constantly dealing with the inherent contradiction of being in a powerful position but at the same time not being what is expected. One area in particular on which the women heads commented (Coleman, 2000) was their isolation as women in an environment where men remained the norm. Another aspect of being a female leader seems to be the way that they are judged physically as well as in terms of how they carry out their job. Hall (1996, p. 100) observes that female headteachers are judged as school leaders but seen also as: 'a woman on show'. Selectors and governors seem to feel free to remark on the physical appearance of the female candidates for headship, particularly on their stature in relation to disciplining boys, but also on their attractiveness (Coleman, 2001). The responses of men show very little of equivalence: when asked about sexism, most of the men related the question to the difficulties faced by women. However, there is an impression among a minority of men that schools prefer to have both a male and a female deputy head and that therefore certain deputy posts are held open for women in a way that may be unfair to male candidates (Coleman, 2002). The figures show that although there is a larger proportion of women deputies than women heads, men still outnumber women at the deputy level in England and Wales by more than two to one (DfEE, 2000).

There is a further important and practical difference between men and women in leadership positions in education and this is the apparent impact of their jobs on family life. In the surveys I conducted, virtually all of the men had wives, many of whom had subsumed their career to that of their husband, and 92 per cent had a child or children. Only two-thirds of the women were married, and divorce and separation was much more common among the women. Very few could rely on their partners to take responsibility for domestic support. Only about a half of the women had a child or children, and childlessness was more common among the younger 40–50 age group than it was among those over 50 (Coleman, 2001; 2002). It does appear that a large proportion of the younger women, in particular, were making a choice to remain childless in view of the demands of the job, something that it was not necessary for the men to do.

Despite the obvious disadvantages of being a woman when it comes to achieving headship, and the negative impact of the job on family life, the women headteachers I surveyed and interviewed did indicate that they perceived some advantages in being a woman educational leader. They felt that they are seen as being more approachable by other women: staff and parents and by girl pupils, and are more likely to be able to 'defuse' an angry male student, teacher or parent. The women headteachers felt able to share emotion in unhappy circumstances and empathise with families where tragedies had occurred, in a way that men might find more difficult. They also felt that they could conduct themselves in ways that are free of the expectations held of their male colleagues. The cultural and social expectations surrounding the leadership of schools and other organisations continues to endorse a very 'male' idea of a formal and autocratic leader. Although male headteachers may not see themselves in this way, they may be trapped in a stereotype from which their female colleagues recognise that they are free. A very small number of men headteachers did comment on their dislike of the constraints imposed on them by the stereotypical expectations of male leaders; a hint of the masculinities debate raised by, among others, Collinson and Hearn (2000).

CONCLUSION

Leadership in education, as in most fields, is identified with men. Although there is a gradual increase in the numbers of women who are reaching leadership positions, the basic social assumptions, based on the distribution of power in society, endorse men as leaders and identify women in subordinate roles. The normatively 'approved' trend of leadership towards a participative and transformational style might appear to favour women, but it seems that these styles are now being equally adopted by men, at least in education. Despite the apparent endorsement of softer styles of management, masculine stereotypes relating to leadership seem to survive, endorsing men as leaders but trapping some of them in a stereotype they find uncomfortable.

The lively debate on whether men and women manage and lead differently has accrued evidence that is equivocal. It is claimed that most leadership studies were carried out on the assumption that there is no difference between the sexes and that research undertaken on a mainly male population can be generalised to women (Shakeshaft, 1989). However, more recently there has been considerable research of a qualitative nature that has focused exclusively on women (Adler, Laney and Packer, 1993; Ouston, 1993; Ozga, 1993). This research seems to indicate that the style of leadership most associated with women is more like the current ideals of leadership than is the male stereotype of leadership (Shakeshaft, 1989). In-depth studies have indicated the range of behaviours and the modelling of 'idealised influence' (Bass and Avolio, 1994; Hall, 1996). Equally, other qualitative work has shown the range of styles that women might use including some styles that could be termed masculine (Reay and Ball, 2000). There have been few equivalent qualitative studies of men. My research has been both qualitative, comprising in-depth interviews with women secondary heads (Coleman, 1996a; 1996b) and quantitative, surveys on all the women secondary heads (Coleman, 2000; 2001) and a sample of male heads (Coleman, 2002) and has provided a 'snapshot' of some of the main dimensions of the life and leadership experience of headteachers, based on their gender. This has shown that there are only small differences between the women and men headteachers in their perceptions of their own leadership styles. At the same time there is considerable difference in how they view their acquisition and occupation of the role of senior manager. There is need for research that would look more deeply at the impact of life experience on the leadership of both women and men and examine in more detail how their gendered experience affects their leadership and management of educational institutions.

REFERENCES

Adler, S., Laney, J. and Packer M. (1993) *Managing Women: Feminism and Power in Educational Management*, Buckingham: Open University Press.

Bass, B.M. and Avolio, B. (1994) *Improving Organizational Effectiveness through Transformational Leadership*, Thousand Oaks, CA: Sage Publications.

Bem, S.L. (1974) 'The measurement of psychological androgyny', *Journal of Consulting and Clinical Psychology*, **42**(2), 155–62.

Bem, S.L. (1977) 'On the utility of alternative procedures for assessing psychological androgyny', *Journal of Consulting and Clinical Psychology*, **45**(2), 196–205.

Blackmore, J. (1989) 'Educational leadership: a feminist critique and re-construction', in I. Smyth, and W. John (eds), *Critical Perspectives on Educational Leadership*, Deakin Studies in Education Series 2, Lewes: Falmer Press.

Blackmore, J. (1994) 'Leadership in "crisis": feminist insights into change in an era of educational restructuring', paper presented at the conference of the American Educational Research Association, New Orleans, April.

Blackmore, J. (1999) *Troubling Women: Feminism, Leadership and Educational Change*, Buckingham: Open University Press.

Blake, R.R. and Mouton, J.S. (1964) *The Managerial Grid*, Houston, TX: Gulf Publishing Co.

Burns, J.M. (1978) *Leadership*, New York: Harper & Row.

Coleman, M. (1996a) 'Management style of female headteachers', *Educational Management and Administration*, **24**(2), 317–32.

Coleman, M. (1996b) 'Barriers to career progress for women in education: the per-ceptions of female headteachers', *Educational Research*, **38**(3), 163–74.

Coleman, M. (2000) 'The female secondary headteacher in England and Wales: leadership and management styles', *Educational Research*, **42**(1), 13–27.

Coleman, M. (2001) 'Achievement Against the Odds: the female secondary head-teachers in England and Wales', *School Leadership and Management*, **21**(1), 75–100.

Coleman, M. (2002) *Women as Headteachers: Striking the Balance*, Stoke-on-Trent: Trentham Books.

Coleman, M., Qiang, H. and Li, Yp (1998) 'Women in educational management in China: experience in Shaanxi Province', *Compare*, **8**(2), 141–54.

Collinson, D. and Hearn, J. (2000) 'Critical studies on men, masculinities and man-agements', in M. Davidson, and R. Burke (eds), *Women in Management: Current Research Issues Volume II*, London: Paul Chapman Publishing.

Davidson, M.J. and Cooper, C.L. (1992) *Shattering the Glass Ceiling: The Woman Manager*, London: Paul Chapman Publishing.

Davies, L. (1998) 'Democratic practice, gender and school management', in P. Drake and P. Owen (eds), *Gender and Management Issues in Education: An International Perspective*, Stoke-on-Trent: Trentham Books.

Department for Education and Employment (DfEE) (2000) *Statistics of Education Teachers in England and Wales*, London: Government Statistical Service.

Evetts, J. (1994) *Becoming a Secondary Headteacher*, London: Cassell.

Ferrario, M. (1994) 'Women as managerial leaders', in M.J. Davidson and R.J. Burke (eds), *Women in Management: Current Research Issues*, London: Paul Chapman Publishing.

Gold, A. (1996) 'Women into educational management', *European Journal of Education*, **31**(4), 419–33.

Goldring, E. and Chen, M. (1994) 'The feminization of the principalship in Israel: the trade-off between political power and cooperative leadership', in C. Marshall (ed.), *The New Politics of Race and Gender*, London: Falmer Press.

Goleman, D. (1996) *Emotional Intelligence: Why It Can Matter More Than IQ*, London: Bloomsbury.

Gray, H.L. (1993) 'Gender issues in management training', in J. Ozga (ed), *Women in Educational Management*, Buckingham: Open University Press.

Grogan, M. (1996) *Voices of Women Aspiring to the Superintendency*, Albany, NY:

State University of New York Press.

Gross, N. and Trask, A. (1976) *The Sex Factor and the Management of Schools*, New York: John Wiley and Sons.

Hall, V. (1996) *Dancing on the Ceiling: A Study of Women Managers in Education*, London: Paul Chapman Publishing.

Hall, V. (1997) 'Dusting off the phoenix: gender and educational leadership revisited', *Educational Management and Administration*, **25**(3), 309–24.

Hill, M.S. and Ragland, J.C. (1995) *Women as Educational Leaders: Opening Windows, Pushing Ceilings*, Thousand Oaks, CA: Corwin Press.

Jirasinghe, D. and Lyons, G. (1996) *The Competent Head: A Job Analysis of Heads' Tasks and Personality Factors*, London: Falmer Press.

Kotecha, P. (1994) 'The position of women teachers', *Agenda* (21) 134–57.

Kouzes, J.M. and Posner, B.Z. (1990) *The Leadership Challenge: How to Get Extraordinary Things Done in Organizations*, San Francisco: Jossey-Bass.

Kruger, M.L. (1996) 'Gender issues in school headship: quality versus power?' *European Journal of Education*, **31**(4), 447–61.

Leithwood, K., Jantzi, D. and Steinbach, R. (1999) *Changing Leadership for Changing Times*, Buckingham: Open University Press.

Mac an Ghaill, M. (1994) *The Making of Men: Masculinities, Sexualities and Schooling*, Buckingham: Open University Press.

Morriss, S.B., Coleman, M. and Low, G.T. (1999) 'Leadership stereotypes and female Singaporean principals', *Compare*, **29**(2), 191–202.

Noddings, N. (1984) *Caring: A Feminine Approach to Ethics and Moral Education*, Berkeley, CA: University of California Press.

Office for National Statistics (ONS) *Social Trends 2001*, London: The Stationery Office.

Ouston, J. (ed) (1993) *Women in Education Management*, Harlow: Longman.

Ozga, J. (ed) (1993) *Women in Educational Management*, Buckingham: Open University Press.

Reay, D. and Ball, S. (2000) 'Essentials of female management', *Educational Management and Administration*, **28**(2), 145–60.

Restine, L. Nan, (1993), *Women in Administration: Facilitators for Change*, Newbury Park, CA, Corwin Press.

Rosener, J.B. (1990), 'Ways women lead', *Harvard Business Review*, **68**(6), 119–25.

Schein, V.E. (1973) 'The relationship between sex role stereotypes and requisite management characteristics', *Journal of Applied Psychology*, **57**(2), 95–100.

Schein, V.E. (1994) 'Managerial sex typing: a persistent and pervasive barrier to women's opportunities', in M. Davidson and R. Burke (eds), *Women in Management: Current Research Issues*, London: Paul Chapman Publishing.

Schick-Case, S. (1994), 'Gender differences in communication and behaviour in organizations', in M.J. Davidson and R.J. Burke (eds), *Women in Management: Current Research Issues*, London: Paul Chapman Publishing.

Schmuck, P.A. (1996) 'Women's place in educational administration: past, present, and future', in K. Leithwood, J. Chapman, D. Corson, P. Hallinger and A. Hart (eds), *International Handbook of Educational Leadership and Administration*, Boston: Kluwer Academic.

Shakeshaft, C. (1989) *Women in Educational Administration*, Newbury Park, CA: Sage Publications.

Shakeshaft, C. (1995) 'Gendered leadership styles in educational organizations', in

B. Limerick and B. Lingard (eds), *Gender and Changing Educational Management*, Rydalmere, NSW: Hodder Education.

Sinclair, A. (1998) *Doing Leadership Differently: Gender, Power and Sexuality in a Changing Business Culture*, Melbourne: Melbourne University Press.

Tannenbaum R. and Schmidt, W.J. (1973) 'How to choose a leadership pattern', *Harvard Business Review*, May–June, 162–80.

Usher, P. (1996) 'Feminist approaches to research', in D. Scott and R. Usher (eds), *Understanding Educational Research*, London: Routledge.

Vinkenburg, C., Jansen, P. and Koopman, P. (2000) 'Feminine leadership–a review of gender differences in managerial behaviour and effectiveness', in M. Davidson and R. Burke (eds), *Women in Management: Current Research Issues Volume II*, London: Paul Chapman Publishing.

Vinnicombe, S. (2000) 'The position of women in management in Europe', in M. Davidson and R. Burke (eds), *Women in Management: Current Research Issues Volume II*, London: Paul Chapman Publishing.

FURTHER READING

Blackmore, J. (1999) *Troubling Women: Feminism, Leadership and Educational Change*, Buckingham: Open University Press.

Coleman, M. (2002) *Women as Headteachers: Striking the Balance*, Stoke-on-Trent: Trentham Books.

Hall, V. (1996) *Dancing on the Ceiling: A Study of Women Managers in Education*, London: Paul Chapman Publishing.

Hall, V. (1997) 'Dusting off the phoenix: gender and educational leadership revisited', *Educational Management and Administration*, **25**(3), 309–24.

Section B: Developing Leaders, Developing Leadership

4

BIOGRAPHY AND THE STUDY OF SCHOOL LEADER CAREERS: TOWARDS A HUMANISTIC APPROACH

Peter Ribbins

INTRODUCTION

Meeting the needs of school leaders, and especially headteachers, for preparation and development has become a substantial industry and big business. Elaborate and expensive programmes of training, assessment and certification have mushroomed in country after country. Whatever the merits of this phenomenon, regarded as an innovation a number of generalisations might be made with some confidence about it.

First, it has been introduced as an 'act of faith' rather than as the result of a substantial, comprehensive and critical examination of such empirical evidence and theoretical discussion as might be available. This is so especially of those countries that have sought to follow where they perceive others to have led. But it is all too often also true of those countries, such as the UK, that have done the leading. Secondly, the debates on this innovation, in so far as these can be said to have taken place at all, have tended to be both constricted and more than a little confused by a lack of clear and shared definitions and understandings of the key concepts and practices involved. Thirdly, the actual functioning and effects of this innovation are by no means always what its advocates have claimed for it and, as some maintain, may be as likely to defeat its stated purposes, in so far as these are made explicit, as to achieve them. Fourthly, the kinds of claims and counter-claims that have been noted above are in part encouraged by the fact that this innovation has rarely been the subject of rigorous and independent review. Furthermore, too often when such a review has taken place, as in the case of a major evaluation of the National Professional Qualification for Headship (NPQH) undertaken by the National Foundation for Educational Research (NFER) for the Department for Education and Employment (DfEE), it has not been made publicly available.

It is not my purpose to attempt to address this formidable agenda of issues as a whole. Rather, I shall focus mainly on the first of the generalisations listed above and in doing so will relate what we know of the careers of school leaders to what this might mean for their development. This will entail a discussion of biography, life history and story, and, most especially, the notion of career. In undertaking this I will make a case for a humanistic approach to the study of leadership careers and preparation of school leaders as against the narrowly instrumental orientation that has dominated a good deal of government-led thinking in this and in related areas.

TOWARDS A HUMANISTIC APPROACH

In a recent paper that seeks to develop a comprehensive map of the field of studies in leaders, leading and leadership in education, Helen Gunter and I have argued for a classification around *six major knowledge provinces* (the conceptual, the descriptive, the critical, the humanistic, the evaluative and the instrumental) differentiated in terms of *seven key groupings of work* (purpose, focus, context, method, audience, communication and impact) (Gunter and Ribbins, 2002; Gunter and Ribbins, 2002a; Ribbins and Gunter, 2002). For the purposes of this chapter I will focus upon the humanistic and instrumental provinces. I do so because it seems to me that in contemporary education the world over too much thinking about leadership and too much of the practice of leadership development has overstressed the possibilities of the instrumental and underrated that of the humanistic.

In this context instrumental research can be seen as concerned essentially with providing leaders and others with effective strategies and tactics for the delivery of group, organisational and system level goals. It is to this form of research and to the suggestions it can offer for the improvement of practice that hard-pressed and sometimes impatient policy-makers and leaders can seem most to yearn for. For some, it appears to be the only truly worthwhile purpose for research. At its best, it must be acknowledged that such research can offer practical assistance about what works and what does not. At its worst, it can contribute to the establishment of a narrowly managerialist outlook and a 'quick fix' mentality in which the people who actually do the leading and those who are led seem to be of little interest.

In contrast, humanistic research in leadership in education, in so far as its primary purpose is to seek to gather and theorise from the experiences of those who are leaders and those who are led, is unlikely to lose sight of the people who are engaged in organisational and other forms of social life. It can take a variety of related forms including life history, life story, prosopography, autobiography and biography. Much of this chapter will deal with the notions of biography and career, as a prelude to this it is worth spending a little time on such associated concepts as life history and life story and of biography and case study.

Usher (1998, p. 18) makes an important distinction in 'the story of the self' between a life lived and a life told. The former 'is what actually happens'. It consists of 'the images, feelings, sentiments, desires, thoughts, and meanings known to the person whose life it is'. A life as told, a life history, 'is a narrative, influenced by the cultural conventions of telling, by the audience, and by the social context' (ibid.). For others the key distinction in the story of the self is that between a life history and a life story. For Miller (2000, pp. 139–40):

> Unlike the life history which can be said to be a (hopefully accurate and reasonably complete) passive reconstruction of a core of factual events, the life story is an active construction of the respondent's view of their life. There is no single 'best' or 'correct' construction. The content of a life story that a respondent will give in an interview will be dependent upon how they see their life at that particular moment and how they choose to depict that life view to the person carrying out the interview . . . the life story is 'true' in that the story the respondent chooses to give at the moment of the interview is, at that place and time, the one they have selected as a genuine depiction of their life.

For Bullough case study research (especially when its focus is upon the depiction of a lived life) and biographical research have much in common. Both:

> are narratives, and both face the challenge of untangling, telling and emplotting a life . . . Both require the creation of a story line that connects the threads of one's life events into a single narrative . . . Both biographers and case study researchers ask the question, What is the story? The story gives meaning and invites meaning making. As part of its appeal, biography encourages boundary crossing. When we read biographies written and lived stories often connect and we 'realise that we are not alone; we can identify with another human being in another age; we can identify with his or her journey through the vicissitudes of life'.

(Oates, 1991, p. 7, cited in Bullough, 1998, p. 25)

What all these forms of research share, and this is especially apparent in the quote from Oates, is 'a strong humanistic impetus' (Miller, 2000, p. 8). As such they have a deep concern for locating individuals within their social, cultural and historical settings. But this can have positive and negative connotations. In an account of the social function of life stories that stress the former Atkinson (1998, p. 10) suggests that they 'can affirm, validate, and support our own experience in relation to those around us. They enforce the norms of a moral order and shape the individual to the requirements of the society. Stories help us understand our commonalties with others, as well as our differences. Stories help create bonds, while fostering a sense of community, by helping us understand the established order around us. Stories clarify and maintain our place in the social order of things'.

But such stories can have a different effect, particularly when regarded from the perspective of an alternative research approach to the instrumental and humanistic as described above. In this, critical research is distinguished by a desire to reveal and emancipate social actors from the various forms that social injustice can take and from the oppression of established but unjustifiable structures of social relationship and power (see Ribbins and Gunter, 2002). In terms of purpose, whilst the first may be said to regard biography as socialisation, the latter seems to see it in terms of its contribution to social emancipation. What else can be said of biography and its purposes?

BIOGRAPHY AND ITS PURPOSES AND FORMS

Biography can have a number of purposes. For Erben (1998, p. 4), at its most general, it seeks 'to provide greater insight than hitherto into the nature and meaning of individual lives or groups of lives. Given that individual lives are part of a cultural network, information gained through biographical research will relate to an understanding of the wider society'. As such, from an ontological perspective, the biographical researcher may be seen as 'adding to the study of groups a sociology of the individual. The formulation, "a sociology of the individual" may seem tautologous but as William Dilthey earlier observed, socio-historical reality can be captured and interpreted through an account of that highly singular and complex repository of the cultural – the single person' (ibid., p. 14).

So much for its general aims, what of the specific purposes of biography and biographical research? On this Erben offers a warning and makes a suggestion in pointing out that 'biographical research data do not claim, or seek the impossibility of the exact replication of a life the requirements is that the research refer to lives in such a way as to illuminate them in relation to a research object' (ibid., p. 12). In stressing that biographical research needs to be clear about what it is seeking to understand, Erben is making a point that has special importance for those who wish to use such an approach to study leadership careers in education. In developing this argument, he stresses that from 'an analysis of a particular life or lives for some designated reason – for example in examining the world of work – it may be appropriate to look at the biographical routes by which individuals become teachers, nurses, prostitutes' (ibid., p. 4).

He could also have argued that such an analysis might enlighten us about the lives of teachers, nurses, prostitutes and the like as they pursue their careers. It might well tell us much about these professions or occupations. Before turning to a discussion of these possibilities and to how they might contribute to an enhanced understanding of the careers of school leaders, let us summarise the three main kinds of biographical research: that which is concerned primarily with seeking to offer an account of the personal life of an individual; that which focuses on the interpersonal life of an individual as he or she relates with other individuals located within the particular social settings which they all interact; and, the life of an individual regarded as one case of a whole set of individuals (such as school teacher) who, while they may never interact socially, nevertheless share a role in common (such as headteacher) or a type of career experience (such as school leader). What, then, can we learn of leadership and leadership careers from biography?

BIOGRAPHY, LEADERSHIP AND CAREERS

In a paper published some years ago, Peter Gronn and I identified three main ways in which biographies can facilitate theorising about leadership. First, as detailed case histories, they may be inspected for evidence of the development and learning of leadership attributes. Second, they can provide what might be described as analytical balance sheets on the ends to which leaders have directed their attributes throughout their careers within the shifting demands on them, and options available to them. Third, a comparative analysis of the career paths of leaders as revealed in biographies can answer broader system and institutional level questions, such as whether 'particular sets of leaders, sanctioned by their societies and organisations as worthy to lead them, share common attributes and whether those same societies and organisations screen their leadership cohorts in any way to guarantee conformity to preferred cultural types or models' (Gronn and Ribbins, 1996, p. 464).

Each of the three ways described above, two explicitly, refer to the notion of a career. In doing so, following Goffmann (1976), like most theorists, we take the view that the concept of career can be used to refer 'to any social strand of any person's course through life' (ibid., p. 119). Applying this to leadership, Gronn (1999, p. 25) suggests 'the notion of a career communicates more than the straightforward idea of task performance . . .[it] has usually signalled the idea of a possibility of, sequenced and planned movement, and therefore, some sense of anticipated trajectory . . . There is also an implied notion of commitment to a course of life'. Given this, 'Career progression is understood generally as a desired, vertical, ladder-like movement through age-related and time-phased stages. The various locations occupied by individuals at any one time generate corresponding expectations and perspectives of career trajectories' (ibid., p. 27).

This may be so, but as others have argued, these expectations and perspectives are shaped by considerations of gender, class and race. Thus while Osler (1997), in a study of *The Education and Careers of Black Teachers*, acknowledges that 'The concept of "career" is often interpreted to mean progression up a hierarchical pyramid' (ibid., p. 125), she also stresses that it 'has been seen as problematic since most people will not reach the top of the pyramid' (ibid.). In addition, she argues 'that men and women often have different understandings of career' and that 'the ways in which individual senior Black educators perceive their careers may enable us to identify how individuals manage the particular structural barriers they are likely to encounter' (ibid.).

Despite their apparent difference, there is a good deal of common ground in terms of the influence of aspects of individual agency and social structure as between the accounts that Gronn and Osler offer of the careers of educational leaders. Thus if Osler (1997), in the quote above, appears to stress the significance of structural considerations, in her concluding remarks she also notes that 'We have seen a variety of approaches to "career" among the ten senior managers' (ibid., p. 127). This would seem to give a greater prominence to aspects of agency. In so far as it does, this resonates with Gronn's (1999, p. 26) view that 'Individuals' careers, as I shall demonstrate in the case of leaders, are indeed structured for them, but those same individuals are still able to negotiate particular identities and pathways of their own choosing from within those structured options available to them'. But what do we know of the careers of educational leaders?

THE CAREERS OF EDUCATIONAL LEADERS

Until comparatively recently we knew little about key aspects of leadership careers in education. As Gronn and Ribbins (1996, p. 465) note 'there is . . . an absence of any systematic understanding in the literature of how individuals get to be leaders, an ignorance of culturally diverse patterns of defining leadership and knowledge of the culturally different ways prospective leaders learn their leadership remains in its infancy'.

Without such an understanding, there is little possibility of a satisfactory answer to Kets de Vries (1993, p. 3) questions, 'What determines who will become a leader and who will not?' A possible response would be to devise a framework that would enable an ordering of the biographical details of leaders' lives. This would have a number of advantages including enabling a comparative analysis of individuals over and against the systems or cultural traditions of leadership that nurture careers given that the latter would offer an appropriate analytical construct on which to build such a framework. It would also allow the kind of longitudinal, comparative analysis of leaders' careers in a variety of cultural and national settings that would go some way to answering the questions from Kets de Vries noted above. In addition, as Gronn and I argued in our paper,

> with 'leadership career' – essentially a mobility pathway or status passage through time – as the conceptual anchorage, there is the added advantage of being able to pinpoint the dialectical interplay between a leader's own sense of agency (fashioned in part *by* her or him) and the social structure (enabling or constraining possibilities *for* her or him) in which that agency is embedded.

> (Gronn and Ribbins, 1996, p. 465, original emphases).

If in educational contexts we are comparatively ignorant about who become leaders and why and how prospective leaders prepare for leadership, we also know relatively little about the lives, careers and continuing developmental needs of those who are school leaders. Gronn (1999, p. 32) believes that

> the field of leadership studies lacks a sound comparative point of reference against which to map leaders' biographical experiences and activities. It is one thing to scrutinise leaders as individuals in isolation, but the field has remarkably few useful benchmarks or parameters for examining the circumstances of leaders' lives in relation to one and another, and also in respect of the cultures and societies from which they emerge. Yet, from the perspective of globalisation and the better appreciation of different, deeply entrenched cultural approaches ... the provision of such a scheme is timely.

For Gronn any scheme that can claim satisfactorily to account for the 'microcosmic details of each individual leader's life' will need to have regard to 'the broad parameters of history, society and culture' within which it is located (ibid.). Taken together, these requirements constitute a demanding agenda. Even so, they do not prevent Gronn from advocating a general leadership career framework; one that is made up of four sequential phases that he term's formation, accession, incumbency and divestiture (ibid.).

In what follows I will consider this and a variety of other frameworks. Drawing upon my own research into the leadership careers of headteachers in England and Wales and principals in a number of other countries, I will outline my own preferred model. Finally, I will attempt to relate all this to ongoing attempts in this country and in other parts of the world to develop a strategic approach to meeting the continuing needs of school teachers and school leaders for professional development.

Weindling (1999, p. 90) in a paper entitled 'Stages of Headship', 'uses socialisation theory to re-examine the NFER (National Foundation for

Educational Research) study of headteachers (Weindling and Earley, 1987; Earley et al., 1990) in order to study the stages of headship transition'. In this he helpfully reviews and summarises the large body of work that has drawn upon stage theories of socialisation in the USA and elsewhere. Much of this reports on research undertaken within a variety of non-educational contexts. Following Hart (1993) he identifies three characteristic periods of organisational socialisation through which leaders commonly pass. In stage one the newly arriving leader must engage in considerable learning as she or he first encounters the people and the organisation. Stage two 'involves the task of attempting to fit in. New leaders must reach accommodation with the work role, the people with whom they interact and the . . . culture (of the institution). They look for role clarity in this new setting and may face resistance from established group members' (ibid., p. 91). In stage three, 'stable patterns emerge but this is only visible in data from longitudinal studies' (ibid.). There is some evidence that not all leaders achieve this stage before they move on to their next post.

Drawing on this model along with the research reported by Gabarro (1987), Parkay and Hall (1992), Day and Bakioglu (1996), Gronn (1993; 1999) and some of my own work (Ribbins, 1997b), Weindling (1999, pp. 98–100) proposes a six-stage model with approximate timings mapping the stages of headship transition/preparation prior to headship as follows: entry and encounter (first months), taking hold (three to 12 months), reshaping (second year), refinement (years three to four), consolidation (years five to seven) and plateau (years eight and onwards).

Most models, especially those that attribute a time dimension, are underpinned by shared assumptions. Parkay and Hall (1992) in a five-stage developmental model (survival, control, stability, educational leadership, professional actualisation) of new high school principals in the USA identify four. First, that principals can begin at different stages and not all do so at stage one. This is especially the case with those not taking up a first principalship. Second, that principals can pass through the stages at different rates. In particular, experienced principals coming to a new principalship, can, but by no means always do, pass through the early stages very quickly. Third, that no single factor, such as their personal characteristics at the time of their succession or the condition of the school at the point at which they take over, determines a principal's stage of development. Fourth, that principals may operate at more than one stage at the same time. Attributing a particular stage in such a case may mean little more than identifying a predominant orientation.

From my research I would make three further assumptions. First, that principals can operate at more than one stage in different aspects of their role and with regard to their relationships with relevant others. Second, that it is possible for a principal to slip back one or more stages or progress by more than one stage in general or in aspects of her or his role or her or his relationship with relevant others. Third, that some principals may never progress to the final stage or even stages, as these have been described above, of principalship. In my search for a career map of headship, I have encountered cases in which each of the seven assumptions has seemed relevant.

A CAREER MAP OF HEADSHIP

In undertaking and interpreting my own research into headteachers and headship, I have found an approach based upon two models helpful. The first, and more general model, developed by Gronn (1993) in part from a biographical study of Sir James Darling, the distinguished headmaster of Geelong Grammar in Melbourne, identifies four main phases (formation, accession, incumbency, divestiture) in the *lives of leaders*. The second model, from Day and Bakioglu (1996), is derived from study of headteachers in England (196 questionnaires and 34 interviews). From this the authors identify four phases (initiation, development, autonomy, disenchantment) in the *career of headteachers*. As a means of studying and describing the lives and careers of teachers and headteachers, I have found it helpful, with qualification, to combine the two models into a single framework. A comprehensive illustration of the merits and possibilities of this framework is beyond the scope of this chapter and is, in any case, available elsewhere (Pascal and Ribbins, 1998; Rayner and Ribbins, 1999; Pashiardis and Ribbins 2003). In what follows I will outline some of its key features. In doing so it may be helpful to rehearse what I have come to think of as two ideal typical pathways or routes to and through headship as follows:

- Formation, accession, incumbency (initiation, development, autonomy, disenchantment), moving on (divestiture).
- Formation, accession, incumbency (initiation, development, autonomy, enchantment), moving on (reinvention).

1   Formation: making headteachers

The process of formation is made up of the influences which, taken as a whole, shape the kinds of people that prospective headteachers become. In this process the headteachers of the future are socialised into deep-rooted norms and values by the action and interaction of such key agencies as the family, school, peer groups, the local community and other reference groups. These agencies, particularly those that exert their influence during the early years (for the importance of these to prospective leaders, see Gardner, 1995; Kets de Vries, 1995), shape the personality of a future headteacher by generating a conception of self, along with the rudiments of a work style, attitude and outlook.

2   Accession: achieving headship

Following formation, those who are to become candidates for headship must first become teachers. They then look for advancement within the profession, seeking experience in one or more leadership roles and, in due course, begin to prepare for promotion to headship. All this means developing their capacity and testing their readiness in comparison with existing headteachers and likely rivals. In doing so, they develop networks of peers, mentors and patrons, and learn to present themselves and jockey for position in the competition for preferment.

I am particularly interested in determining how heads regard their earlier careers and the extent to which they see this as a preparation, planned or otherwise, for headship. In reflecting upon the almost 100 interviews with heads and principals with which I have been engaged in six countries, I have found two things especially remarkable. First, how few British headteachers and to a lesser extent principals elsewhere have enjoyed deputy headship or have seen it as a useful preparation for headship (Ribbins, 1997a). Second how very few see themselves as having deliberately pursued a planned course leading to headship (Gronn and Ribbins, 2003). This can be so even among those who like Valerie Bragg knew that she wanted to be a headteacher 'almost as soon as I started teaching'. She sees herself as having taken

> a very traditional route. I obtained an early promotion to head of department, went on to be head of a sixth form which gave me plenty of pastoral contact, then on to a deputy headship and then to a headship. I attended carefully selected courses on timetabling, pastoral care, curriculum development . . . I suppose the whole thing looks carefully planned but I did not have a conscious checklist.
>
> (Ribbins and Marland, 1994: p. 64)

In this her account reflects the view expressed so forcefully by Franklyn (1974, p. x) that

> There is no plot in this story because there have been none in my life or in any other life which has come under my notice. I am one of a class of the individuals which have not the time for plots in their life but have all they can do getting their work done without indulging in such a luxury.

3   Incumbency: enacting headship

Incumbency marks the period or periods of actual headship and runs from the time a head is first appointed to headship to the time he/she finally leaves headship. There are, of course, many headteachers who have experienced a second, a third or even further headships. In doing so they may face each time starting again on the first of the four phases of incumbency described below. With this caveat in mind, over the whole course of a headship career, from my research it seems to me that incumbency can take one of two main routes, each with four successive sub-phases. Following the Day and Bakioglu (1996) model, the first three sub-phases common to both routes may be entitled *initiation*, *development* and *autonomy*. The fourth sub-phase of a headship career can take one or other of two directions, one negative (*disenchantment*) the other positive (*enchantment*).

- *Initiation*: following appointment there is an immediate period of induction or initiation. During this time new heads become familiar with the organisational and workplace norms of their new school and its community and of the roles they will be expected to fulfil. The evidence suggests that this first phase normally takes at least three years before a new head feels fully initiated in post. During this phase most heads experience a broadly similar range of emotions – beginning with feelings of initial elation and enthusiasm quickly followed by a growing sense of realism and adjustment to what the real parameters of the job will be. More generally new heads felt ill prepared and uncertain about what was expected of them. Unsurprisingly, they view these first years as exhausting and demanding. Some claim to have enjoyed a relatively smooth transition into post; others faced great difficulties. The quality of this experience seems to be influenced by factors such as: self-belief, depth and breadth of previous experience, relevance of previous experience, the ability to transfer previous experience, the breadth and relevance of prior-preparation and training, the ability to transfer prior-preparation and training; learning from working with appropriate and inappropriate role models; ability to learn on the job, and the quality of the institutional and local support structures in place.

- *Development*: this phase is characterised by enthusiasm and growth and normally takes some four to eight years. By this time the head feels in control, has the measure of the job and has made good progress in developing the wide range of capacities and competencies that it requires. Such heads have developed confidence in their ability to manage their schools. This allows them to maintain self-belief in the face of the stress and pressure which is a head's lot today. A growing sense of assurance is often expressed in a new vision for the school and/or the development of novel ways of working. This tends to be the phase that heads recall as the period of their careers in which they were most effective and made the most progress.

- *Autonomy*: this phase usually comes into play after eight years or more in the job. By this time such heads are generally very confident and competent. A combination of experience and survival has given them a sense of control and the knowledge that they have largely mastered the demands of headship. They have learnt a variety of strategies to cope with the stresses and strains of the job and can take a more open and longer-term perspective on the problems they face. Some believe this can make them even more effective as leaders. Their day-to-day professional life is usually much easier than it was. They regard themselves as 'management experts'. Having put in place appropriate management posts and teams, and delegated responsibilities to them, the school may appear to run smoothly without much apparent hands-on management from the head. Such headteachers tend to advocate a collegial or teamwork approach to managing the school as both right and good. Of course, not all heads in post for eight years and more achieve all of this. Furthermore, there is evidence that even among those who do, some may take very different routes in the final phase of headship.

- *Disenchantment*: the final phase of incumbency, as has been described by Day and Bakioglu (1996), is a transitional time for the mainly long-serving and highly experienced heads who come into this category. For some there is the prospect of disenchantment; the seeds of disillusion and loss of commitment may stem back to the previous phase. They may seem to be at the very height of their power and authority, but it is at just such a time that feelings of stagnation and loss of enthusiasm can set in. This can be a point at which heads reassess their life goals. If they have not achieved much of what they had wished, they might begin to feel trapped in post with nowhere to go. Day and Bakioglu (1996) depict a downwardly spiralling process leading finally towards disillusion and, in Gronn's term, divestiture. In passing, I should perhaps note that Gronn, in response to the above suggestions, has claimed that 'If indeed Day and Bakioglu's notion of disenchantment does imply "a pattern of creeping negativism" the same cannot be said for divestiture' (Gronn, 1999: 41). For my part, I cannot see what positive meaning can be given to 'disenchantment'. In addition, while I accept that Gronn did not wish 'divestiture' necessarily to be construed in negative terms, such an interpretation would surely be usual. Thus, for example, in defining what it is to 'divest' the *Oxford English Dictionary* does so in such terms as 'strip', 'deprive', 'dispossess' and 'rid'. Furthermore, in his account of the reasons why divestiture takes place, Gronn (1999, p. 39) notes that 'At some point in their lives, due to factors associated with ageing, illness, lack of fulfilment or incapacity, leaders have to divest themselves of leadership by releasing their psychological grip'. And while he goes on to distinguish between voluntary and involuntary departure and their potentially very different meanings for those involved, it is hard to see any of the factors identified above in positive terms. Gronn may need a more appropriate term for this final phase of a leader's career. I certainly felt this need, and while he has reservations (ibid., p. 41) about the notion of 'moving on' that Christine Pascal and I have resorted to, it could be that in his reference to the concept of 'letting go', Gronn may perhaps have identified just such a term (ibid.).

However that may be, Day and Bakioglu (1996) in their account of disenchantment describe such headteachers as increasingly autocratic in style and reluctant to respond to any kind of demand for change, especially where externally mediated. There were hints of this among one or two of the longest-serving of the headteachers I have been involved in interviewing but, as I shall argue below, most remain much more positive.

- *Enchantment*: some long serving heads do seem discouraged and disenchanted, but others are not. We spoke to several who despite their long years in post remain enchanted with headship. If anything they appear even more confident and optimistic about what is possible than some of those in the previous phase. As such they express feelings of having much left to do, of new challenges to face, of looking forward to this. They still see their work as focusing on children and their achievements and they still speak with a passionate commitment about the profession of teaching and of the life of the headteacher. Huberman (1993) identifies four conditions for sustaining high levels of continuing professional satisfaction: enduring commitment; manageable job expectations; good relations with colleagues; and, a balanced home and school life. I would add two more: a balance between leisure and work-related activities; and, worthwhile opportunities for continuing professional development.

Not all heads enjoy all these conditions. Among those with long experience and who continue to value and enjoy the post, by no means all are happy with every aspect of contemporary headship. Two examples must suffice to illustrate this view. First, John Evans, head of a large comprehensive in Cornwall, notes that 'Some of my best headteacher friends have retired because of illness or stress. I am talking about people I rate highly who are not just looking for a way out. To survive you've got to be much tougher than in the past. I'm diabetic with serious stomach problems and think this is stress related. It's part of the job'. Second, Sir David Winkley, at the time head of a primary school in Birmingham, on being asked if he still enjoyed headship, responded with some caution: 'I don't know. In a sort of way I must enjoy it, or I wouldn't do it . . . whether I'd come back to do it again, I'm not sure. At the moment I think that the stresses involved are enormous . . . there is no question about its "worthwhileness", but I think it's a terribly difficult job to do'.

Whatever their reservations, John Evans and David Winkley regard headship as worthwhile and even exciting. Others were less reserved. The following brief quotations are all from headteachers who had been in post for 16 years or more: 'it (being a headteacher) still gives me a buzz' (Michael Marland); 'I feel very good about it (the prospect of several more years of headship) . . . There is plenty to look forward to with excitement' (Brian Sherratt); 'it's a superb job . . . It's still the most rewarding job there is' (John Evans); 'I love my job. I'm a very happy headteacher . . . I love it. It's been a marvellous joy to me to have been appointed to this job at Ash Field. There has been, and there still is, so much to do' (Anne Hinchcliffe); and, 'It's good to be a head . . . There is nothing that has happened in my life as a head that has made me think I really shouldn't have come into this line of work' (Liz Paver).

4 Moving on: leaving headship

This final phase focuses on leaving headship. It deals with how heads anticipate and divest themselves of office, whether to a new occupation or to retire. The manner of this transition can depend on the way in which they experienced the final phase of incumbency. The *disenchanted* face the prospect of *divestiture* while the *enchanted* can look forward to *reinvention*.

Michael Ashford, a primary school headteacher of long experience, expresses what I mean by the latter possibility:

When I came here I told the governors I'd give them ten years, because it is such a big job. Last year I started to think about what I would do when I became 55 . . . I probably thought I ought to move on and let somebody else have a go at this job. But there is so much to do still . . . when I am 55, I will say 'Right, thank you, I have got 30-odd years in. I've got a reasonable pension, a nice home, things are OK.' I'll go into some form of management training, if anybody wants me. If they don't I'll be a gardener. Can you think of a better second occupation for an educator?

Earlier in our discussion I had asked Ashford how he had prepared for headship. He responded:

I was an effective deputy . . . I worked incredibly hard, had a good classroom and good relationships with the children, and tried to manage things in a way which made sure everybody could operate effectively. I attended the professional development course I thought relevant to the curriculum I was working in but was never schooled for headship in a formal course.

By this he meant a degree, perhaps an MBA. Those seeking headship in England and Wales today would be as likely to consider the programme of courses currently offered through the National College for School Leadership. It is with the attempt to develop a strategic programme of courses for school leaders and with the contribution that this has made to our understanding of the careers of school leaders that I will now turn.

TOWARDS A STRATEGIC PROGRAMME FOR THE DEVELOPMENT OF SCHOOL LEADERS

Many of the frameworks that have been proposed, especially within the UK, have been related directly to ongoing attempts to devise a worthwhile and comprehensive strategic approach to meeting the continuing professional and management development needs of school teachers and leaders. Achieving this has not been straightforward. The James Committee as long ago as 1972 was the first public body to suggest that an effective teaching profession would require initial *and* substantial ongoing in-service training (James Report, 1972). Although, its ideas were at the time largely ignored, they did exercise a significant influence upon subsequent thinking and policy.

Thus in 1974 the Advisory Committee on the Supply and Training of Teachers put forward a five-phase, career-long, approach that was designed to meet the continuing in-service needs of teachers (induction, consolidation, reorientation, advanced training and refreshment). In the late 1980s a School Management Task Force was set up to improve school management in England and Wales. It also advocated a career-long approach from initial training to retirement, with all teachers entitled to be treated as managers and encouraged to widen their experience and deepen their understanding of management at every stage. This entailed a commitment to the provision of preparation and induction for all those who were preparing to assume major new managerial responsibilities rather than restricting this just to those who had already been appointed to a headship (Stayn, 1992).

After 1995, under the leadership of the Teacher Training Agency (TTA), things began to change. In its *Initial Advice to the Secretary of State on the Continuing Professional Development of Teachers* the TTA (1995) proposed the development of agreed national standards setting targets for career progression designed to establish clear and explicit expectations of teachers in key roles. It wished to develop criteria for four key points in the profession defined as Newly Qualified Teachers; Expert Teachers; Experts in Subject Leadership; Experts in School Leadership. Whatever its limitations, the development and implementation of this framework is an impressive effort. However that may be, this effort, impressive or not, did not prevent the government from extracting responsibility for these programmes from the TTA and passing them to the National College for School Leadership. The 'Foreword' to the initial prospectus for the proposed National College, signed by Tony Blair and David Blunkett, contains two paragraphs that seem dismissive of the efforts of the TTA, and earlier attempts, to produce an effective and comprehensive strategic programme for the development of school leaders:

> The National College is among the most radical and innovative proposals in our Teachers Green Paper. Rooted in outstanding practice, it will offer heads, deputies and other school leaders *for the first time* the professional support and recognition they deserve . . .
>
> Up to now leadership development has lacked coherence, direction and status. *For the first time* the college will provide a single national focus for leadership development and research, offering school leaders the quality support other professions take for granted.
>
> (DfEE, 1999, p. 2, emphases added).

During its brief existence, the College has striven to produce a comprehensive theoretical framework for leadership development (NCSL, 2001). In doing so, it has proposed a model based upon five stages in a school leader's career. Around this model it intends to plan its future provision: the stages are made up of emergent leadership, established leadership, entry to headship, advanced leadership and consultant leadership (ibid., pp. 9–10). It will be interesting to see how this 'new' approach will be interpreted and evaluated in practice.

TOWARDS THE FUTURE

In this chapter I have attempted to consider the possibilities of biographical and associated methods for enabling the development of a better understanding of the careers of school leaders in general and of headteachers in particular. In doing so I have examined a number of models, including one of my own, that seek to identify the key stages involved. In the previous part of the chapter I considered the role of a number of national agencies and bodies in determining and seeking to provide for the developmental needs of school leaders. In bringing my remarks to a conclusion, I will focus upon the latest of these agencies, the National College for School Leadership, and with some thoughts on the possibilities and limitations of its efforts to date.

Among its achievements over the last year, the college has as noted above produced a five-stage model representing the career of a typical schools leader. Although it is not evident how these stages were generated or how they build upon the extant literature, in one important respect, the college does seem to have shown itself to be more willing than some of its predecessors sometimes appeared to be to consider the place of research in shaping how it thinks and in determining what it does. In particular, it has supported financially and practically recent attempts to develop a comprehensive map of the field of leadership (Southworth, 2002) against which it would be able, presumably, to locate its future endeavours. Indeed, its five-stage framework may well represent an attempt to play an active role in the development of such a map. All this is to be welcomed, especially if, in interpreting its efforts, it shows a sustained willingness to go beyond the narrowly instrumental and to embrace the possibilities of the kinds of critical and humanistic approaches that were discussed earlier (see Ribbins and Gunter, 2003).

REFERENCES

Atkinson, R. (1998) *The Life Story Interview*, London: Sage Publications.

Bullough, R. (1998) 'Musing on life writing: biography and case studies in teacher education', in C. Kridel (ed.), *Writing Educational Biography*, New York: Garland, pp. 9–33.

Day, C. and Bakioglu, A. (1996) 'Development and disenchantment in the professional lives of headteachers', in I. Goodson and A. Hargreaves (eds), *Teachers' Professional Lives*, London: Falmer Press.

Department for Education and Employment (DfEE) (1999), *National College for School Leadership*, London: DfEE.

Earley, P., Baker, L. and Weindling, D. (1990) *Keeping the Raft Afloat: Secondary Headship Five Years On*, Slough: NFER.

Erben, M. (1998) 'Biography and research method', in M. Erben (ed.), *Biography and Education: A Reader*, London: Falmer Press, pp. 4–18.

Franklyn, M. (1974) *My Brilliant Career*, Sydney: Angus and Robinson.

Gabarro, J. (1987) *The Dynamics of Taking Charge*, Boston: Harvard Business School.

Gardner, H. (1995) *Leading Minds: An Anatomy of Leadership*, New York: Basic Books.

Goffman, E. (1976) *Asylums*, Harmondsworth: Penguin.

Gronn, P. (1993) 'Psychobiography on the couch: character, biography and the comparative study of leaders', *Journal of Applied Behavioural Science*, **29**(3), 41–62.

Gronn, P. (1999) *The Making of Educational Leaders*, London: Cassell.

Gronn, P. and Ribbins, P. (1996) 'Leaders in context', *Educational Administration Quarterly*, **32**(2), 452–73.

Gronn, P. and Ribbins, P. (2003) 'Evolving Formations' in *International Studies in Educational Administration*, **31**(2), forthcoming.

Gunter, H. and Ribbins, P. (2002) 'Leadership studies in education: towards a map of the field', *Educational Management and Administration*, **31**(1) 387–417.

Gunter, H. and Ribbins, P. (2002a) 'Challenging orthodoxy in school leadership studies: old maps for new directions?' Opening keynote given at the first meeting on ESRC seminar series on *Challenging the Orthodoxy of School Leadership*: Towards a new Theoretical Perspective, November, Warwick University.

Hart, A. (1993) *Principal Succession: Establishing Leadership in Schools*, New York: SUNY Press.

Hubermann, M. (1993) *The Lives of Teachers*, London: Cassell.

James Report (1972) *Teacher Education and Training*, London: HMSO.

Kets de Vries, M. (1993) *Leaders, Fools and Impostors: Essays on the Psychology of Leadership*, San Francisco: Jossey-Bass.

Kets de Vries, M. (1995) 'The leadership mystique, *Leading and Managing*, **1**(3), 193–211.

Miller, R. (2000) *Researching Life Stories and Family Histories*, London: Sage Publications.

National College for School Leadership (NCSL) (2001) *Leadership Development Framework*, Nottingham: NSCL.

Oates, S. (1991) *Biography as History*, Waco, TX: Mankham Press Fund.

Osler, A. (1997) *The Education and Careers of Black Teachers*, Buckingham: Open University Press.

Parkay, F. and Hall, G. (eds) (1992) *Becoming a Principal*, Boston: Allyn & Bacon.

Pashiardis, P. and Ribbins, P. (eds) (2003) *The Making of Secondary School Principals on Selected Small Islands*, a special edition of *International Studies in Educational Administration*, **31**(2).

Pascal, C. and Ribbins, P. (1998) *Understanding Primary Headteachers*, London: Cassell.

Rayner, S. and Ribbins, P. (1999) *Headteachers and Leadership in Special Education*, London: Cassell.

Ribbins, P. (1997a) (ed.) *Leaders and Leadership in the School, College and University*, London: Cassell.

Ribbins, P. (1997b) 'Heads on deputy headship', *Educational Management and Administration*, **25**(3), 295–308.

Ribbins, P. and Gunter, H. (2002) 'Mapping leadership in education: towards a typology of knowledge domains', *Educational Management and Administration*, **30**(4), 359–87.

Ribbins, P. and Gunter, H. (2003) 'Leadership studies in education: maps for EPPI reviews?', in L. Anderson and N. Bennett (eds) *Evidence Informed Policy and Practice in Educational Leadership*, London: Paul Chapman Publishing, in press.

Ribbins, P. and Marland, M. (1994) *Headship Matters*, London: Longman.

Southworth, G. (2002) 'Mapping the field of school leadership', draft paper from a Seminar organised by the Standing Conference for Research in Educational Leadership and Management, held at the University of Reading in December 2001.

Stayn, D. (1991) 'Developing educational managers', in P. Ribbins, R. Glatter, T. Simkins and L. Watson (eds.), *Developing Educational Leaders*, London: Longman, pp. 330–45.

Teacher Training Agency (1995) *Initial Advice to the Secretary of State on the Continuing Professional Development of Teachers*, London: TTA.

Usher, R. (1998) 'The story of the self: education, experience and autobiography, in M. Erben (ed.), *Biography and Education: A Reader*, London: Falmer Press, pp. 18–32.

Weindling, D. (1999) 'Stages of headship', in T. Bush, L. Bell, R. Bolam, R. Glatter and P. Ribbins (eds), *Educational Management: Redefining Theory, Policy and Practice*, London: Paul Chapman Publishing, pp. 90–102.

Weindling, D. and Earley, P. (1987) *Secondary Headship: The First Years*, Windsor: NFER-Nelson.

FURTHER READING.

Bush, T., Bell, L., Bolam, R., Glatter, R. and Ribbins, P. (eds) (1999) *Educational Management: Redefining Theory, Policy and Practice*. London: Paul Chapman Publishing.

Gronn, P. (1999) *The Making of Educational Leaders*, London: Cassell.

Gunter, H. and Ribbins, P. (2002) 'Leadership studies in education: towards a map of the field', *Educational Management and Administration*, **31**(1), 387–417.

Pascal, C. and Ribbins, P. (1998) *Understanding Primary Headteachers*, London: Cassell.

Rayner, S. and Ribbins, P. (1999) *Headteachers and Leadership in Special Education*, London: Cassell.

Ribbins, P. and Gunter, H. (2002) 'Mapping leadership in education: towards a typology of knowledge domains', *Educational Management and Administration*, **30**(4), 359–387.

Pashiardis, P. and Ribbins, P., (eds) (2003) *The Making of Secondary School Principals, on Selected Small Islands*, a special edition of International Studies in Educational Administration, 31(2).

5

MODELS OF LEADERSHIP DEVELOPMENT: LEARNING FROM INTERNATIONAL EXPERIENCE AND RESEARCH

Ray Bolam

INTRODUCTION

In many countries around the world, headteachers are widely perceived to be critically important in achieving school effectiveness and improvement and, as reforms designed to raise standards are introduced, their roles are changing significantly. As a result, policy-makers are compelled to develop and modify their national training strategies to equip headteachers and other school leaders with the knowledge and skills required to carry out these changed roles. The relative commonality of these trends raises the obvious question: are there any emerging national models of how best to organise and deliver leadership development and training from which policy-makers and practitioners in other countries can learn?

The purpose of this chapter is to explore possible answers to this question, and to clarify some of the underlying policy and professional issues, by reviewing selected research and practical experience. It focuses initially on the changing roles of school leaders and on the consequential changes in leadership development programmes, using two detailed vignettes – of Poland and of England and Wales – to demonstrate the uniqueness of such programmes. The final section proposes a provisional, typological framework for the comparative analysis of international models of leadership development and considers the relative difficulty of adapting selected sub-models, using training methodology and needs assessment as examples, from other countries. It concludes with some suggestions for policy, practice and research.

A few words about the chapter's terminology and parameters are worth stating at the outset. First, the terms principal and headteacher are used more or less interchangeably and, second, with respect to the terms leadership and management: 'I take "educational leadership" to have at its core the responsibility for policy formulation and, where appropriate, organisational transformation; I take "educational management" to refer to an executive function for carrying out agreed policy; finally, I assume that leaders normally also have some management responsibilities' (Bolam, 1997). Third, the working definition of leadership development used here is that it is:

- an ongoing process of education, training, learning and support activities
- taking place in either external or work-based settings
- proactively engaged in by qualified, professional teachers, headteachers and other school leaders
- aimed primarily at promoting the learning and development of professionally appropriate knowledge, skills and values
- to help school leaders to decide on and implement valued changes in their leadership and management behaviour
- so that they can promote high quality education for their students more effectively
- thus achieving an agreed balance between individual, school and national needs.

As we shall see in the final section, this definition is by no means unproblematic or one that is widely adopted in practice.

Fourth, the term 'model' is used somewhat loosely to refer primarily to the overall national leadership development strategies and policies adopted in any one country and the term sub-model to the components of that model. 'Model' is, thus, not intended to denote quality of an exemplary nature and so, in principle, it can be either effective or ineffective for achieving its purposes. Finally, space does not permit consideration of several important issues, for example the training needs of middle managers (see Bush and Jackson, 2002; Turner, 2002), leadership development for particular types of school (e.g., special schools – see Rayner, Gunter and Powers, 2002) or gender and school management (see Hall, 1999).

CHANGING LEADERSHIP ROLES AND DEVELOPMENT NEEDS

There is now an extensive research literature on school effectiveness and improvement within which, of the various factors cited as correlating with educational achievement, strong leadership always figures prominently (e.g., Gray and Wilcox, 1995; Stoll and Mortimore, 1995). However, given that the concept of 'effectiveness' is problematic, not least because it is rooted in specific national and cultural values, there can be no single answer to the question: what is effective school leadership and management? Nevertheless, a considerable amount of research has been published on the roles, tasks and training needs of headteachers, on school culture and on strategies for school improvement, and there is broad agreement about some main conclusions. For example, one study, based on a sample of 57 schools in England and Wales (Bolam et al., 1993), concluded that effective schools are likely to display certain common management features, including strong, purposive leadership by headteachers; broad agreement and consistency between headteachers and teachers on school goals, values, mission and policy; headteachers and their deputies working as cohesive management teams; a collaborative professional and technical sub-culture; norms of continuous improvement for staff and students; a leadership strategy which promotes the maintenance and development of these and related features of the school's culture. In their essentials, these conclusions are consistent with those from other developed countries (e.g., van Wieringen, 1992). However, by way of caution, it is important to recognise that recent studies have also concluded that the impact of principals and headteachers on student outcomes, although positive, is indirect (Hallinger and Heck, 1999), being mediated through a range of complex factors (Silins and Mulford, in press). Moreover, some scholars (e.g., Ouston, 1999) are doubtful about whether the emphasis on the role of the headteacher in school effectiveness and school improvement is warranted.

There is considerable evidence that national reforms in many countries have resulted in substantial changes in the roles of school principals. For example, an Organisation for Economic Cooperation and Development (OECD) study of school management in nine countries – Belgium, Greece, Hungary, Japan, Mexico, Netherlands, Sweden, the UK and the USA – argued that:

> Schools everywhere are being asked to do more than ever before. They face a complex world and a seemingly endless set of pressures. Those who manage schools must take responsibility for an arduous task. [This can lead to a] ... sense of crisis and despair that can easily affect educational management ... yet ... school systems and individual schools are experimenting with management.
>
> (CERI, 2001, p. 13)

Experience elsewhere is similar. For instance, in the United Arab Emirates (UAE), Al-Araj (1999) conducted a survey of 164 secondary headteachers and interviewed a sub-sample which included deputy heads. Within a highly centralised system the headteachers had limited power and authority, acting mainly in an executive capacity to implement central directives on work with a dominant administrative core. She concluded that methods of headteacher selection were inappropriate, that deputies were not being adequately prepared for headship and that headteachers received inadequate in-service training. Wen-haur Shieh (2001) predicted that the Integrated Curriculum Project, to be implemented in all schools in Taiwan, would have huge impact on schools, on principals' role in the change process and, therefore, on their training needs.

Also writing from an Asian perspective, Cheng (in press) argued that the changing role of education in national development has created serious challenges for school leaders who must respond positively to changes in the aims, content, process and practice of their schools. Two examples – school-based management and community involvement – illustrate his argument. In Hong Kong, Korea, Malaysia, Singapore and mainland China, there have been powerful moves towards varying degrees and forms of de-centralisation and school-based management to facilitate school development and effectiveness. School autonomy and the participation of local community are now being encouraged and, although there is a tradition of parental involvement in some developed countries, Cheng argued that this tradition was largely absent in most Asian countries.

A comparative study of the roles and training needs of a sample of new headteachers in five European countries – Hungary, the Netherlands, Norway, Spain and Wales – produced findings in the same vein (Bolam, Dunning and Karstanje, 2000). About 700 new headteachers, all in their first three years of service, responded to the survey in the mid-1990s. Their evidence indicated that new headteachers everywhere in the 'new', post-1989, Europe faced difficult challenges. Of course, some issues were undoubtedly specific to each individual country, and even to each Spanish region, in part because of differing political and cultural values, institutions and policy trends. Thus, in Hungary, the inheritance of communism was still evident; in Spain, the tradition of democratic elections for school leaders and strong regional identities were powerfully influential; the Welsh language and culture were increasingly important in Wales; rurality and remoteness were major issues in Norway; and the increasing size and organisational complexity of schools, as well as immigration, were particular factors in the Netherlands.

Notwithstanding these national variations, three overall explanations accounted for the majority of difficulties identified by the heads: the complexity of their roles and tasks; changing external pressures and demands; poor access to professional training, development and support, both before and after appointment. A clear picture of needs emerged. It was evident that internal problems had greater impact than external problems. Although 'consequences of national policy' was perceived as having a high level of impact, in reality this issue tended to be an underlying cause of a cluster of internal problems, since national policy was promoting a package of changes in policy and practice. Interestingly, headteachers in all countries (with the exception of two Spanish regions) reported the most marked difference between their task priorities and those of their predecessors as being a shift from 'concern for administration' to 'concern for achievement of school goals' or the 'well-being of teachers and students'. This shift was interpreted as reflecting the greater responsibility for educational developments now devolved to the school level, usually as a consequence of greater school autonomy. This was also the most likely explanation for the preponderance of self-management problems in the lists of the highest-ranking internal problems, notably 'managing own time' and 'coping with a wide range of tasks'.

Compared to most OECD countries, the approach in England and Wales was noteworthy for the scale and scope of the post-1988 reform programme, which covered all 27,000 schools, and for the shift towards centralisation at a time when many other countries were introducing de-centralising measures (Karstanje, 1999). The reforms inevitably resulted in extensive and radical changes in the roles and responsibilities of headteachers and other senior staff. From 1988, headteachers were required to have strategic leadership, planning, marketing, evaluation and development skills; to focus much more directly than hitherto on student learning and assessment targets; to operate as a quasi-chief executive in relation to school governors; to deal with and respond to external inspections; and to co-operate, as well as compete, with neighbouring schools.

These developments and issues were the focus of considerable research (Wallace and Weindling, 1999). For instance, a unique, ten-year, longitudinal study (see Weindling, 1999) offered insights into the cumulative impact of the reform process on a cohort of British secondary headteachers. In 1987, 80 per cent of the sample said their role was very different from when they had started the job in 1982 and, in 1993, 90 per cent said their role had continued to change significantly over the previous five years. The main areas of difference concerned the introduction of local management of schools, which had pushed finance-related issues up their list of concerns, together with the other mandated changes. Interestingly, the European study found that Welsh heads were much more likely than their counterparts in the Netherlands, Norway and Spain to see government reforms as causing them substantial problems (Dunning, 2000).

Some commentators (e.g., Clarke and Newman, 1997; Levačić, 1999) have argued that the policies summarised above were adopted by many governments across the public sector. Thus, reforms in health, social services and housing, as well as education, have a common technical/ideological core, often referred to as managerialism, rational management or new public management. A comparative study of school leadership in Denmark, Scotland, England and Australia (Moos and Dempster, 1998) concluded that, although the precise configuration and the degree of implementation of such managerialist reforms had varied from country to country, they had undoubtedly impacted, albeit differentially, on school leadership in all four countries.

THE IMPACT ON LEADERSHIP TRAINING AND DEVELOPMENT

There is widespread acceptance that these, often radical and extensive, policy and role changes also impacted considerably on the training needs of school principals, which in turn produced strategic shifts in national policies for leadership development and training. Often, the rationale was the one referred to by the Commonwealth Secretariat (1996), with respect to Africa, that 'the head plays . . . the most crucial role in ensuring school effectiveness'. Responses to these changes were varied. The OECD study (CERI, 2001, p. 21) concluded that there was a wide diversity of approaches to leadership and management development in terms of content, delivery mode, timing and institutional framework. Some leadership preparation programmes were dominated by universities, notably in the USA, whereas others, for example in the UK, were significantly influenced by practitioners, with considerable consequences for the university sector (Furlong, 2000). Indeed, a comparative study of preparation programmes in the UK and the USA concluded that there were, in effect two parallel systems operating in England and Wales – in universities and in the nationally funded programmes (Brundrett, 2001).

Other countries have adopted a more balanced strategy. Supported by Dutch government funding, the University of Amsterdam has pioneered a method of integrating theory and practice, first in Hungary and the Czech Republic, which was adapted in Romania (NSO, 2001). A consortium of the Romanian principals' professional association and six universities put together a team of trainers made up equally of practitioners and academics. They offer a nation-wide masters programme, aimed at enhancing professional knowledge and skills, which will be 25 per cent field-based, including on-the-job coaching, and 25 per cent applied work within an academic course framework. The Hungarian and Czech approaches had been broadly similar. Interestingly, policy in China has also apparently sought to integrate theory and practice by involving universities in principal training (Wenchang and Daming, 2002).

The dilemmas and challenges in formulating a national strategy for leadership development are considerable and, inevitably, vary from country to country, as do the solutions. Moreover, these features are dynamic and thus change over time, as the following two detailed examples illustrate. First, in Poland, the year 1989 was the crucial turning point for the nation and, consequently, for headteacher training and development. After 1989, most of the many headteachers who had previously been selected and trained according to Communist Party rules were replaced. This posed two major problems: quantitatively, how to organise and pay for the training of the 50,000 new heads and deputy heads across the country; qualitatively, how to develop the right programme. Four important contextual factors were among the changes: from the role of headteacher as bureaucrat to autonomous professional; from a national curriculum for headteacher training to regional curricula; from theoretical to practical courses; from top-down to bottom-up needs assessment.

In 1990, 49 regional centres for teacher and headteacher training were established, taking as their starting points the earlier external in-service courses, which had led to a diploma:

- for new heads and deputies – two, one-week courses, interspersed with 10 days' shadowing of experienced heads, and assessed by a written essay
- for experienced heads and deputies – 30 days of lectures over one year culminating in a written examination and a thesis.

Elsner's account is based on one of them, the Katowice Centre, of which she was director and where alternative approaches were developed in response to the criticism that the diploma programme was too theoretical. The centre set up a Headteachers' Club where experienced heads held monthly meetings for their own self-development and to help new colleagues. A newsletter on school management issues was circulated to over 2,000 schools in Upper Silesia and a prestigious competition was held to find the most creative approaches to the management of change, as judged by a panel of experts. By 1991, this club had evolved into a formally recognised professional association for primary and secondary headteachers.

Ekiert-Grabowska and Elsner (1993) referred to the continuing lack of trust between professional educators, including headteachers and teachers, which was a legacy of the totalitarian regime. As a result, headteachers were very reluctant to be open about their own training and development needs and new ways of encouraging them to be frank had to be devised, trialled and modified. They reported on a survey of 34 headteachers, based on 27 competency statements, in which the self-perceived weaknesses were seen as time management, creative problem-solving, budgeting and managing change and the strengths as being negotiation and conflict resolution, collaboration with parents and creating a positive climate.

These findings were then used as the basis for programme design although the writers said that, in reality, they learned little that was new. Even though the response rate was higher than hitherto, the headteachers did not display any initiatives and appeared to want to be told what to learn and even how to learn it. Similar behaviour patterns were revealed for lecturers and trainers. The writers concluded that this was to be expected, given the long history of totalitarian rule and the continuing hierarchical structures within which schools continued to operate, and that it would take time to change people's beliefs and behaviour. Accordingly, they decided to train the lecturers and trainers on their own, using technology and distance learning materials adapted from abroad, especially from England.

Oldroyd (1993) described these materials and their underlying rationale. He argued that *intermediate* technology is more appropriate than *high* technology in former communist countries where resources are in short supply and there is a weak infrastructure to support training across the country. Furthermore, what schools need in such circumstances is a support strategy that will enable them to create and sustain change from within. He saw low cost, distance learning materials that promote action learning and collaborative reflection, via purpose-designed academic materials, as the way forward.

The second example concerns England and Wales where a distinctive leadership development system now operates. This system is best understood in the context of wider policy developments over a period of about 20 years. During this time there was research and experimentation with different forms of organisation, funding and provision for in-service training for teachers in general and for school management training in particular (see Bolam, 1997) and a distinctive and supportive professional infrastructure emerged, key features of which are as follows. Two headteachers' unions (the National Association for Headteachers and the Secondary Heads Association) have, for many years, been active in promoting and delivering training and development programmes for headteachers. The Universities' Council for the Education and Training of Teachers (UCET) has also been active in this field for many years. The National Foundation for Educational Research has carried out numerous relevant studies. The British Educational Research Association has published and disseminated relevant research. The British Educational Leadership, Management and Administration Society (BELMAS) has actively promoted networking and the dissemination of information, sought to influence government policy, organised national and international conferences for policy-makers, headteachers, academics, consultants and researchers, promoted research and published articles and books in this field. Most recently, a General Teaching Council was established in each of England and Wales, the equivalent one for Scotland having been in place for some years, to strengthen the professionalism of teachers and headteachers.

Against this background, in the mid-1990s, the Teacher Training Agency introduced a comprehensive structure for leadership development with three components – preparation, induction and in-service training. The first is covered by the National Professional Qualification for Headship (NPQH) and the third by the Leadership Programme for Serving

Headteachers (LPSH). The second is covered by the recently reviewed HEADLAMP Programme in England and by the Professional Headship Induction Programme (PHIP) in Wales. All three are now co-ordinated by the National College for School Leadership (NCSL) which has formulated a Leadership Development Framework (NCSL, 2002; Newton, Chapter 6 in this volume) encompassing five stages:

- emergent leadership, which includes subject and specialist leadership roles
- established leadership, comprising experienced deputy and assistant heads who do not wish to be headteachers
- entry into headship, which embraces the revised HEADLAMP programme and NPQH
- advanced leadership, for heads with four or more years' experience
- consultant leadership.

Thus, over a generation, what is possibly the most comprehensive and sophisticated school leadership development model in the world has been gradually, and incrementally, developed in the unique circumstances of England and Wales. In sharp contrast to the Polish experience, this system is a high cost one: for example, the NCSL's annual budget is £60 million (NCSL, 2002, p. 26).

DISCUSSION AND CONCLUSIONS

This chapter's central argument is that the roles of school leaders and models of preparatory training, certification, selection, evaluation and professional development are necessarily rooted in the particular context of a single country. They are the product of unique, and dynamically changing, sets of circumstances – political, economic, social, cultural, historical, professional and technical – in that country. It follows that those of us seeking to learn and adapt from international experience must be cautious. This is also true when trying to learn from international theory and research, as two Hong Kong-based writers (Walker and Dimmock, in press) argue:

> The field is also constrained by an overreliance on theories and practices predominantly developed by a relatively culturally homogeneous cadre of scholars from English-speaking backgrounds. Our salient argument . . . is that societal culture is a significant influence on school organization and leadership in different societies because it helps shape school leaders' thoughts about concepts such as leadership, followership, communication and learning and teaching.

As well as, one might add, leadership development.

Attempts to promote international understanding about such matters must take seriously what we know from experience and research about complex innovations across cultures (Hallinger, 2001). The process of devising, adapting and implementing new models of leadership development may usefully be conceptualised as a complex innovation consisting of several components and, thus, it may be more productive to recognise that national leadership training and development models actually are each made up of several sub-models. Building on earlier approaches (e.g., Bolam, 1992; Bush and Jackson, 2002; CERI, 1982; 2001), the following list of key issues and questions provides the basis of a typological framework to analyse the main sub-models within any national model:

- Does leadership development for headteachers include preparatory, induction and in-service components? Are other leadership roles covered (e.g., subject leaders)? What are their broad features (e.g., how many hours/weeks do they take)? (The scope sub-model)
- Are the programmes compulsory? Do they carry accreditation and, if so, from whom (e.g., university, government, professional associations)? (The regulatory framework sub-model)
- How are they funded (e.g., nationally, locally, by individual grants or loans to principals, by requiring principals to contribute money or time)? How large is the budget? (The funding sub-model)
- How are they co-ordinated (e.g., by government, by a national college, by universities)? (The organisational sub-model)
- How are development and training needs established? Is the process linked to performance management and/or national standards? What concept of professional leadership underpins these procedures? (The needs identification sub-model)
- How are programmes evaluated and held accountable? (The evaluation and accountability sub-models)
- Who are the providers or suppliers (e.g., national and local administrators and inspectors, consortia, universities, professional associations, 'privatised' agencies and consultants)? Do they have the capacity to 'deliver'? (The suppliers sub-model)
- What are the main content areas of training programmes (e.g., leadership, communication, curriculum)? What part does theory play? (The curriculum sub–model)
- What methods do they use (e.g., course-based training, work-based training, mentoring, internships, industrial attachments)? What role is played by information and communications technology and e-learning? (The methodology sub-models)

Space does not permit detailed consideration of each of these sub-models but it is surely the case that some are easier to adapt than others, as can be illustrated in relation to two of them. The methodology sub-model is made up of components that provoke relatively few of those resistance problems which are based on conflicts of values and attitudes and which can be critical barriers to successful implementation. Thus, mentoring can be relatively easily adapted from one setting – England and Wales (Bolam et al., 1995) – to another – Singapore (Low, 2001) – and e-learning is being used in leadership programmes across the world (NCSL website; Tomlinson 2001). On the other hand, the needs identification sub-model is highly complex and generates difficult issues that are often culture specific, as demonstrated below.

One fundamental issue concerns the underlying rationale and goals of national programmes. It is clear from earlier parts of this chapter that models of leadership development are often being devised in political contexts in which external, 'restructuring' changes, initiated by national, state or local authorities to raise standards of achievement, exert priority over school leaders' own vision of needed improvements. Moreover, many developed countries use the same broad 'steering' strategies, often based on dedicated or categorical funding, to couple leadership development tightly to the implementation of their reform policies in what is now the dominant paradigm for systemic change in OECD member countries (Halasz, 2000). The implications for needs identification are evident.

A second issue concerns the underlying concept, or theory, of leadership that informs needs identification. My own position is that contingency, situational or pluralist theories of leadership (see Bush, 1995, p. 154) are the most useful for *describing and explaining* the behaviour of leaders. Essentially these argue that, empirically, there appears to be no single or 'correct' way either to lead or structure an organisation since the 'leaders', the 'led' and the organisation itself each have distinctive, even unique, characteristics, as do the tasks of leadership and management, in what is invariably a changing, turbulent environment. Given the unavoidably contingent and unpredictable nature of their work, effective leaders and managers must necessarily, therefore, adopt strategies and methods consistent with their own knowledge and skills, and appropriate to their particular organisations, tasks, staff and contexts – institutional, local and national. The practical consequence is that they must learn and use a repertoire of styles and techniques and exercise informed professional judgement to operate effectively within the constraints and opportunities of their unique situation (see Bolman and Deal, 1997). The implications for a training and development programme are obvious. However, if the quite different position is taken that headteachers must behave according to external prescription, for example, that they should lead and manage their schools to implement centrally determined policies and programmes or, alternatively, that they should aim to be 'transformational' or 'instructional' leaders or to promote 'distributed' leadership, then quite different implications follow for needs identification and thus, of course, for programme design and content.

A third key issue concerns the extent to which the definition of leadership development either implicit or explicit in a programme or model is linked to a notion of being a *professional* educator. An important rider to the working definition presented in the Introduction is that:

> The notion of appropriateness must itself be based on shared and public value judgements about the needs and best interests of their clients . . . The essence of professional development for educators must surely involve the learning of an independent, evidence-informed and constructively critical approach to practice within a public framework of professional values and accountability, also open to critical scrutiny.

(Bolam, 2000, p. 272)

The position taken on professional values in any overall model of leadership development can have profound practical consequences for needs identification. For example, it is notable that the Scottish national scheme, unlike the English NPQH, takes professional values as its starting point. The first standard is called 'Professional Values' and requires headteachers: 'to hold, articulate and argue for professionally defensible educational values . . . based on the professional obligations of headteachers to serve the interests of children and young people in schools'. (SQH Development Unit, 1998, p. 4). The implications for the implementation of a work-based training programme for school leaders in Scotland are well described by Reeves et al. (2001)

A fourth issue concerns the extent to which an overall model is based on national standards, as has been the case in England (TTA, 1998) where they are integrated closely with a wider system of national standards for all teachers and, most recently, with a new system of performance management and performance-related pay. The latter is based on five key career milestones: preparation for initial qualification, induction for beginning teachers, a career stage reaching a performance threshold for most teachers, advanced skills teachers who must first pass the performance threshold and headship. Each stage uses competency-style standards and various forms of appraisal or assessment to measure performance and is linked to the pay structure (DfEE, 2000). These developments are by no means unique to Britain. Thus, the USA has developed inter-state standards for principals (Murphy, Yff and Shipman, 2000) but these are far from being controversial even in one country (see Waite, 2002). A needs identification process tied closely to such standards and performance management structures will obviously take on a different character to one that is not.

In conclusion, what broad lessons can be drawn from this analysis? For policy-makers and practitioners the main one is to be cautious and circumspect in seeking to adapt from international experience. More specifically, it is to support the approach of those who seek to adapt selectively from international experience. Assessing the relevance of sub-models will almost certainly be of greater potential value than assessing the overall model operating in any particular country. The reason is both simple and common sense: the more complex overall model is much more likely to be the product of the specific culture in which it operates, as illustrated by the Polish and British vignettes, and, therefore, much less easy to import, or indeed adapt, to another country. However, as the case of needs identification illustrates, even sub-models can be highly problematic. The most difficult task is to assess the value of the precise configuration of sub-components which go to make up the overall model of leadership development in any one country. In England these include the National College, the three main stages of training – preparatory, induction and in-service – the national standards and the emphasis on e-learning. One important potential contribution for researchers is to conduct comparative research and development studies designed to address these issues and to produce practical guidelines to illustrate the strengths and weaknesses of the overall model, and the possibilities for adaptation of their associated training strategies, approaches and methods. A more refined typological framework, perhaps building on the one outlined above, would be an important first step in this process.

REFERENCES

Al-Araj, F.M.S. (1999) 'Selection and training of secondary school headteachers in the UAE', unpublished PhD thesis, Cardiff University: School of Social Sciences.

Bolam, R. (1992) 'Curricula in educational management', in A.M.L. van Wieringen (ed.), *Training for Educational Management in Europe*, Die Lier: Academic Book Centre.

Bolam, R. (1997) 'Management development for headteachers: retrospect and prospect', *Educational Management and Administration*, **25**(3), 265–83.

Bolam, R. (2000) 'Emerging policy trends: some implications for continuing professional development', *Journal of In-service Education*, **26**(2), 267–79.

Bolam, R., Dunning, G. and Karstanje, P. (eds) (2000) *New Headteachers in the New Europe*, Munster and New York: Waxman Verlag.

Bolam, R., McMahon, A., Pocklington, K. and Weindling, R. (1993) *Effective Management in Schools*, London: HMSO.

Bolam, R., McMahon, A., Pocklington, K. and Weindling, R. (1995) 'Mentoring for new headteachers: the British experience', *Journal of Educational Administration*, **33**(5), 29–44.

Bolman, L,G., and Deal, T.E. (1997). *Reframing Organizations: Artistry, Choice, and Leadership*, (2nd ed,), San Francisco, CA: Jossey-Bass.

Brundrett, M. (2001) 'The development of school leadership preparation programmes in England and the USA', *Educational Management and Administration*, **29**(2), 229–45.

Bush, T. (1995) *Theories of Educational Management*, (2nd edn), London: Paul Chapman Publishing.

Bush, T. and Jackson, D. (2002) 'Preparation for school leadership: international perspectives', *Educational Management and Administration*, **30**(4), 417–30.

Centre for Educational Research and Innovation (CERI) (1982) *In-service Education and Training of Teachers: A Condition for Educational Change*, Paris: OECD.

Centre for Educational Research and Innovation (CERI) (2001) *New School Management Approaches*, Paris: OECD.

Cheng, Y.C. (in press) 'The changing context of school leadership: implications for a paradigm shift', in K. Leithwood and P. Hallinger (eds), *The Second International Handbook of Research on Educational Leadership and Administration*, Dordrecht: Kluwer.

Clarke, J. and Newman, J. (1997) *The Managerial State*, London: Sage Publications.

Commonwealth Secretariat (1996) *Better Schools: Resource Materials for Heads: Introductory Module*, London: Commonwealth Secretariat.

Department for Education and Employment (DfEE) (2000) *Professional Development: Support for Teaching and Learning*, London: DfEE.

Dunning, G. (2000) 'New heads in Wales', in R. Bolam, G. Dunning and P. Karstanje (eds), *New Headteachers in the New Europe*, Munster and New York: Waxman Verlag.

Ekiert-Grabowska, D. and Elsner, D. (1993) 'Barriers to effective headteacher development', in K. Hamalainen and F. van Wieringen (eds), *Reforming Educational Management in Europe*, Die Lier: Academisch Boeken Centrum.

Furlong, J. (2000) *Higher Education and the New Professionalism for Teachers: Realising the Potential of Partnership*, London: CVCP.

Gray, J. and Wilcox, B. (1995) *'Good School, Bad School': Evaluating Performance and Encouraging Improvement*, Buckingham: Open University Press.

Halasz, G. (2000) 'System regulation changes in education and their implications for management development', unpublished keynote paper for the Annual Conference of the European Network for the Improvement of Research and Development in Educational Management (ENIRDEM), 23 September, Tilburg University, Netherlands.

Hall, V. (1999) 'Gender and education management: dual or dialogue?', in T. Bush, L. Bell, R. Bolam, R. Glatter and P. Ribbins (eds), *Educational Management: Re-defining Theory, Policy and Practice*, London: Paul Chapman Publishing.

Hallinger, P. (2001) 'Leading educational change in East Asian schools', *International Studies in Educational Administration*, **29**(2), 61–72.

Hallinger, P. and Heck, R. (1999) 'Can leadership enhance school effectiveness?', in T. Bush, L. Bell, R. Bolam, R. Glatter and P. Ribbins (eds), *Educational Management: Re-defining Theory, Policy and Practice*, London: Paul Chapman Publishing.

Karstanje, P. (1999) 'Decentralisation and deregulation in Europe: towards a conceptual framework', in T. Bush, L. Bell, R. Bolam, R. Glatter and P. Ribbins (eds), *Educational Management: Re-defining Theory, Policy and Practice*, London: Paul Chapman Publishing.

Levačić, R. (1999) 'Managing resources for school effectiveness in England and Wales: institutionalising a rational approach', in R. Bolam and A.M.L. van Wieringen (eds), *Research on Educational Management in Europe*, Munster and New York: Waxmann.

Low, G.T. (2001) 'Preparation of aspiring principals in Singapore; a partnership model', *International Studies in Educational Administration*, **29**(2), 30–37.

Moos, L. and Dempster, N. (1998) 'Some comparative learnings from the study', in

J. MacBeath (ed), *Effective School Leadership: Responding to Change*, London: Paul Chapman Publishing.

Murphy, J., Yff, J. and Shipman, N. (2000) 'Implementation of the inter-state leaders' licensure consortium standards', *International Journal in Educational Leadership in Education*, **3**(1), 17–39.

National College for School Leadership website: http://www.ncsl.org.uk.

National College for School Leadership (NCSL) (2002) *Corporate Plan 2002/06*, Nottingham: NCSL.

Netherlands School of Educational Management (NSO) (2001) 'Transformation of educational management in Romania: School Managers Training Programme', Amsterdam: NSO, University of Amsterdam (mimeo).

Oldroyd, D. (1993) 'School-based management development: an "intermediate technology" for the self-managing school', in R. Bolam and A.M.L. van Wieringen (eds), *Educational Management across Europe*, Die Lier: Academisch Boeken Centrum.

Ouston, J. (1999) 'School effectiveness and school improvement: critique of a movement', in T. Bush, L. Bell, R. Bolam, R. Glatter and P. Ribbins (eds), *Educational Management: Re-defining Theory, Policy and Practice*, London: Paul Chapman Publishing.

Rayner, S., Gunter, H. and Powers, S. (2002) 'Professional development needs for leaders in special education', *Journal of In-service Education*, **28**(1), 79–94.

Reeves, J., Casteel, V., Morris, B. and Barry, P. (2001) 'Testing a standard for headship: outcomes from the initial evaluation of the Scottish Qualification for Headship Programme', *International Studies in Educational Administration*, **29**(2), 38–49.

SQH Development Unit (1998) *The Standard for Headship in Scotland*, Stirling: University of Stirling, Institute of Education.

Silins, H. and Mulford, B. (in press) 'Leadership and school results', in K. Leithwood and P. Hallinger (eds), *Second International Handbook of Research on Educational Leadership and Administration*, Dordrecht: Kluwer.

Stoll, L. and Mortimore, P. (1995) 'School effectiveness and school improvement: viewpoint 2', London: Institute of Education, University of London (mimeo).

Teacher Training Agency (TTA) (1998) *National Standards for Headteachers*, London: TTA.

Tomlinson, H. (2001) 'Leadership development and e-learning', *Management in Education*, **15**(5), 6–10.

Turner, C. (2002) 'Subject heads of department in secondary schools in Wales: improving the standards of teaching and learning', unpublished PhD thesis, Cardiff: Cardiff University, School of Social Sciences.

van Wieringen, A.M.L. (ed) (1992) *Training for Educational Management in Europe*, Die Lier: Academic Book Centre.

Waite, D. (2002) 'The "Paradigm Wars" in educational administration: an attempt at transcendence', *International Studies in Educational Administration*, **301**(1), 66–81.

Walker, A. and Dimmock, C. (in press) 'Moving school leadership beyond its narrow boundaries: developing a cross-cultural approach', in K. Leithwood and P. Hallinger (eds), *The Second International Handbook of Research on Educational Leadership and Administration*, Dordrecht: Kluwer.

Wallace, M. and Weindling, D. (1999) 'Overview of a group of research projects with relevance to school management', in T. Bush, L. Bell, R. Bolam, R. Glatter and P. Ribbins (eds), *Educational Management: Re-defining Theory, Policy and Practice*, London: Paul Chapman Publishing.

Weindling, D. (1999) 'Stages of headship', in T. Bush, L. Bell, R. Bolam, R. Glatter and P. Ribbins (eds), *Educational Management: Re-defining Theory, Policy and Practice*, London: Paul Chapman Publishing.

Wenchang, L. and Daming, F. (2002) 'Principal training in China: models, problems and prospects', *International Studies in Educational Administration*, **29**(2), 13–19.

Wen-haur, Shieh (2001) 'Implications of site-based curriculum reform for principals' change leadership development', in L. Wen-liuh Lin (ed) *International Conference on School Leader, Preparation, Licensure/Certification, Selection, Evaluation and Professional Development*, Taipeh: National Taipeh Teachers' College.

FURTHER READING.

Bolam, R. (1997) 'Management development for headteachers: retrospect and prospect', *Educational Management and Administration*, **25**(3), 265–83.

Bolam, R. (2000) 'Emerging policy trends: some implications for continuing professional development', *Journal of In-service Education*, **26**(2): 267–79.

Bolam, R., Dunning, G. and Karstanje, P. (eds) (2000) *New Headteachers in the New Europe*, Munster and New York: Waxman Verlag.

Bolam, R., McMahon, A., Pocklington, K. and Weindling, R. (1993) *Effective Management in Schools*, London: HMSO.

Bolam, R., McMahon, A., Pocklington, K. and Weindling, R. (1995) 'Mentoring for new headteachers: the British experience', *Journal of Educational Administration*, **33**(5): 29–44.

Bolman, L,G., and Deal, T.E. (1997) *Reframing organizations: Artistry, choice, and leadership*, 2nd edn, San Francisco: Jossey-Bass.

Brundrett, M. (2001) 'The development of school leadership preparation programmes in England and the USA', *Educational Management and Administration*, **29**(2), 229–45.

Brundrett, M. (1999) *Beyond Competence: the Challenge for Educational Management*, Dereham: Peter Francis.

Murphy, J. (1992) *The Landscape of Leadership Preparation: Reframing the Education of School Administrators*, Newbury Park, CA: Corwin Press.

Murphy, J. and Forsyth, P.B. (eds) (1999) *Educational Administration: A Decade of Reform*, Thousand Oaks, CA: Corwin Press.

6

THE NATIONAL COLLEGE FOR SCHOOL LEADERSHIP: ITS ROLE IN DEVELOPING LEADERS

Peter Newton

INTRODUCTION

Unlike the USA, systematic leadership and management development for schools in the UK has a comparatively short history. It was, nonetheless, as long ago as the 1960s when the first calls were made for the provision of more systematic training of headteachers. The intervening years have seen the construction and elaboration of school leadership programmes by higher education institutions and, more recently, 'national programmes' under the direction of government organisations. It was, however, only in the late 1990s that the decision was made by the UK government to establish a National College for School Leadership that would take a strategic overview of leadership training and would seek to develop a 'coherent national framework' (DfEE, 1999, p. 4) for school leadership programmes.

This chapter outlines briefly the growing calls for a more synchronous and planned approach to leadership training and development, culminating in the creation of the National College itself. The chapter then proceeds to elucidate the vision that now underpins the college's plans for future developments in the field.

THE CALL FOR MORE SYSTEMATIC TRAINING AND DEVELOPMENT OF HEADTEACHERS AND THE CREATION OF THE NATIONAL COLLEGE FOR SCHOOL LEADERSHIP

The Plowden Report (1967), which influenced so much of the English education system for the period of a generation, was one of the first governmentally inspired documents to state that there was inadequate provision of training courses to prepare either prospective headteachers or deputy headteachers for their future duties. The importance of the availability of in-service training to teachers in schools throughout their careers in order to produce a high-performance teaching force was subsequently recognised in the James Report (DES, 1972).

Almost coterminous with these developments, the idea of management development was probably first applied to education in this country by Glatter (1972), and by the mid-1970s Lyons (1976) began to provide an accurate picture of the various aspects of school management. By the early 1980s two key studies by Lloyd (1981) and Nias (1981) revealed that schools could be managed successfully using very divergent styles of leadership and made plain the pivotal role of headteachers in developing the 'ethos' of a school. With this growing body of knowledge about the nature of headship and its centrality in developing the very nature of the school as an organisation it is perhaps not surprising that it was at this juncture that the largely ignored recommendations of the Plowden Report about the need for systematic training of school leaders were taken up once again. For instance Wood (1982) made a strong case for such enhanced training opportunities to be created and, in particular, he advised that a 'training college' for heads should be created. Wood argued for a course which was 'something unique, and new, and explicitly designed to meet an identified need' (ibid., p. 288).

An exegesis of the subsequent progress in school leadership training and development in agencies including higher education, local education authorities (LEAs) and by national government has been offered by a number of scholars (see, for instance, Bolam, 1997; Brundrett, 1999). The arrival of the first 'national programmes' that found specific government imprimatur came with the Headteachers' Leadership and Management Programme (HEADLAMP) (TTA, 1995); soon to be followed by the National Professional Qualification for Headship (NPQH) (TTA, 1997a) and the Leadership Programme for Serving Headteachers (LPSH) (TTA, 1998). With the construction of these three programmes, originally under the aegis of the Teacher Training Agency, England and Wales had, for the first time, a clear set of systematic training programmes for the development of school leaders from aspirant to highly experienced headteachers.

It was not, however, until the White Paper, *Teachers Meeting the Challenge of Change* (HMSO, 1998) that the government expressed its intention of taking the step of establishing a national college to address the development needs of school leaders, the vision for which was set out in an ensuing initial prospectus (DfEE, 1999).

In November 2002 the Prime Minister, Tony Blair, subsequently launched the National College for School Leadership. The creation of the college demonstrates the government's commitment to improving leadership in education. This commitment has grown from an increasing recognition that the quality of leadership in schools is directly responsible for the quality of educational outcomes for pupils. The evidence for what is now taken as common sense can be found scattered liberally throughout the educational press. The government challenged the college to make itself: 'a driving force for world class leadership in our schools' (DfEE, 1999, p. 3). To this end the college has been set four main targets:

- To provide a single focus for school leadership development and research.
- To be a driving force for world class leadership in our schools and the wider education service.
- To be a provider and promoter of excellence; a major resource for schools and a catalyst for innovation.
- To stimulate national and international debate on leadership issues (NCSL, 2002a, p. 9).

The college is now housed on a £25 million state of the art conference centre, which was completed on the Jubilee Campus at the University of Nottingham, in the summer of 2002. From this conference centre the college will run headship training programmes, short skills programmes, its virtual presence and research-led learning.

Richard Greenhalgh, Chairman of Unilever, and Chair of the Governing Council of the college said in his introduction to the college's *Corporate Plan*: 'We know from other sectors – both business and public – that in changing organisations, the difference between success and failure is often the quality of the leadership.' His aspiration for the college was that, by the year 2006, it would be: 'a world class leadership centre, recognised internationally both inside and outside education' (NCSL, 2002a, p. 5). The UK Prime Minister, Tony Blair, was also in no doubt about the importance of the initiative:

> leadership and vision are crucial to raising standards and aspirations across our nation's schools . . . We cannot leave them to chance . . . our best heads are superb – but we need more of them – and that means offering them the best available training; the chance to share their experience of what works; the opportunity to learn from the best in leadership whether in the public or private sectors in this country or abroad; and time for reflection, refreshment and inspiration.

(DfEE, 1999, p. 2)

This clear goal setting and reaffirmation of support from the highest levels of government has been extremely important in ensuring that the college has been enabled to progress swiftly with it strategic plan for the development of school leadership. These plans are embodied in the *Leadership Development Framework* (NCSL, 2001a) produced after wide consultation with all sectors of the educational community.

THE LEADERSHIP DEVELOPMENT FRAMEWORK

In October 2001 the college launched a new leadership framework (NCSL, 2001a), offering it to the profession for consultation. The framework is a comprehensive plan to ensure a coherent programme of training and development throughout the career of a school leader. The framework came about as a result of considerable consultation with many thousands of school leaders and many hundreds of key organisations. Heather Du Quesnay, Chief Executive and Director of the college has said: 'this framework is designed to be the backbone for leadership development in this country's schools. We want it to form a coherent and flexible whole which will make a real difference to our education system.' (NCSL, (2001a).

The underpinning educational principles for the framework came about as a result of extensive work by a think tank, led by the then Professor of Education at the University of Nottingham, David Hopkins (see NCSL, 2001a, p. 4–6). The think tank, with extensive, national and international representation, helped the college to conceptualise its work. The think tank generated ten propositions around the nature of school leadership, principles of learning underpinning those propositions and recommendations as to the characteristics of any activity that should sit within a leadership development framework.

The ten school leadership propositions run as follows. School leadership must:

- be purposeful, inclusive and values driven
- embrace the distinctive and inclusive context of the school
- promote an active view of learning
- be instructionally focused
- be a function that is distributed throughout the school community
- build capacity by developing the school as a learning community
- be futures orientated and strategically driven
- be developed through experiential and innovative methodologies
- be served by a support and policy context that is coherent and implementation driven
- be supported by a national college that leads the discourse around leadership for learning (NCSL, 2001a, p. 4).

The implications of this work for the college are many. A clear link is made between research about high-quality learning and the leadership curriculum. At the same time the needs of the individual must be met. This will enable a productive involvement in training that seeks to help leaders to shape, interpret and implement a government agenda that seeks to transform the nation's education service. Not only must leadership training take into account career-long aspirations, but also the unique context of the school.

The think tank paved the way for the college to promote leadership training as a series of building blocks, intermingling training in instructional skills, organisational and strategic management and the development of personal and interpersonal skills. A heavy burden rests on the training providers, who should not only understand what constitutes the best adult learning, but also how to ensure the development of appropriate skills and the acquisition of innovative and enquiring leadership minds.

The work of the think tank and its recommendations sit alongside other foundations for leadership learning. These include the *National Standards for Headteachers* (and other groups of leaders and teachers) published by the Teacher Training Agency in the latter part of the 1990s (TTA, 1997b) as well as a developing strategy for continuing professional development being constructed within the Department for Education and Skills (DfES). Furthermore a major training programme for prospective headteachers, the NPQH, and the two other major national development programmes, HEADLAMP and the LPSH, both described earlier, are already well established. In addition, local education authorities, diocesan boards, professional associations, leadership centres and universities across the country offer a host of other leadership and management programmes to schools.

HEADSHIP TRAINING PROGRAMMES

The college already runs all three of the national headship programmes. The revised NPQH is being undertaken by well over 5,000 candidates across the country. This programme balances training and development with work-placed learning. It combines private study, school-based assessment, residential training, face to face learning and a strong element of information and communication technology (ICT).

The Headteachers' Leadership and Management Programme has been running for a number of years. Headteachers have access to over £2,500 worth of funding to spend on training and development activity commensurate with their needs. This has been provided by well over 150 training providers nationally. In its review of HEADLAMP (NCSL, 2001b), published alongside the *Leadership Development Framework*, the college recommends a tighter structure for the programme, tying provisions to individual needs, core modules of a training and development programme, mentor support, learning networks and a tighter relationships between continuing professional development and a personal leadership development profile.

THE FIVE STAGES OF SCHOOL LEADERSHIP

In order to make sense of training provision for school leaders on a national basis and provide a structure around which the college and its numerous partner providers can organise leadership training and development activity, the college has proposed that there are essentially five stages of school leadership (NCSL, 2001a, p. 7–12).

Emergent leaders are those beginning to take on formal leadership roles within the system, managing teams, co-ordinating the work of other teachers in a single subject, pastoral or special needs area. Many would think of teachers in this group as 'middle managers'. The National College has been charged with developing a training programme for subject and specialist leaders to be applied on a national basis. Early piloting work of elements of this programme, 'Leading from the Middle' began in April 2002 and the programme was due to begin to roll out fully in autumn 2002. Meeting the needs of underrepresented groups, such as Asian and Black teachers is also crucial to the future of our schools.

Established leaders are those who are experienced deputy and assistant headteachers and expert heads of subject and specialist areas who have decided that they do not wish to become headteachers. Meeting their training and development needs is vital for the continuing health of the profession.

Those *entering into headship* are well catered for in the NPQH and the Headteachers' Induction Programme, both available to support school leaders as they move into the more senior positions (see NCSL, 2002a). Following the implementation of its review recommendations the college aims to significantly increase the take-up of the induction programme. The college is working with the DfES on a consultation to explore the implications of making NPQH compulsory.

Those in *advanced leadership* positions have significant and important continuing training needs. The LPSH has traditionally filled this area and the college is developing a range of additional programmes in relation to change management, school renewal and the effective management of people. The college is also providing a platform for serious consideration of future schools and the implications for the organisation of schooling. School leadership faces challenges and difficulties as new conceptions emerge as to the purpose and nature of schooling in the future. Research into the future schools agenda and dissemination of our knowledge of e-learning and innovative teaching strategies will underpin the college's work.

The richest resource in the profession is undoubtedly those *consultant leaders* who have moved through all the other stages and are now highly experienced and proficient in their roles. The knowledge, skills and experience of these individuals are a rich resource and the college is seeking ways to harness this resource both for the benefit of the individuals concerned and the profession as a whole.

The College recognises that the value and status of leadership training will be enhanced by accreditation arrangements that provide progression to other higher education programmes and recognition within a national framework of qualifications. To this end the college is currently working with partner universities to secure that recognition.

To effectively reach the many thousands of potential and actual leaders that constitute its clientele the college also needs a strong regional presence. To that end it is seeking to establish a network of affiliated centres around the country both to provide programmes from the national agenda and develop and offer distinctive local and regional provision.

A VIRTUAL PRESENCE

One of the commonest feelings of those in leadership positions in schools is one of isolation and loneliness. NCSL Online – the National College for School Leadership's virtual arm – is determined to address this problem by exploiting the power and potential of new technology. Through this new technology the college's intention is to make accessible to school leaders the knowledge they need to help their staff and their pupils exploit the power of technology to the full and transform learning for the majority.

The college already hosts two groundbreaking new online communities – Talking Heads (for serving headteachers) and Virtual Heads (for NPQH candidates). Both of these sites has been extremely well received by the profession and around 10,000 school leaders are registered to use them. The sites are used for the exchange of ideas, problem-solving, debating issues with colleagues and learning about leadership and leadership methodology. Talking Heads provides communities for practising headteachers as well as access to key figures such as Professor Michael Barber, Professor Tim Brighouse, Professor Stephen Hepple and others. Virtual Heads, the NPQH training arm, provides a convenient and flexible method of studying for NPQH candidates.

The National College's website (NCSL, 2002b) and online communities are vehicles for developing a living and continuous debate within the profession on all aspects of school improvement and practice. A major challenge facing the profession is managing the impact of new technology on the curriculum on teaching and learning and on the organisation and management of schools. It is vital that the leadership of schools fully understands the implications of ICT for learning and organisational effectiveness. In order to support headteachers in acquiring this learning, NCSL is providing a range of training opportunities both face to face and through its online communities.

A major development, which will have important implications for teachers and school leaders, is the rise and development of a digitally available and digitally delivered curriculum. The BBC with Granada Learning have been awarded a contract to design, develop, produce and make widely available six GCSE subjects and these will be delivered to learners through home personal computers (PCs) at school and home, possibly through digital television and in time through other devices that can access the World Wide Web. The increasing opportunity for pupils to learn 'virtually' and independently has massive implications for the future of formalised schooling.

The college is a major player in understanding how to manage pupil's learning when much of it will be taking place away from the conventional school. The college recognises a need for a healthy debate by what is meant by e-learning and e-pedagogy and its implications for the future organisations of schools. Managing 'distributed learning' will have massive implications for the timing of the school day, the organisation of the formal timetable and the deployment of staff. The potential benefits that this technology offers are massive and the college is keen to involve school leaders in creating this future for themselves.

RESEARCH AND SCHOOL IMPROVEMENT

Underpinning the work of the college and all its activities for school leaders is a strong research base. Through its research group the college will be engaged in a process of knowledge creation, knowledge formulation and knowledge transfer (see NCSL, 2002c). The college considers it vital that the use of this knowledge, and the customisation of the knowledge so that it is accessible, constantly underpins its work. Through the Research and School Improvement Group the college will come to better understand the characteristics of learning leaders, learning schools and a knowledge rich system. The college is committed to working directly with school leaders, thereby promoting enquiry based leadership models and facilitating the formulation of knowledge from practice. Through working with groups and networks of schools, connections can be made between school leaders, e-networks set up and other partners such as LEAs involved at all levels of the system.

The college is committed to working within the research community in universities and has already extensively engaged with the Evidence for Policy and Practice (EPPI) reviews (see EPPI, 2002); the Standing Conference for Research on Educational Leadership and Management (SCRELM) (see SCRELM, 2002); the British Educational Leadership, Management and Administration Society (BELMAS) (see BELMAS, 2002) and other groups. In order to ensure that research significantly underpins the college's work a number of strands are being developed. These include researching successful leadership in urban and challenging contexts:

- focusing research on the best national and international evidence concerning operation for and support for newly appointed headteachers
- work designed to understand how to increase the capacity of schools to improve by engaging new and emerging knowledge within their development
- bringing learning communities together as networks to apply, study and contribute to emerging knowledge about effective schools
- learning from best practice worldwide through links with international leadership centres, universities internationally, international conference circuits and the British Council.

A CHALLENGING FUTURE

The *Leadership Development Framework* (NCSL, 2001a) and the *Corporate Plan 2002/06* (NCSL, 2002a) demonstrate clearly the range and depth of work that the college will be undertaking. In particular the college is committed to delivering high-quality leadership development opportunities to its 25,000 schools, developing, piloting and researching new and innovative approaches to meeting the leadership development needs of school leaders, and learning from the profession and partners and using this emerging knowledge and experience to help shape future policy and strategy both for the college and the education system as a whole.

The canvas the college has to work on is extensive. It will focus its activities in the first few years to ensure the greatest impact. Networked communities of learners will help create both professional knowledge and learning. The online community will grow; particularly as e-learning discussion communities are given priority. The college will work closely with government to support urban improvement initiatives, such as Excellence in Cities and its Transforming Secondary Education strategy. The two national training programmes will continue to evolve and grow and the college will particularly emphasise the role of consultant leaders as a significant force in transforming the profession. New leaders trained through the Leading from the Middle programme will be the bedrock of new members of the leadership profession and a central part of the college's work in the future.

REFERENCES

British Educational Leadership, Management and Administration Society (BELMAS) (2002) http://www.belmas.org.uk/

Bolam, R. (1997) 'Management development for headteachers', *Educational Management and Administration*, **25**(3), 265–83.

Brundrett, M. (1999) *Beyond Competence: The Challenge for Educational Management*, Dereham: Peter Francis.

Department of Education and Science (DES) (1972) *Teacher Education and Training* (James Report), London: HMSO.

Department for Education and Employment (DfEE) (1999) *National College for School Leadership: A Prospectus*, London: DfEE.

Evidence for Policy and Practice (EPPI) (2002) http://eppi.ioe.ac.uk

Glatter, R. (1972) *Management Development for the Education Profession*, London: Harrap.

Her Majesty's Stationery Office (HMSO) (1998) *Teachers Meeting the Challenge of Change*, London: HMSO.

Lloyd, K. (1981) Primary school headship types – a study of the primary head's leadership role perceptions, M.Ed thesis, University of Birmingham, in M. G. Hughes (1982) *Professional Development for Senior Staff in Schools and Colleges, Educational Management and Administration* **4**(1), 29–45.

Lyons, G. (1976) *Heads' Tasks: A Handbook of Secondary School Administration*, Windsor: NFER.

National College for School Leadership (NCSL) (2001a) *Leadership Development Framework*, Nottingham: NCSL.

National College for School Leadership (NCSL) (2001b) *Review of the Headteachers' Leadership and Management Programme*, Nottingham: NCSL.

National College for School Leadership (NCSL) (2002a) *Corporate Plan 2002/06*, Nottingham: NCSL.

National College for School Leadership (NCSL) (2002b) *NCSL Homepage*, http://www.ncsl.org.uk

National College for School Leadership (NCSL) (2002c) *Research and Development: R and D Programmes*, http://www.ncsl.org.uk/index.cfm?pageid=randd-pro-grammes-index

Nias, J. (1981) 'Leadership styles and job satisfaction in primary schools', in T. Bush, R. Glatter, J. Goodey, C. Riches (eds), *Approaches to School Management*, London: Harper & Row.

Plowden Report (1967) *Children and their Primary Schools*, 2 vols, Report of the Central Advisory Council for Education in England, London: HMSO.

Standing Conference for Research in Educational Leadership and Management (SCRELM) (2002) http://www.screlm.btinternet.co.uk/

Teacher Training Agency (TTA) (1995) *HEADLAMP 3/95*, HEADLAMP Programme Document, London: TTA.

Teacher Training Agency (TTA) (1997a) *National Professional Qualification for Headship*, London: TTA.

Teacher Training Agency (TTA) (1997b) *National Standards for Headteachers*, London, TTA.

Teacher Training Agency (TTA) (1998) *National Leadership Programme for Serving Headteachers*, London: TTA.

Wood, A.D. (1982) 'A training college for headteachers of secondary schools; some thoughts and consideration', *School Organization*, **3**(3), 287–96.

FURTHER READING

NCSL (2001) *Leadership Development Framework*, Nottingham: NCSL.

NCSL (2002) *Corporate Plan 2002/06*, Nottingham: NCSL.

NCSL (2002) *Leading the Management of Change – Building Capacity for School Development*, Nottingham, NCSL.

NCSL (2002) *National Professional Qualification for Headship (NPQH) Guide for Applicants*, Nottingham: NCSL.

NCSL (2002) *NCSL Homepage*, http://www.ncsl.org.uk

NCSL (2002) *NCSL Online Showcase*, Nottingham: NCSL.

NCSL (2002) *Research and Development: R and D Programmes*, http://www.ncsl.org.uk/index.cfm?pageid=randd-programmes-index

Section C: Teachers as Leaders

7

TEACHER LEADERSHIP: ITS NATURE, DEVELOPMENT, AND IMPACT ON SCHOOLS AND STUDENTS

Kenneth Leithwood

INTRODUCTION

Over the past four years, my colleagues, students and I have conducted a series of six studies on teacher leadership. Three of these studies, grounded in design (Strauss and Corbin, 1990), relied on qualitative data to describe the nature of informal teacher leadership in both elementary and secondary schools (Anderson, 2002; Leithwood, Jantzi and Steinbach, 1999; Ryan, 1999). The remaining three studies inquired about the effects of teacher leadership on selected aspects of school organisation, as well as on students (Leithwood and Jantzi, 1999; Leithwood and Jantzi, 2000); in these three studies, which tested a framework for understanding leadership effects using quantitative methods, teacher leader effects were compared with the effects of principal leadership. Throughout the chapter some or all of these studies are referred to as the 'CLD research' (CLD is the acronym for the Centre for Leadership Development, our institutional home within OISE/UT).

Each of the six studies conceptualised leadership as an influence process (Yukl, 1989) that depends on a person's behaviour being recognised as, and at least tacitly acknowledged to be, 'leadership' by others who thereby cast themselves in the role of followers consenting to be led (Greenfield, 1995; Lord and Maher, 1993). From this perspective, leadership is 'the process of being perceived as a leader' (Lord and Maher, 1993: p. 11) through the social construction of meaning on the part of followers (Meindl, 1995).

This chapter summarises evidence and implications from the six studies to briefly answer three questions: What is 'teacher leadership'? How much does it contribute to a school's effectiveness? And how can it be

103

developed? In light of the answers to these questions, the paper concludes by briefly considering whether teacher leadership is actually a useful concept.

WHAT IS 'TEACHER LEADERSHIP'?

Background

Leadership, suggest Sirotnik and Kimball (1996), does not take on new meaning when qualified by the term 'teacher'. It entails the exercise of influence over the beliefs, actions, and values of others (Hart, 1995), as is the case with leadership from any source. What may be different is how that influence is exercised and to what end. In a traditional school, for example, those in formal administrative roles have greater access than teachers to positional power in their attempts to influence classroom practice, whereas teachers may have greater access to the power that flows from technical expertise. Traditionally, as well, teachers and administrators often attempt to exercise leadership in relation to quite different aspects of the school's functioning, although teachers often report a strong interest in expanding their spheres of influence (Reavis and Griffith, 1993; Taylor and Bogotch, 1994).

Teacher leadership may be either formal or informal in nature. Lead teacher, master teacher, department head, union representative, member of the school's governance council, mentor – these are among the many designations associated with formal teacher leadership roles. Teachers assuming these roles are expected to carry out a wide range of functions. These functions include, for example: representing the school in district-level decision-making (Fullan, 1993); stimulating the professional growth of colleagues (Wasley, 1991); being an advocate for teachers' work (Bascia, 1997); and improving the school's decision-making processes (Malen, Ogawa and Kranz, 1990). Those appointed to formal leadership roles also are sometimes expected to induct new teachers into the school, and to positively influence the willingness and capacity of other teachers to implement change in the school (Fullan and Hargreaves, 1991; Whitaker, 1995).

Teachers exercise informal leadership in their schools by sharing their expertise, by volunteering for new projects and by bringing new ideas to the school. They also offer such leadership by helping their colleagues to carry out their classroom duties, and by assisting in the improvement of classroom practice through the engagement of their colleagues in experimentation and the examination of more powerful instructional techniques. Teachers attribute leadership qualities, as well, to colleagues who accept responsibility for their own professional growth, promote the school's mission and work for the improvement of the school or the school system (Harrison and Lembeck, 1996; Smylie and Denny, 1990; Wasley, 1991).

CLD research

Functions reported for teacher leaders in this literature created expectations about what we might find were the functions of teacher leaders in our study. But the three studies specifically inquiring about the nature of informal teacher leadership were guided by the principles of grounded theory development. Methodologically, all three studies were conducted in two stages. During the first stage, all teachers in selected schools were asked to respond to a one-page, confidential questionnaire requesting them to nominate people in their schools, exclusive of administrators, who provided leadership. At the second stage, the three people receiving the most nominations by their colleagues in each school, along with the nominators, were interviewed. Questions focused on what it was that caused the nominees to be viewed as leaders and what they did to provide leadership.

Based on the application of 'constant comparative' coding methods recommended for the development of grounded theory, results suggested that teachers' perceptions of informal teacher leadership could be described in terms of traits, capacities, practices, and outcomes. Results from Leithwood, Jantzi and Steinbach (1999) illustrate much of what has been learned about each of these categories.

Traits. In these studies of teacher leaders in six secondary schools, 75 specific traits were identified from a total of 341 units of coded text. These traits were further classified as mood, values, orientation to people, physical characteristics, responsibility, personality, and work-related traits. The most frequently mentioned specific trait was 'quietness'; being unassuming and soft-spoken was highly valued by these teachers. The next most frequently mentioned specific traits were: having a sense of commitment to the school and/or the profession; having a sense of humour; being a hard worker; and possessing an appreciative orientation to others.

Personality characteristics were mentioned 69 times. This category of trait included being unselfish, intelligent, genuine, humble and energetic. Values were mentioned 58 times and included commitment to the school and/or profession, having strong beliefs and being fair. Mood, mentioned 53 times, included being quiet, having a sense of humour, and being even-tempered. Work ethic also was mentioned 53 times, a category which included: being determined; not appearing to be 'empire-building'; being a visionary; and having high standards. Responsibility was discussed 34 times. This category included: being a hard worker; being steady; and being dependable. Physical characteristics, being tall or big, were mentioned only three times.

Capacities. This category encompasses a leader's knowledge, skills and/or abilities. One hundred and fifty-nine items coded in this category were organised into seven dimensions: procedural knowledge; declarative knowledge; relationships with staff; problem-solving ability; relationships with students; communication skills; and self-knowledge.

The most frequently mentioned skills were associated with procedural and declarative knowledge. Procedural knowledge had to do with a teacher's knowledge of how to carry out leadership tasks, e.g., making tough decisions, knowing how to run a meeting, and dealing with administration. As teachers said: '[she] can put out fires without too much trouble'; '[he] knows how to handle a situation without implicating anyone else'; or '[she] knows how to evaluate our students, modify programs, develop report cards'.

The declarative knowledge category refers to knowledge about specific aspects of the profession, e.g., knowledge about government education policy; knowledge about education in general; knowledge about the school, students and the community; knowledge about specific subjects; and knowledge about union issues.

Teachers' ability to work well with their colleagues included statements about how a particular teacher can motivate staff, work effectively with others and be willing to moderate disagreements. Being a good problem-solver was seen as an important leadership capacity. For example, one teacher said, '[she] can listen to a discussion and, in the end, filter it all down to what the real problems are'. Getting to the heart of the matter or being able to synthesise information was mentioned five times. Dealing with difficulties well and being able to think things through are other examples of statements coded as problem-solving skills.

The capacity to relate well with students, particularly being able to motivate them and being able to understand them, was valued among teacher leaders, as was having good communication skills (being articulate and persuasive). Statements coded as self-knowledge referred to a leader's ability to change, and to 'know what she is doing'. '[She] knows she can't win all of her battles.'

Practices. What leaders actually do is what we coded as 'practices' in our studies. These functions, tasks, and activities, were organised into nine dimensions. The most frequently mentioned dimension was that the teacher performs administrative tasks, such as working administrative periods in the office, being on committees, and organising specific events (e.g., running the commencement programme and spearheading the implementation of special courses). Modelling valued practices was the next most frequently mentioned dimension. This included leading by example, interacting with students, being a motivator for staff and students, and never missing a day of work. One teacher said, 'he sets the example that there are many teachers who have taught for a long time and who are excellent teachers'. Another said, 'he reminds us of our objectives'.

Formal leadership responsibilities were frequently mentioned. This dimension reflects the number of times teachers were nominated as leaders because of their position, e.g., being a department head or being head of a particular committee. Supporting the work of other staff was associated by many respondents with leadership; this referred to the help the teacher provided to his or her colleagues (e.g., helps young teachers, helps with course outlines, helps with a difficult class) or the support given to staff (e.g., 'kind of stroking people and saying you can do it', 'speaks out on our behalf whether we agree or disagree', 'allows people to vent').

Teachers felt being visible in the school was an important dimension of leadership. Examples of this practice include: presenting information at staff meetings and being a leader in the school not just in the department. Specific teaching practices (e.g., having lessons well prepared and being a good teacher) often were mentioned. Confronting issues directly, sharing leadership with others, and personal relationships were the last three dimensions of practices mentioned by the interviewees.

Outcomes. The outcomes associated with leadership provide important clues about the basis for leader attributions under circumstances in which leadership is experienced long enough to draw inferences from leader effects on the organisation, not simply on existing leader stereotypes. Outcomes of leadership identified by 'followers' tell us something about the needs people have that they hope leadership can meet. One hundred and sixty-two statements were coded as nine different dimensions of outcomes. Most frequently mentioned was gaining the respect of staff and students. Next most frequently identified as a leadership outcome was that activities involving the leader were invariably implemented well ('it went off very well' or 'things always work out in the end' or 'he and [T] have taken the track team to extreme heights'). The fact that people listen to the leader was mentioned frequently; one interviewee said, for example, 'when she speaks up, people listen'.

Being widely perceived as a leader was mentioned often. One teacher said, 'people turn to him for leadership in the school'. Another said, 'I think he's someone they would turn to if they were looking for avenues to proceed'. A desire to emulate the leader was mentioned: 'She makes you want to put as much effort forth as she does'; 'You're just saying, hey, if I could be like that'. Having a good effect on students, contributing to the culture of the school ('he adds to the heart of the school'), enhancing staff comfort level and meeting high expectations were other types of outcomes associated with those teachers nominated as leaders by their peers.

TEACHER LEADERSHIP EFFECTS ON SCHOOLS AND STUDENTS

Background

Empirical evidence concerning the actual effects of either formal or informal teacher leadership are limited in quantity and report mixed results. For example, many of the more ambitious initiatives establishing formal teacher leadership roles through the creation of career ladders have been abandoned (Hart, 1995). And Hannay and Denby's (1994) study of department heads found that they were not very effective as facilitators of change largely due to their lack of knowledge and skill in effective change strategies. On the other hand, Duke, Showers and Imber (1980) found that increased participation of teachers in school decision-making resulted in a more democratic school. Increased professional learning for the teacher leader also has been reported as an effect of assuming such a role (Lieberman, Saxl and Miles, 1988; Wasley, 1991).

Empirical evidence about school effects, in general, and principal leader effects, in particular, is helpful in establishing realistic expectations for what is likely to be found in empirical studies of teacher leader effects. Recent reviews of empirical research on school effectiveness suggest that educational factors for which data are available explain, in total, something less than 20 per cent of the variation in student cognitive outcomes; very little evidence is available concerning such non-cognitive outcomes as the one used in our studies. Reynolds et al. (1996) suggest 8–12 per cent for research carried out in the UK, while Creemers and Reetzigt (1996, p. 203) suggest 10–20 per cent for studies carried out 'in the Western Hemisphere . . . after correction for student intake measures such as aptitude or social class'. Variation within this range across studies may be explained by such variables as school size, type of student outcome serving as the dependent measure, nature of students, as well as department and subject matter differences.

While these relatively small amounts of explained variation are now considered to be both meaningful, and practically significant, a school is not a single variable. It is an aggregate of variables, the 'correlates' of effective schools, or the organisational conditions used as mediating variables in our own studies, for example. Some of these variables most likely contribute more strongly than others to a school's effects, although they have yet to be unpacked empirically, except for distinguishing between classroom and school level factors (Creemers and Reetzigt, 1996; Scheerens, 1997). Efforts to do the unpacking, however, realistically begin with very modest amounts of variation to be explained, especially if it is assumed, as seems reasonable, that at least a handful of factors contribute to explained variation. This was Ogawa and Hart's (1985) argument in claiming importance for their finding that principal leadership explained

2–8 per cent of the variation in student performance, the range of variation common to the leadership effects studies reviewed by Hallinger and Heck (1996; 1998).

CLD research

All three CLD studies inquiring about teacher leader effects assessed the relative effects on selected aspects of school organisation and on students of both teacher and principal sources of leadership (Leithwood and Jantzi, 1999). The framework for these studies conceptualised the two sources of leadership as independent variables, family educational culture as a moderating variable, and a cluster of school (e.g., culture, vision, structure) and classroom (e.g., instructional practices) characteristics as mediating variables. The dependent variable was student engagement with school, a variable with two dimensions – identification and participation.

Data to test this framework were collected from large samples of teachers and students in two large school districts in Ontario and Nova Scotia using two survey instruments. One survey asked teachers about the status of school organisation conditions, as well as the relative influence of principal and teacher sources of leadership. The second survey asked students about their engagement with school (participation and identification), and the status of their family educational culture. Regressions and path modelling techniques (LISREL 8; see Joreskog and Sorbom, 1993) were the primary methods of data analysis used to test the framework.

Results of the three studies are very similar. Figure 7.1, from Leithwood and Jantzi (1999), reports the results of testing (using LISREL) the framework for the study adapted in response to a factor analysis in which all items measuring school conditions loaded on the same factor. The model as a whole, explains 84 per cent of the variation in student participation and 78 per cent of the variation in student identification. Significant relationships, with differing strengths, are reflected in the total effects of family educational culture (.88), school conditions (.13 and .18), and principal leadership (.07 and .09). The total effects of teacher leadership are not significant.

Figure 7.1 also indicates strong, significant relationships (.56) between principal leadership and school conditions, a much stronger relationship than is the case with teacher leadership (.29) or family educational culture (.28). School conditions are weakly related to both student variables; the relationship with student identification is, nevertheless, statistically significant (.18).

An additional series of regression analyses were completed to determine the strength of the relationships between teacher and principal leadership and each of the five variables included as part of school conditions. Both principal and teacher leadership were significantly related to all school

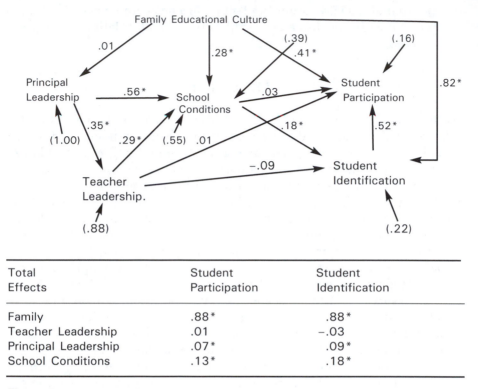

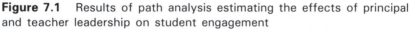

Total Effects	Student Participation	Student Identification
Family	.88*	.88*
Teacher Leadership	.01	−.03
Principal Leadership	.07*	.09*
School Conditions	.13*	.18*

Figure 7.1　Results of path analysis estimating the effects of principal and teacher leadership on student engagement

Source: Leithwood and Jantzi (1999)

conditions, although with a uniform pattern of stronger relationships with principal leadership. Principal leadership has its greatest effects on culture (.26) and structure and organisation (.27). The weaker effects of teacher leadership do not vary much among school conditions (.05 to .10).

　　With student engagement in school as the dependent variable, results of the study indicate that teacher leadership effects are statistically non-significant whereas, principal leadership effects, although not strong, do reach statistical significance. As well, teacher leadership had smaller effects on school conditions as compared with principal leadership. More teacher leadership has been advocated over the past decade for several reasons but without much evidence that it has the potential its advocates claim. While Heller and Firestone (1995) concluded from their data that principal leadership does not stand out as a critical part of the change process, our results suggest that teacher leadership is not likely to stand out either, at least not for change processes aimed at increasing student engagement with school.

HOW CAN TEACHER LEADERSHIP BE DEVELOPED?

Background

In spite of the modest effects that CLD research has found for teacher leadership on schools and students, many will still want to know how it might be fostered. Both the development and exercise of teacher leadership is inhibited by a number of conditions. Time taken for work outside of the classroom likely interferes with time needed for students (Smylie and Denny, 1990). When extra time is provided for leadership functions, it is usually not enough (Wasley, 1991). Furthermore, the lack of time, training and funding for leadership roles (Cooper, 1988; White, 1992) interferes with teachers' personal lives, as well as their classroom work.

Cultures of isolationism common in schools inhibit the development of teacher leaders and their work with teaching colleagues, as do the associated norms of egalitarianism, privacy, politeness, and contrived collegiality (Duke, Showers and Imber, 1980; Griffin, 1995; Hargreaves, 1994; Sirotnik, 1994). Teacher leaders' effectiveness, some claim, is constrained by lack of role definition (Smylie and Denny, 1990) and by requiring them to take on responsibilities outside their areas of expertise (Little, 1995).

CLD research

Our research about this question has focused on the development of informal teacher leadership, although much of what is suggested in this section also is appropriate for the development of those assuming such formal teacher leader roles as department head and lead teacher (see Leithwood, Jantzi and Steinbach, 1999, ch. 8; Ryan, 1999). Teachers in our qualitative studies were asked to describe the practices of principals which made an important contribution to the development of teacher leadership in their schools. While some teachers claimed that their 'principal has the greatest impact on [who assumes] leadership roles', others claimed that people become leaders because of what they do. Still others believed that it's a 'combination of being tapped on the shoulder and self-identifying'.

Regardless, most teachers claimed that some principal practices can significantly influence how teacher leadership develops. These responses are summarised here in five categories, the first four of which reflect dimensions from our model of transformational school leadership (Leithwood, Jantzi and Steinbach, 1999).

Providing individualised support. One of the most frequently mentioned ways that principals influence the development of distributed leadership is by supporting and encouraging specific staff initiatives and leadership in general. For example, one teacher said, 'the administration has been very supportive of any initiatives that we take; at times people are encouraged, they sort of get a little push'. One form that this support takes is through the encouragement of risk-taking. When asked how the principal developed leadership among others, one teacher replied, 'he builds the ability for people to take risks; he doesn't criticise for failures'. Creating a comfortable and safe environment for trying out leadership roles and for encouraging the free expression of ideas was seen as an important practice for principals.

Another form of support mentioned by many teachers was the emotional support provided by the principal's appreciation for and recognition of a job well done. Pats on the back and other forms of praise were interpreted as encouragement to tackle leadership roles. As one teacher said, 'If the top of the administration believes in you, then I think you'll find people are willing to take leadership roles on themselves'. The principal can also show support by 'pump[ing] you up when you're getting discouraged'.

Building collaborative cultures. Along with creating a risk-free environment, many teachers spoke about the contribution to developing teacher leadership development of the principal's efforts to build collaborative cultures and the structures required for collaboration to take place. Establishing and/or maintaining a tradition of shared decision-making was seen to be crucial by many teachers. As one teacher said: 'The principal influences the distribution of leadership with encouragement to get involved. I think for the most part there's just been the atmosphere of encouraging input on anything.'

Setting up a committee structure in the school was frequently mentioned as one way to accomplish this because of the leadership opportunities it provided for staff. One caveat mentioned by many teachers regarding the establishment of a committee structure was the importance of awarding some authority or autonomy along with the leadership responsibility. The principals in our studies did that. Said one teacher, '[principal] was really good at delegating responsibility to others and then allowing them the freedom to do whatever they want to do, providing that they didn't get totally out of control'. Having some freedom of action was seen as as an incentive for taking on leadership responsibilities.

Providing intellectual stimulation. Being open to new initiatives and encouraging a culture of continuous improvement was mentioned as important for developing teacher leadership. Providing professional development opportunities and giving people the 'space to grow' were also viewed as fostering such leadership. Two teachers described how their principals provided intellectual stimulation as follows:

> The principal is really good at listening and he's smart. He'll say, have you thought of ... and he can be really quick at coming up with possible paths to take, and that's good because sometimes you're so close to it that you don't see it.

We've had a lot of administrators come out of this school, go to the board; we have a lot of people in this school who are known around the board for their work in curriculum. That's because he's very conscious of saying, why don't you go to that conference? Or he'll say why don't you do a presentation on this to that group?

Other teachers indicated that their principals fostered teacher leadership by encouraging staff to take courses and get advanced degrees.

Modelling. This category of practice includes those principals' personality traits that teachers found particularly conducive to developing their leadership. Being professional, having a high energy level, being gregarious and positive were among the traits mentioned. The willingness to share leadership (not being threatened by giving up some control or power) was claimed to be an important way for principals to model a sincere belief in teacher leadership.

Teachers also spoke about principals creating an 'environment here that's very receptive to people taking on leadership', including being approachable and open to diverse opinions from staff.

Identifying and selecting potential teacher leaders. Many teachers reported that their principals developed teacher leadership in the school through their choice of people for various leadership opportunities in the school. One teacher said, for example, 'the development of school leaders is entirely in [the principal's] court and whether he serves the ball to you or not [determines] if school leaders develop'. Mostly the way this was done was described as subtle: 'the principal asks if someone would consider volunteering for something that needs to be done'. But sometimes it was more direct: one teacher described the principal's influence as 'simply a case of sitting down with people and talking a little bit about what he has in mind and what he hopes will happen and then asking you to consider how you might participate in that'. There is never intimidation or coercion to accept a position.

The most important aspect of the selection process, though, is the principal's knowledge of each teacher (e.g., what the teacher is capable of doing but may be reluctant to tackle), what would be beneficial for the teacher to for his or her professional development. The selection or request for participation emerged out of an established relationship. One teacher said, 'he knew what to suggest, but he never assigned or anything like that'. Another teacher said, of a different principal,

He can spot budding leaders. He has a good sense of who is ready to take on a different role, who is able and who is ready. He will give it to somebody who he thinks is ready to take it on even knowing that the first time it might get screwed up. *So he isn't just delegating; he is picking and choosing people and nurturing leadership along.*

That was seen as a crucial practice on the part principals. Another teacher described the role as 'probably more of a parent, to be able to find out emotionally, physically, mentally, spiritually where you are and be able to try to get you to the next level'. This has important implications for expanding the teacher leadership available within a school. Formal school leaders are by no means the only influence on who is selected for teacher leader roles in the school. This is especially the case when those roles are of an informal nature, or when self-selection is possible. But when formal school leaders are able to participate in determining the choice of people for teacher leader roles, our study recommends a preference for teachers who already display the traits associated with teacher leaders from among those who display comparable levels of development with respect to practices and capacities.

CONCLUSION: IS TEACHER LEADERSHIP A USEFUL CONCEPT?

Results of our research are consistent in many respects with evidence provided by other large-scale, quantitative studies of principal leadership effects. To date, however, there have been very few such large-scale studies of teacher leadership effects. So the representativeness of our findings concerning such effects remains to be tested by others. Advocates of teacher leadership may find these results disappointing. They do not confirm the beliefs of such advocates or the implications typically drawn from qualitative studies of teacher leadership. However, the results should not be viewed as surprising. Most areas of inquiry touching on school effects have proceeded through an initial phase of enthusiastic advocacy, followed by a phase of largely qualitative research in small numbers of exceptional cases aimed at better understanding the phenomena, to a more mature phase which includes quantitative testing of effects on a large scale. This third phase is always hard on the initial advocates, because effects are very difficult to produce on a large scale, and even more difficult to detect quantitatively. It is probably time the concept of teacher leadership moved into this third phase. Our research provides a point of departure for the move.

Somewhat indirectly, results of our research also have prompted us to reconsider the motivation for grafting the concept of 'leadership' onto the concept of 'teacher'. Some of this motivation, no doubt, is to enhance the status of the occupation in an effort to further professionalise it. But the meaning of leadership remains murky, and its present status is highly dependent on a set of possibly fleeting, modern, Western values. In contrast, the concept of teaching is relatively clearer, and teaching is a long and honoured practice in most cultures. From this perspective, does not grafting leadership onto the concept of teaching actually devalue the status of teaching in the long run? Does not this grafting imply that being a teacher, and all that entails in the classroom and the wider organisation, is really not enough to warrant a respected role in bettering the human condition? Indeed, it seems likely that this marriage of concepts will do a disservice to the concept of leadership, as well. If everyone is a leader, for example, does not the concept lose all value as a legitimate distinction among social and organisational practices, separating it even further from its genesis in organisational administration?

REFERENCES

Anderson, K. (2002) 'Shared decision-making, school improvement and educational leadership in schools', PhD thesis, OISE University of Toronto.

Bascia, N. (1997) 'Invisible leadership: teachers' union activity in schools', *Alberta Journal of Educational Research*, **43**(2/3), 69–85.

Cooper, M. (1988) 'Whose culture is it anyway?', in A. Lieberman (ed.), *Building a Professional Culture in Schools*, New York: Basic Books, pp. 45–54.

Creemers, B.P.M. and Reetzigt, G.J. (1996) 'School level conditions affecting the effectiveness of instruction', *School Effectiveness and School Improvement*, **7**(3), 197–228.

Duke, D., Showers, B. and Imber, M. (1980) 'Teachers and shared decision-making: the costs and benefits of involvement', *Educational Administration Quarterly*, **16**, 93–106.

Fullan, M. and Hargreaves, A. (1991) *What's Worth Fighting For: Working Together for your School*, Toronto: Ontario Public School Teachers' Federation.

Fullan, M. (1993) *Change Forces*, Toronto: Falmer Press.

Greenfield, W.D. (1995) 'Toward a theory of school administration: the centrality of leadership'. *Educational Administration Quarterly*, **31**(1), 61–85.

Griffin, G. (1995) 'Influences of shared decision-making on school and classroom activity: conversations with five teachers'. *The Elementary School Journal*, **96**(1), 29–45.

Hallinger, P. and Heck, R. (1996) 'Reassessing the principal's role in school effectiveness: a review of empirical research 1980–1995'. *Educational Administration Quarterly*, **32**(1), 5–44.

Hallinger, P. and Heck, R.H. (1998) 'Exploring the principal's contribution to school effectiveness: 1980–1995'. *School Effectiveness and School Improvement*, **9**(2), 157–91.

Hannay, L.M. and Denby, M. (1994) 'Secondary school change: the role of department heads', paper presented at the annual meeting of the American Educational Research Association, New Orleans, April.

Hargreaves, A. (1994) *Changing Teachers, Changing Times: Teachers' Work and Culture in the Postmodern Age*, New York: Teachers College Press.

Harrison, J.W. and Lembeck, E. (1996) 'Emergent teacher leaders', in G. Moller and M. Katzenmeyer (eds), *Every Teacher Is a Leader: Realizing the Potential of Teacher Leadership*, San Francisco: Jossey-Bass.

Hart, A.W. (1995) 'Reconceiving school leadership: emergent views', *Elementary School Journal*, **96**(1), 9–28.

Heller, M.F. and Firestone, W.A. (1995) 'Who's in charge here? Sources of leadership for change in eight schools', *The Elementary School Journal*, **96**(1), 65–86.

Joreskog, K.G. and Sorbom, D. (1993) *LISREL: Structural Equation Modeling with*

SIMPLIS Command Language, Chicago, IL: Scientific Software.

Leithwood, K. and Jantzi, D. (1999) 'The relative effects of principal and teacher sources of leadership on student engagement with school', *Educational Administration Quarterly*, **35** (supplemental), 679–706.

Leithwood, K. and Jantzi, D. (2000) 'Principal and teacher leadership effects: a replication;, *School Leadership and Management*, **20**(4), 415–34.

Leithwood, K., Jantzi, D. and Steinbach, R. (1999) *Changing Leadership for Changing Times*, London: Open University Press.

Lieberman, A., Saxl, E.R. and Miles, M.B. (1988) 'Teacher leadership: ideology and practice', in A. Lieberman (ed.), *Building a Professional Culture in Schools*, New York: Basic Books, pp. 148–66.

Little, J.W. (1995) 'Contested ground: the basis of teacher leadership in two restructuring high schools', *The Elementary School Journal*, **96**(1), 47–63.

Lord, R.G. and Maher, K.J. (1993) *Leadership and Information Processing*, London: Routledge.

Malen, B., Ogawa, R. and Kranz, J. (1990) 'What do we know about school-based management? A case study of the literature', in W. Clune and J. Witte (eds), *Choice and Control in American Education Volume 2: The Practice of Choice, Decentralization and School Restructuring*, New York: Falmer Press.

Meindl, J.R. (1995) 'The romance of leadership as a follower-centric theory: a social constructionist approach', *Leadership Quarterly*, **6**(3), 329–41.

Ogawa, R. and Hart, A. (1985) 'The effects of principals on the instructional performance of schools, *Journal of Educational Administration*, **23**(1), 59–72.

Reavis, C. and Griffith, H. (1993) *Restructuring Schools: Theory and Practice*, Lancaster, PA: Technomic.

Reynolds, D., Sammons, P., Stoll, L., Barber, M. and Hillman, J. (1996) 'School effectiveness and school improvement in the United Kingdom', *School Effectiveness and School Improvement*, **7**(2), 133–58.

Ryan, S. (1999) 'Teacher leadership: a qualitative study in three secondary schools', PhD thesis, OISE/University of Toronto.

Scheerens, J. (1997) 'Conceptual models and theory-embedded principles on effective schooling', *School Effectiveness and School Improvement*, **8**(3), 269–310.

Sirotnik, K. (1994) 'Curriculum: overview and framework', in M.J. O'Hair and S. Odell (eds), *Educating Teachers for Leadership and Change*, Thousand Oaks, CA: Corwin Press, pp. 235–42.

Sirotnik, K. and Kimball, K. (1996) 'Preparing educators for leadership: in praise of experience', *Journal of School Leadership*, **6**, 180–201.

Smylie, M.A. and Denny, J.W. (1990) 'Teacher leadership: tensions and ambiguities in organizational perspective', *Educational Administration Quarterly*, **28**(2), 150–84.

Strauss, A. and Corbin, J. (1990) *Basics of Qualitative Research: Grounded Theory Procedures and Techniques*, Newbury Park, CA: Sage Publications.

Taylor, D.L. and Bogotch, I.E. (1994) 'School level effects of teachers' participation in decision-making', *Educational Evaluation and Policy Analysis*, **16**(3), 302–19.

Wasley, P.A. (1991) *Teachers as Leaders: The Rhetoric of Reform and the Realities of Practice*, New York: Teachers College Press.

Whitaker, T. (1995) 'Informal teacher leadership: the key to successful change in the middle school', *NASSP Bulletin*, January, pp. 76–81.

White, P. (1992) 'Teacher empowerment under "ideal" school-site autonomy', *Evaluation and Policy Analysis*, **14**(1), 69–84.
Yukl, G. (1989) *Leadership in Organizations*, Englewood Cliffs, NJ: Prentice Hall.

FURTHER READING

Harrison, J.W. and Lembeck, E. (1996) 'Emergent teacher leaders', in G. Moller and M. Katzenmeyer (eds), *Every Teacher is a Leader: Realizing the Potential of Teacher Leadership*, San Francisco: Jossey-Bass.
Leithwood, K. and Jantzi, D. (1999) 'The relative effects of principal and teacher sources of leadership on student engagement with school', *Educational Administration Quarterly*, **35** (supplemental), 679–706.
Leithwood, K. and Jantzi, D. (2000) 'Principal and teacher leadership effects: a replication', *School Leadership and Management,* **20**(4), 415–34.
Leithwood, K., Jantzi, D. and Steinbach, R. (1999) *Changing Leadership for Changing Times*, Buckinham: Open University Press.
Ryan, S. (1999) 'Teacher leadership: a qualitative study in three secondary schools', PhD thesis, OISE/University of Toronto.

8

TEACHER LEADERSHIP: PROSPECTS AND POSSIBILITIES

Helen M. Gunter

INTRODUCTION

The study and practice of educational leadership continues to be a busy terrain, particularly since the realities of professional work are often in tension with the current demands for modernisation. How teachers in their everyday work live their professional identities, make choices and take action, within a structuring context that seeks to confirm or challenge what they do and do not do, is central to this chapter. I will be asking questions about the stabilities and fractures in teachers' work, and examining the acceptability and possibilities for enabling teachers to reveal what they do as educational leadership. In doing this I will be drawing on published research and I intend to position myself as public intellectual (Gunter and Ribbins, 2002). In contrast with other professional practice (such as trainer, teacher, consultant, expert) where I may seek to locate myself, to different degrees as neutral facilitator, in this chapter I take up a committed commentator position. The implications of this are that in providing evidence and argument I am aiming to promote intellectual engagement and practical action around fundamental questions about society. Issues about teachers' work are inextricably connected with how we engage with the public good, and how we understand the purposes of schools and schooling. Such matters are simultaneously close to and distant from everyday practice. Closeness comes from recognising the dilemmas that teachers have every day in the choices they make in how to handle the tough issues of caring for and working with children; distance comes from the need to create the space to reflect upon the implications of our actions for how we want to live and work together.

FROM SEDITION TO SEDATION

For the past 30 years teachers have been positioned in print and in minds as the problem in education. There are two fabricated images that have been reworked and overlain until they have become so simple as to make professional irresponsibility obvious to all. Teachers have either made parents and children the victims of progressive ideologies and have used misguided notions about how schools should be organised, and/or teachers have waved placards and thrown eggs at ministers and so are unfit to be in charge of impressionistic minds. Teachers it seems have too much time to think because of the privilege of a short working day and long paid holidays. It seems that teachers have been cartooned as seditious by working contrary to parental interests. Consequently, teachers have had to be brought under control, and this is being done by cleansing the profession in England:

- Economically: low wages limits recruitment and retention.
- Intellectually: competencies prescribe acceptable values, behaviours, tasks and knowledge.
- Physically: illness and disillusionment means that particular types of teachers and talent exit.
- Practically: routinisation limits creativity and the opportunities to think otherwise.
- Socially: admitting to being a teacher in public is a defensive embarrassment and hence might be best left unsaid.

The combined effect of this has been to simultaneously sedate and stimulate the teacher and so the core activity of teaching and learning is being reconfigured around comparative measurement within and between 'performing schools' (Gleeson and Gunter, 2001; Gunter, 2001a). On the one hand the teacher is calmed through the provision of ringbinder scripts for the what, why and how to teach, and on the other hand is exhorted to be excited about their performance delivery. Two trends are illustrative of how the preferred teacher is being storied: language and evidence.

The language of education is shaping how we are allowed to think in ways that make the problems of schools and schooling look simple and hence capable of being easily solved. Staff rooms, performance threshold applications for salary enhancement and training assessment portfolios are awash with effectiveness, improvement, standards, auditing, vision, teams, stakeholders and outcomes. We might ask where has the dialogue gone around issues of pedagogy, learning, social justice, caring, democracy and theory? The modernisation of the teacher means that these words along with the complex and contested matters underpinning them have been consigned to the dustbin of history. A teacher who wants to survive at work has to stop talking about the realities of doing the job and instead image the self in line with the need to perform.

Not only is the language banal because it is preventing the endemic issues undermining teaching and learning to be surfaced, but it is also making out that resolution is easy by having a school development action plan or by improving the average points score in the national examination league tables. Teachers must evidence what they do and why they are doing it. Interventions in social relationships that are long term, complex and the product of collective activity are being scripted into short-term individualised encounters where cause and effect are close together. Teachers must be outcome orientated where their eye is on delivery, and so accountability is through being able to demonstrate that what they have done is not based on professional judgement and courage but on their fit with external training requirements. Furthermore, the culture of self-compliance (or self-absence/exit, as illustrated above) means that asking questions, promoting alternative debates, confronting tough matters, is difficult. It is hard to stand up and say that you have questions about why schools, as the prime target, should improve or be effective, and yet this is the type of enquiry that we need if we are to escape and provide alternatives to the current mediocrity that besets modernisation. Furthermore, as Smyth (1995, p. 5) argues children who witness this close up learn that in problem resolution 'institutional authority has more currency than the moral authority and credibility that attach to peer and collegial professional judgement on what is important about teaching'. This modernisation is almost feudal in both intent and impact, as the teacher is positioned as follower to the all-visioning headteacher as leader. Role incumbents either as senior or middle managers are also victims of modernisation as their identity is being shifted away from the professional matters of learning, and the needs of children and teachers, towards the disciplinary control of external accountability. Failure to perform in ways that are approved of means that heads and managers (and their families) have found themselves being publicly named and shamed.

It seems that in the last 30 years we have shifted from restructuring to retasking to reculturing and this has stripped the educational out of leadership as business sector models have come to dominate (Gunter, 2001a). Consequently, in spite of the rhetoric of leadership in education we have moved to performativity where the individual teacher or headteacher is on their own in demonstrating their worth and worthiness (Ball, 1999). By drawing on Sennett's work, Smyth (2001a) argues that we are witnessing a 'corrosion of character' in schools and we need to ask 'why do teachers do things with which they disagree?' Compliance can be secured through the logic of economic need in which education must produce the outcomes demanded by the globalising economy, and arguing for other educational goals located in citizenship and community is difficult because it is idealistic (the causal link with profit and profitability is difficult to make) and easily marginalised as dangerously ideological.

FROM SACRIFICE TO SIGNIFICANCE

Where do we go from here? Research shows that there is a 'refusal' to do things in ways that are being strictly prescribed (Nixon, 1995). Heads and teachers are trying to retain education within learning rather than submit to the dead hand of tests and more tests. In spite of the continued fabrication of long holidays, teachers have continued to use their time in ways that are educationally productive such as summer school, preparing sessions and working with students as examination results are published. We should not confuse this commitment to children, parents and the community with a compliance with modernisation. Teachers have always given of themselves, it is embodied in who they are, and it is a concern that it is not given the positive recognition it deserves (Hargreaves, 1998). Indeed, it has been turned into a type of martyrdom in which the invisibility of intrinsic rewards has been either sentimentalised, or often ridiculed around vocation and putting up with poor pay and working conditions. A legacy of Thatcherism is that this served powerful economic interests as the failure of teachers to make an effective case for more status, and hence worthiness of investment, affected recruitment and retention. The personal and personalising nature of teaching which means that you cannot walk away from tough issues means that the cost of educational reform has been borne by teachers and their families. Private business has always looked longingly at the public sector and tried to reproduce the capacity to work beyond the terms and conditions of the job description. It has done this through teams and profit incentive schemes, but it has largely failed because in the end entrepreneurship is elitist and hollow. The irony lies in the obsession with destroying public sector values by the use of private sector techniques at a time when the latter would benefit from a collective approach to economic problems.

The crisis in the recruitment and retention of teachers opens up possibilities for reconceptualising the significance of teachers and teaching. This has to be more than recognising that teachers have been so far largely ignored, except as implementers, in much of the reform agenda. It also has to go beyond the need to create only financial incentives to train and stay. We need to look at how and why teachers go about their work, what it means and the possibilities for development. In doing this we need to take a long hard look at leadership and how current preferred models may position teachers in ways that prevent the type of profession that learners need. Is it sufficient to argue for leadership to be 'distributed' (Gronn, 2000, p. 317), 'shared' (Moos and Dempster, 1998, p. 108), 'dispersed' or 'dense' (Sergiovanni, 2001, p. 112–16)? As Blackmore (1999. p. 222) argues: 'It also means problematising leadership as a key concept in educational administration and policy – redefining it and even rejecting it – for perhaps the focus upon leadership is itself the biggest barrier to gender equality.' Hence our task is not just to stimulate future and current teachers in ways that generate job satisfaction, but we need to look at the conditions of that satisfaction and engage with issues that challenge the power structures which seek to do the satisfying.

A current trend in the modernisation process is to reprofessionalise teachers as organisational leaders. Teachers are followers of and are integrated within the vision and mission created, and sustained by the headteacher and senior management. Teacher capabilities are harnessed and utilised through both a cognitive and emotional commitment to school goals, and they can demonstrate their empowerment through teamwork and the use of problem-solving strategies. This transformational leadership is about winning hearts and minds in order to realise organisational goals, and participation in processes such as development planning, long-term strategic thinking, as well as day-to-day efficiency and effectiveness, gives the teacher the opportunity to use new skills and knowledge. This trend in both policy and globalised models of leadership enables teachers with particular dispositions towards organisational compliance to gain leadership experience that is consistent with the type of formal leadership that post-holders in schools are being trained in (Gunter, 1999). However, while the rhetoric is of teams and empowerment, this is a very top-down model, or as Allix (2000, p. 18) argues: 'implies a pattern of social relations structured not for education, but for domination'. It assumes that in the division of labour the direction of control from top to bottom remains, and can be reinforced by models such as instructional leadership where the headteacher:

> is responsible for improving instruction and developing teachers' practice. It is the principal who must be trained to recognise good teaching, often by learning a prescribed five-step model of teaching. It is the principal who will teach the teachers about teaching practice. Instructional leadership will be accomplished through evaluation of teachers by principals using a standardised version of teaching

> (Garman, 1995: p. 151)

Consequently empowerment is the acceptance of organisational hierarchy and professional judgement is replaced by recipes devised by those at distance from practice. Garman (1995, p. 32) goes on to argue that the calls for empowerment have not come from teachers themselves, they are the 'silenced practitioners' because it is difficult to argue against the power structures that position the voice of teachers and children as being contrary to the drive for standards.

We might therefore ask where are the possibilities for teacher leadership that is both about education and is itself educative? Fruitful terrain for exploring this is by acknowledging the importance of teachers as researchers, mentors, learners and, ultimately, as teachers. By embarking on this journey there is the need to acknowledge that all of these teacher identities can be incorporated and sanitised through the current model of transformational leadership, and so I would like to note that my approach here is to investigate the issues around teachers' work that assumes professionality. As Nixon et al. (1997, p. 12) argue: 'the shift . . . is away from "professionalism" as the ideology of service and specialist expertise; away from "professionalisation" where the status of the occupation is at stake; and towards "professionality" which focuses on the quality of practice in contexts that require radically altered relations of power and control'. Consequently, if we are really serious about teacher leadership then we need to create the conditions for the exercise of agency and give recognition to teachers who may think otherwise to the mainstream vision and mission. The challenge lies both with those who are practitioners and their dispositions to engage in practice as intellectual and not just technical work, and with those who research school practice and the extent to which they reveal this in action (Gunter, 2001a).

Teacher research has a long history and, it could be argued, has always been a part of practice through trial and error approaches to developing and implementing new strategies. However, formalising teacher enquiry within the classroom and/or the school as a whole could be used to silence ideas if it is only based on audit and technicist evaluation. The possibilities still exist for an alternative conceptualisation through action research that seeks to be emancipatory by interventions that lead to sustainable change. Grimmett argues that action research is central to enabling professionality:

> Teachers face many of the dilemmas encountered by elite athletes and chronically ill patients. They frequently hold high aspirations for their own classroom performance; their own person is integrally part of their practice, placing their self-esteem constantly at risk; and their need for skills to help them cope with inordinate pressures created by the changing societal context is fairly evident. Like elite athletes, teachers clearly need mental skills that enable them to engage in reframing the everyday dilemmas they face in teaching and in the implementation of a new programme. However, they also need interpersonal support, stability and intellectual challenge in a community of inquirers. Teacher research provided a structure that permitted such an enabling environment to flourish.

> (Grimmett, 1995, p. 118)

Clearly a teacher cannot engage in professionality on their own, and how teachers work with children, with each other and in wider networks, in the generation and use knowledge, is central to an exercise of agency in which they can act upon what they know is worth knowing. Illustrative of this is the drive to formalise teachers as mentors, particularly with teachers in training, newly qualified teachers and, increasingly, with children. The danger in the creation and widespread adoption of mentoring is that it could be implemented as an integrating top down process of induction into established and/or preferred ways of working. Cochran-Smith and Paris (1995) argue that in order to move away from the conservative and smooth process of co-option into established norms then we need to begin with the epistemology of teachers and enable power to operate as a shared resource:

> If teaching is regarded as an intellectual activity and teachers are among those who have the authority to generate knowledge about teaching, then a central task involved in mentoring is supporting beginners as they learn to be knowers. This means learning to be not only critical consumers and interpreters of other people's knowledge but also knowledge-makers who formulate analytical frameworks, pose problems of practice and develop conjoined ways of collecting and connecting evidence in order to make decisions about teaching.

(Cochran-Smith and Paris, 1995, pp. 184–5).

This has implications for teacher learning and how individual biographies and organisational experiences support this type of thinking. We are all aware of the 're-entry' problem of having had access to new ideas and having them discounted back in the organisation. Also we can all possibly cite evidence of the cynicism that can surround teacher experiences of intensive learning required by the come-and-go of internal and external initiatives. As Hursh (1995) argues, teachers need to challenge the normality of teaching and learning, and see it as a product of political struggles that they have an entitlement to be a part of. Within school the operation of performance review with lesson observations does not have to follow a strict line management process based on abstracted criteria that is presented as good practice. Peer and pupil review are possibilities, but as work on teacher appraisal in the 1990s shows, such radical changes cannot be imposed or legislated without work that enables questions to be asked about the nature of teaching and learning, and how best might we research it for ourselves (Gunter, 2001b).

The arguments presented so far do present contradictions and, like Blackmore (1999), I remain troubled by the use of the word 'leadership' and how it has been defined and used to position teachers. The appropriation of leadership as the functions and behaviours of post holders means that the professionality imbued in relationships between teachers, and with children, parents and the community, is being elided. I would want to argue that we need to engage with the extensive work that exists about teachers' working lives in order to promote teachers as teachers. Leadership is within this conceptualisation but if we are really serious about improving teaching and learning then it cannot be structured by enduring hierarchical power structures. Teachers will continue to have technical competence, and will develop craft knowledge through experience, but they also need to position themselves within practice in such a way that they are able to 'confront strangeness' (Smyth, 2001b, p.

171). In this way they can draw on a range of resources, including theories gathered from study and reading, and theories developed within practice, which I call conceptually informed practice (Gunter, 2001a). As Atkinson (2000) argues, we cannot ignore that teachers do base their work on theories and so we need to open this up so that this is critically engaged with. I do not underestimate the challenge in all of this, and it is about working for rather than establishing a vision of an end result to be achieved. There is much that will enhance it and it has been revealed through research that shows teachers can and do exercise professional courage in the choices over teaching and learning (Crowther, 1997). Furthermore, such work shows that schools need not adopt traditional hierarchies and cultures which prevent authentic teacher participation, and so those who may benefit from a top-down model need not accept the practice that is associated with it (Smyth, 2001b). On the other hand, there are long traditions within the teaching community of allying their interests in ways that may run contrary to the prime purposes of teaching and learning. We have to address this, and perhaps a good place to begin is to discuss what we mean by competency to teach, what this means, who defines it, and why particular practice is experienced and labelled as such.

FROM SILENCE TO STEREO

Studying and practising teaching is essentially sociological. If we are to open up our understandings and to look at possibilities for change then we need to approach researching teacher work through conceptualising agency and structure (Gunter, 2001a). For example, Gronn (1996; 2000), in his scholarly analysis of leadership theory, has argued that we need to view distributive or shared leadership by asking different types of questions about organisations. Understanding a division of labour in which there is the leader and the followers is unhelpful because of the neo-Taylorist approach to the separation of the design from the implementation of work. Dressing this up in the more seductive language of the 1990s with empowerment and collaboration does not really deal with the dualisms of leader–follower, visioner–deliverer. If we are to begin with the realities of practice, and that the work of teaching and schools is distributed, then, as Gronn (2000) argues, we need to have a more sophisticated analysis of who or what does the distribution than just the leader empowering the follower. Similarly, Wallace (2001, p. 165) has shown that the contextual setting of headship in the UK means that while it may be normatively desirable to share, the realities of accountability do 'justify British headteachers proceeding with caution towards the most extensive, equal sharing of leadership possible to maximise potential for synergy, while allowing for contingent reversal to hierarchical operation to minimise the risk of disaster'. What we are facing is how the arguments for site-based management in the 1980s, which put emphasis on delegating decisions and choices to those who had to live with the consequences, have been lost because of the endurance of the headmaster tradition. For site-based management to deliver its democratic possibilities for authentic participation in schools, there needed to be a follow through in discussions about traditional hierarchies. Not only has this not happened but hierarchy has been strengthened through the emphasis on headteachers as organisational and transformational leaders, and by the excessive demands for public accountability through narrow indicators of school performance. Nevertheless, the debate about democratic development is timely since there is research evidence of increasing demands by teachers, parents and pupils for more involvement in decision-making (Moos and Dempster, 1998).

How might we proceed as practitioners and researchers? The questioning of the existence of leadership because there are 'substitutes' for leaders only takes us part of the way. Gronn (2000, p. 319) describes these arguments as: (a) there is 'evidence in numerous studies of a lack of demonstrated leader effects in explaining organisational outcomes'; (b) there are 'the personal attributes of organisational members (e.g. their self-motivation to perform)'; (c) there is a momentum to work or 'organisational processes (e.g. autonomous work group norms)', and (d) there are regularities to work or 'the characteristics in the work itself (e.g. its routine or programmed nature'. Giving recognition to teacher agency within the division of labour is helpful in this analysis, but labelling it as a 'substitute' only creates a push–pull debate over whether leaders do or do not deny teacher professionality. If we conceptualise leadership as what leaders as role incumbents do when they are leading, then looking for places and spaces where their influence and power does not reach is an interesting activity. If, however, leadership is conceptualised as a dynamic relationship that all in school and the community can engage in, then we need to develop a sociologically informed approach to the interplay between agency and structure. What we need is theory and theorising that is able to recognise the complexities of how agency and structure work within practice, and so teacher motivation to act is revealed or cloaked because of the shaping influence of structures such as organisational culture which approves of or criticises such activity. In this way the emphasis is less on being or not being an official in-post leader, and more on what agents do, and how we seek to capture and understand it within real time and real-life practice.

Bourdieu's constructivist social science removes the dichotomy between agency and structure through providing the tools of field and habitus to describe and explain the dynamics of leadership (Gunter, 2000). A field is a dynamic 'space of relations within which agents evolve' (Bourdieu, 1990, p. 192), and so Bourdieu is interested in exploring how and why:

'types of behaviour can be directed towards certain ends without being consciously directed to these ends, or determined by them' and he argues, 'the notion of habitus was invented, if I may say so, in order to account for this paradox' (ibid., pp. 9–10). Habitus or dispositions to act reveal positioning of the self, and how the practitioner can be positioned by others:

> The habitus, as the system of dispositions to a certain practice, is an objective basis for regular modes of behaviour, and thus for the regularity of modes of practice, and if practices can be predicted (here, the punishment that follows a certain crime), this is because the effect of the habitus is that agents who are equipped with it will behave in a certain way in certain circumstances. That being said, this tendency to act in a regular manner, which, when its principle is explicitly constituted, can act as the basis of a forecast (the specialised equivalent of the practical anticipations of ordinary experience), is not based on an explicit rule or law. This means that the modes of behaviour created by the habitus do not have the fine regularity of the modes of behaviour deduced from a legislative principle: the habitus goes hand in glove with vagueness and indeterminacy. As a generative spontaneity which asserts itself in an improvised confrontation with ever-renewed situations, it obeys a practical logic, that of vagueness, of the moreor-less, which defines one's ordinary relation to the world.

(Bourdieu, 1990, pp. 77–8)

The school as a field of study and practice is a place of struggle over purposes, processes and products. The staking of cultural and symbolic capital through entering and positioning within a field provides a dynamic conceptualisation through which the location and exercise of power can be understood. Conflict is not a product of human nature but it is the structure of unequal distribution of capital which 'by generating the rarity of certain positions and the corresponding profits, favours strategies aimed at destroying or reducing that rarity, through the appropriation of rare positions, or conserving it, through the defence of those positions' (Bourdieu, 2000, pp. 183–4). A headteacher having a vision and/or presenting a visioning process is a position, and a teacher who positions the self or is positioned in ways that deny or enhance agency can be understood as a part of a complex process of habitus being disclosed within the context of an arena of struggle. As Bourdieu (2000, p. 180) argues, 'habitus is not destiny' but is generative because 'habitus is that presence of the past in the present which makes possible the presence in the present of the forth-coming' (ibid., p. 210). Whether and how this plays out within everyday practice enables us to have the opportunity to understand how by attributing leadership to a role incumbent is not just a product of an organisational flow chart but is integral to how teacher habitus has been structured over time, and how this experience structures future action. Consequently, the division of labour is a structuring process, but how agents engage with this is related to their 'feel for the game' that they may or may not enter. Therefore, it is less helpful to talk in terms of distributing leadership and more productive to think in terms of how teachers take up positions in relation to those who seek to do the distributing.

What Bourdieu's theory of practice does for us is to enable position to be related to existing power structures both institutionally (Bourdieu, 1988) and politically (Bourdieu, 1993) in which claims about objectivity can be related to political and economic interests that can shape and determine such activity. When role incumbents take on the charismatic role of visionary and hence position the teacher as follower we can ask ourselves how this has been structured by agency or by the impact of modernisation structures which require headteachers to have a vision to be both appointable and accountable. The impact of the changing political economy of where 'relevant' leadership can and should be produced means that Bourdieu's theorising of the impact of neo-liberalism on structures and practices in what counts as leadership can enable us to gain new insights into the contradictions in working lives (Bourdieu, 2000; Bourdieu et al., 1999).

Teachers worry about the current modernisation process but may not be able to take action without fulfilling the caricature of the trendy lefty radical. However, teachers clearly cannot work for alternative leadership practices on their own. For teachers to change the labelling of their leadership as sedition then they also need children and parents to resist the folklore positioning of teachers as subversives in how they communicate their support for schools within the wider community. In this way, while the issues are lived every day in schools, the wider context of how we conceptualise and practise the public good is central. What is our contribution as researchers and commentators on schools and schooling? Unfortunately the economising of research and professional practice of those in higher education who work with teachers means that the opportunity to speak out is also increasingly limited (Gunter, 2002). Nevertheless as knowledge workers who work with teachers in reflecting on and developing their practice, then the role of the social sciences comes into play. As Bourdieu (1990) argues, by making the conditions in which the researcher produces knowledge about knowledge production explicit then we are freed from the illusion of adopting technical method as a guarantor of freedom.

Emancipation like empowerment always has been and continues to be problematic. Just as we can question the top-down models of empowerment based on the illusion that people can only be 'switched on' by external structural forces such as development planning and the charismatic leader, then we also need to question the ideological goals of seeking to liberate by standing outside of so called 'false consciousness'.

We need to understand the settings in which people work, and that their dispositions are real and reasonable for them. The consequences are that as Delanty argues we need to work through the complexity of the public intellectual role with living in an emergent world of 'indeterminacy' (Delanty, 1997, p. 141). There is very little point in writing this chapter if it only mattered to me; on the other hand, if others raise questions then the resulting dialogue is such that there should be opportunities to speak out. This is not an indulgence because our work as social scientists is to problem pose because 'social science cannot itself provide answers to social problems' (Delanty, 1997, p. 141). This can easily be characterised, in a climate of problem-solving, as irrelevant and, so, just as teachers need to rework their role as mediators within knowledge production, then so do we.

REFERENCES

Allix, N.M. (2000) 'Transformational leadership: democratic or despotic', *Educational Management and Administration*, **28**(1), 7–20.

Atkinson, E. (2000) 'In defence of ideas, or why "what works" is not enough', *Management in Education*, **14**(3), pp. 6–9.

Ball, S.J. (1999) 'Performativities and fabrications in the education economy: towards the performative society?', keynote address to the AARE Annual Conference, Melbourne.

Blackmore, J. (1999) *Troubling Women: Feminism, Leadership and Educational Change*, Buckingham: Open University Press.

Bourdieu, P. (1988) *Homo Academicus*, Cambridge: Polity Press in association with Blackwell Publishers, Oxford.

Bourdieu, P. (1990) *In Other Words: Essays Towards a Reflexive Sociology*, trans. M. Adamson, Cambridge: Polity Press in association with Blackwell Publishers, Oxford.

Bourdieu, P. (1993) *The Field of Cultural Production*, Cambridge: Polity Press.

Bourdieu, P. (2000) *Pascalian Meditations*, trans R. Nice, Cambridge: Polity Press in association with Blackwell Publishers, Oxford.

Bourdieu, P., Accardo, A., Balazs, G., Beaud, S., Bonvin, F., Bourdieu, E., Bourgios, P., Broccolichi, S., Champagne, P., Christin, R., Faguer, J., Garcia, S., Lenoir, R., Œuvrard, F., Pialoux, M., Pinto, L., Podalydès, D., Sayad, A. Soulié, C. and Wacquant, L.J.D. (1999) *The Weight of the World*, Cambridge: Polity Press, in association with Blackwell Publishers, Oxford.

Cochran-Smith, M. and Paris, C.L. (1995) 'Mentor and mentoring: did Homer have it right?' in J. Smyth (ed.), *Critical Discourses on Teacher Development*, London: Cassell.

Crowther, F. (1997) 'The William Walker Oration, 1996. Unsung heroes: the leaders in our classrooms', *Journal of Educational Administration*, **35**(1), pp. 5–17.

Delanty, G. (1997) *Social Science: Beyond Constructivism and Realism*, Buckingham: Open University Press.

Garman, N.B. (1995) 'The schizophrenic rhetoric of school reform and the effects on teacher development', in J. Smyth (ed.), *Critical Discourses on Teacher*

Development, London: Cassell.

Gleeson, D. and Gunter, H.M. (2001) 'The performing school and the modernisation of teachers', in D. Gleeson and C. Husbands (eds.), *The Performing School*, London: Routledge Falmer, pp. 139–58.

Grimmett, P. (1995) 'Developing voice through teacher research: implications for educational policy', in J. Smyth (ed.), *Critical Discourses on Teacher Development*, London: Cassell.

Gronn, P. (1996) 'From transactions to transformations', *Educational Management and Administration*, **24**, 7–30.

Gronn, P. (2000) 'Distributed properties: a new architecture for leadership', *Educational Management and Administration*, **28**(3), 317–38.

Gunter, H. (1999) 'Contracting headteachers as leaders: an analysis of the NPQH', *Cambridge Journal of Education*, **29**,(2), 249–62.

Gunter, H. (2000) 'Thinking theory: the field of education management in England and Wales', *British Journal of Sociology of Education*, **21**(4), 623–35.

Gunter, H.M. (2001a) *Leaders and Leadership in Education*, London: Paul Chapman Publishing.

Gunter, H.M. (2001b) 'Teacher appraisal 1988–1998: a case study', *School Leadership and Management*, **53**(3), 241–50.

Gunter, H.M. (2002) 'Purposes and positions in the field of education management: putting Bourdieu to work', *Educational Management and Administration*, **30**(1), 3–22.

Gunter, H.M. and Ribbins, P. (2002) 'Leadership studies in education: towards a map of the field'. *Educational Management and Administration*, **30**(4), 387–416.

Hargreaves, A. (1998) 'The emotional politics of teaching and teacher development: with implications for educational leadership', *International Journal of Leadership in Education*, **1**(4), 315–36.

Hursh, D. (1995) 'It's more than style: reflective teachers as ethical and political practitioners', in J. Smyth (ed.), *Critical Discourses on Teacher Development*, London: Cassell.

Moos, L. and Dempster, N. (1998) 'Some comparative learnings from the study', in J. MacBeath (ed.), *Effective School Leadership: Responding to Change*, London: Paul Chapman Publishing.

Nixon, J. (1995) 'Teaching as a profession of values', in J. Smyth (ed.), *Critical Discourses on Teacher Development*, London: Cassell.

Nixon, J., Martin, J., McKeown, P. and Ranson, S. (1997) 'Towards a learning profession: changing codes of occupational practice within the new management of education', *British Journal of Sociology of Education*, **18**(1), 5–28.

Sergiovanni, T.J. (2001) *Leadership: What's in it for Schools?* London: Routledge Falmer.

Smyth, J. (1995) 'Introduction', in J. Smyth (ed.), *Critical Discourses on Teacher Development*, London: Cassell.

Smyth, J. (2001a) 'Reflections on a "Damaged Life", the "hidden injuries" of teaching within the self-managing school', paper presented to the Annual Meeting of the American Educational Research Association, Seattle, 10–14 April.

Smyth, J. (2001b) *Critical Politics of Teachers' Work: An Australian Perspective*, New York: Peter Lang.

Wallace, M. (2001) 'Sharing leadership of schools through teamwork: a justifiable risk?' *Educational Management and Administration*, **29**(2), 153–67.

FURTHER READING

Gronn, P. (1996) 'From transactions to transformations', *Educational Management and Administration*, **24**, 7–30.

Gronn, P. (2000) 'Distributed properties: a new architecture for leadership', *Educational Management and Administration*, **28**(3), 317–38.

Gunter, H. (1999) 'Contracting headteachers as leaders: an analysis of the NPQH', *Cambridge Journal of Education*, **29**(2), 249–62.

Gunter, H.M. (2001) *Leaders and Leadership in Education*, London: Paul Chapman Publishing.

Gunter, H.M. (2002) 'Purposes and positions in the field of education management: putting Bourdieu to work', *Educational Management and Administration*, **30**(1), 3–22

Gunter, H.M. and Ribbins, P. (2002) 'Leadership studies in education: towards a map of the field'. *Educational Management and Administration,* **30**(4), 387–416.

Moos, L. and Dempster, N. (1998) 'Some comparative learnings from the study', in J. MacBeath (ed.), *Effective School Leadership: Responding to Change*, London: Paul Chapman Publishing

Nixon, J. (1995) 'Teaching as a profession of values', in J. Smyth (ed.), *Critical Discourses on Teacher Development*, London: Cassell.

Sergiovanni, T.J. (2001) *Leadership: What's in it for Schools?* London: Routledge Falmer.

Smyth, J. (2001) *Critical Politics of Teachers' Work: An Australian Perspective*, New York: Peter Lang.

9

EFFECTIVE LEADERSHIP FOR WAR AND PEACE

Clive Harber and Lynn Davies

INTRODUCTION

Recent global events have underlined the argument of this chapter, that educational leadership has to enter a new phase – a phase that will require very different thinking. This shift is not the same as simple incremental changes to allow for new technology or the 'knowledge economy'. Nor is it an expansion of the usual nods in the direction of contingency and regard for contextual difference. Much is indeed already made in the leadership literature of the need to take into account the context of the educational institution. Sergiovanni (2001) for example starts his recent book on leadership by quoting Barth's critique of the 'list approach' to factors in effective leadership, i.e., that the same things applied to different contexts and to different situations typically produce different results. However, our chapter argues that such an acknowledgement of context is often no more than lip-service. By chapter 5, Sergiovanni is arguing for a 'system of layered standards in school', with the first one being 'uniform standards for all schools in basic reading, writing and math (maybe civics)' (ibid., p. 93). The assumption of unchanging and undifferentiated goals for formal education remains the same.

There are three major problems with current educational leadership literature. The first is that it is mainly about conventional schools – fixed-site buildings where pupils go at regular times on a daily basis and learn a planned curriculum manifested in a timetable. Schooling does not equal education and there are many different forms of education as well as many different forms of schooling. A second problem is that of real contextuality, in that the published literature largely stems from, and is written about, the industrialised north of the planet. Educational organisations in developing countries and in unstable societies exist in very different contexts, as we have argued in detail elsewhere (Harber and Davies, 1997).

The third and most significant problem, related to the first two, is the lack of acknowledgement of ideology. Education is intimately bound up with goals based on open or hidden values, and forms of education policy and provision reflect these values. Leadership cannot be discussed as if it existed in a moral or political vacuum, as if there were 'principles' of leadership regardless of the goals of the educational institution. Yet if we merely take a model of educational effectiveness and leadership effectiveness as based on the principle of congruence between inputs, processes and desired outputs, this can end up being morally relativist. Consider the following example.

Let us imagine a terrorist training camp which is, above all else, an educational institution. How would we judge its effectiveness? First, we would need to understand the goals it had set itself, then we could judge its effectiveness in terms of the appropriateness of its inputs and processes and how they did or did not contribute to success or failure in achieving desired outcomes. Leadership of the terrorist training camp would be a key process variable. Let us say its goals are to produce 50 highly disciplined and dedicated terrorists a year, willing to sacrifice their own lives and capable of making bombs and using and handling automatic guns. Inputs required would include experienced terrorists to carry out the training, a secret and secluded training camp and a good supply of necessary materials and weaponry. Outputs might be judged in relation to both the successful 'graduation' of 50 terrorists and the extent to which they wreaked havoc on the designated enemy. Process variables might include intense indoctrination in the cause, strict discipline, a rigorous regime of physical training and practical lessons in bomb-making and firing a machine gun. What would be the characteristics of an effective educational leader in this context? He or she would need to be authoritarian, unbending, harsh, closed-minded, violent and full of hatred for the enemy.

This example of educational leadership is effective in terms of the goals it sets itself. However, who are the goals themselves effective for? Are all goals equally morally acceptable? One of the criticisms made of the school effectiveness literature is that it skates over the issue of the diversity of possible goals for education. However, recognising that such diversity exists immediately raises the issue of acceptability. Even our example is not straightforward. While not likely to find much support in the atmosphere of the 'international war against terrorism' in which we are writing, it nevertheless has to be pointed out that in recent history liberation movements in Africa (for example, Zimbabwe, Namibia and South Africa) have had to organise along very similar lines in order to overcome undemocratic, oppressive and violent regimes. Training and education were very much part of their organisational structure (Harber, 1989;1997). This chapter, then, deliberately sets out to provide an antidote to the more conventional literature on leadership by exploring the diversity of educational organisation and goals, and the implications for effective educational leadership. In particular, it explores the growing arena of educational leadership in times of political conflict and crisis.

ARE ALL EDUCATIONAL GOALS EQUALLY MORALLY ACCEPTABLE?

In Nazi Germany an effective school leader was a party member, a believer in racist doctrine, a supporter of military expansion and blindly obedient to the party and the state. In this way he or she would help to produce young fascists for the Reich. This example brings home the issue of the moral purpose of education in a rather stark manner, but it is far from being alone. From 1948 to 1994, South African schools existed to try to make apartheid 'normal' and 'acceptable' in the minds of young South Africans. From the apartheid government's point of view the role of education was to help perpetuate and reproduce a racist system and to encourage obedience and conformity to that system. Again authoritarian and racist leaders would be ideal heads.

Perhaps these examples, though real enough, are too clear cut. In Denmark there is a Private Independent Schools Act which allows for schools to be established on any chosen ideological basis. Twelve pupils are needed to start a school and the school is then subsidised by the state. In 1998 the Danish neo-Nazi party, the Danish National-Socialist Movement, intended to set up a school of its own. The Ministry of Education would assess the school's purpose, including potential breaches of the law on racism, 'but breach of the law is not in itself enough to deny a school a subsidy' (De Laine, 1998). Is the educational leadership likely to be exercised in this school at odds with the sort of educational leadership that should be exercised by the state in this case? Is neo-Nazism just another ideology or do its tenets, for example racism, depart from the very basis of democracy? Does the greater goal of democracy therefore exclude this particular version of diversity?

At the time of writing this chapter, the British government was calling for more faith-based schools. Here is one example. The Head of Kilskeery Independent Christian School in County Tyrone, Northern Ireland, claims that whenever she has a teacher recruitment crisis she does not advertise but gets down on her knees and prays for help. Staff at the school must share the doctrine of the Free Presbyterian faith that they are God's true servants in an immoral world, that the theory of evolution is wrong and that all children are natural sinners who must be taught to conform to God's law. The head's leadership style consists of doctoring *Macbeth* to cut out the 'immoral' bits, showing how the Bible proves evolution to be wrong, rejecting sex education of any kind and using corporal punishment to restrict the innate sinful tendencies of children (Ghouri, 1998). Can the leadership of such a school be judged to be effective solely in terms of the goals that it has set for itself or are some of its aims harmful and therefore its leadership also harmful? Ironically, at the same time the government was attempting to promote more faith-based schools, reports on race riots in Oldham, Burnley and Bradford over the summer of 2001 suggested that part of the problem was that schools had become too racially segregated and that there should be more mixing of faiths. Should forms of educational organisation be judged on the extent to which they contribute to the strength and sustainability of democracy?

BASIC PRINCIPLES: PEACE, SUSTAINABLE DEVELOPMENT AND DEMOCRACY

It will be clear from the above examples that we do not believe in a moral relativism in discussions of educational leadership and school effectiveness. We start from a number of linked propositions:

1 That one of the major goals of education should be peace.
2 That sustainable development of a society is integral to that peace.
3 That goals of literacy or productivity should be a sub-set of goals of peace and sustainable development.
4 That democratic organisation and education for democracy are the most likely ways to achieve the above ends.
5 That schools and leadership in many contexts remain authoritarian, and hence unlikely to achieve the above ends.

Many (since the early 1990s, most) countries internationally pay lip-service to the need to operate a democratic system of government. So the key national goal set by political leaders is democracy and, indeed, the word 'democracy' often features in government policy documents on education. Yet one insufficiently remarked aspect of school and classroom leadership internationally is that it is authoritarian leadership. Elsewhere one of the writers has summarised evidence from a wide range of countries in South and Central America, Africa, Asia, North America and Europe as to the authoritarian nature of school and classroom relationships (Harber, 1997). Educational leaders set the tone and nature of such relationships. Yet if democracy is supposed to be the foremost political goal of education, should not this be reflected in the ways in which schools are led if schools are to be judged effective? This is the opposite argument to the one explored in the section above. Instead of what forms of leadership should be excluded from a consideration of 'effectiveness' because they are not morally effective in their own right, this section argues that there ought to be one overriding consideration in terms of goals, given the stated commitment of governments to democracy. Education should produce democratic citizens committed to equality of human rights, to mutual respect between individuals and groups and to free participation and informed choice in political decision-making.

Where research has been done on the views of pupils, the lack of democracy in their lives at school is a salient theme. A survey of 3,600 students in schools in Canada found widespread evidence of what Fullan and his colleagues (1991, p. 171) called the 'alienation theme'. Students were consistently critical of a lack of communication, dialogue, participation and engagement in the process of learning. In Britain a recent survey of 15,000 pupils found that among what they would like would be,

- a listening school with children on the governing body, class representatives and the chance to vote for teachers
- a flexible school without rigid timetables or examinations, without compulsory homework, without a one-size-fits-all curriculum, so that they could follow their own interests and spend more time on what they enjoy
- a respectful school where they are not treated as empty vessels to be filled with information, where teachers treat them as individuals and where children and adults can talk freely to each other, and the pupils' opinions matter.

What is clear is that, given that the children were asked to write about 'The school that I'd like', they did not feel that these were currently features of schooling in Britain (Birkett, 2001).

There are a range of issues here. One appears to be inefficiency: Smith and Andrews (1989) studied over 2,500 teachers and 1,200 principals and found that effective principals were engaged in four areas of leadership interactions with teachers: (1) as 'resource provider', (2) as 'instructional resource', (3) as 'communicator' and (4) as 'visible presence'. Of these the 'instructional leader' role was found to be particularly important in identifying the effective head. However, only 21 of the 1,200 were actually effective instructional leaders. Two other studies found that only 10 per cent of headteachers functioned effectively according to their criteria (Fullan, 1991, p. 151).

More sinister even than alienation is how schools actually harm pupils. In some parts of the world there is increasing evidence of the psychological and physical harm – manifested in stress, anxiety and resulting physical symptoms – which is done to children and teachers by increasingly controlled, regulated, ordered, inspected, competitive and test-driven schooling systems which are aimed at classification and ranking in order to serve markets in education. A survey in 2000 of 8,000 pupils in England and Wales, for example, found that stress is damaging pupils and resulting in sleeping and eating disorders. The cause of this was endless testing, with the report entitled 'Testing to Destruction'. It was calculated that by the time the average sixth former leaves school he or she will have taken

75 or more external tests (Smithers, 2000). One in five primary children in Bavaria is taking medication for stress or to improve 'performance' (Sharma, 2001). In a study in America, it was found that students were stressed out and regularly participated in devious, deceptive and cruel behaviour to get the best grade (Hill, 2001). In India, in 2000 at least four suicides were reported because of pressure on students for college entry (Behal, 2000). Back in the UK, one survey found that 58 per cent of teachers had sought medical help for stress. This can have consequences for pupils, in that: 'the daily classroom experiences of a child whose teacher is under stress will certainly be less than positive. Shouting, verbal put-downs, short temper, poor quality assignments, poorly planned, unimaginative lessons, work not marked' (Cosgrave, 2000, pp. 117–18).

The issue for leadership is grave. While we have concentrated here on stress and anxiety as an example, there is considerable evidence of the many ways in which schooling can cause violence to pupils and reproduce violence in the wider society (Harber, 2002a). It is not merely a problem of schools being vaguely undemocratic within themselves, but that educational leaders may have little power to change the inexorable testing and regulatory regimes imposed by governments or little capacity to challenge acceptance of violent solutions to problems. If educational leaders accede to the pressure for 'standards' without providing ways in which their pupils and staff can live in a dignified and humane fashion, then their schools will be contributing to conflict (Davies, 2001b). The schools may be effective in the narrow sense of academic achievement, but they will also be effective in turning out damaged and aggressive individuals.

SHIFTS TOWARDS DEMOCRATIC LEADERSHIP

Nonetheless, we do have examples internationally of education systems that organise, or are attempting to organise their schools on a more democratic basis. Davies and Kirkpatrick (2000) studied schools in Denmark, Holland, Sweden and Germany, and found that England was lagging behind the rest of Europe in terms of pupils' rights and their participation in educational decision-making. Legislation in these countries ensured not just the presence of school councils, but also pupil representation on school boards, on curriculum committees and on appointments or promotions panels. Very effective pupil unions – financed and supported by the state – enabled forums for consultation of young people about education by government or local authority as well as ways of training pupils in the practice of democracy.

In some developing countries undergoing transition to democracy there is also a clear recognition of the importance of education in building a sustainable democracy. In South Africa all secondary schools must now by law have a Learner Representative Council (LRC) elected by the student body and representatives from the LRC sit on school governing bodies which have considerable powers over the running of schools. Similar policies have been adopted in neighbouring Namibia, and Uganda is also making considerable efforts in regard to education for democracy (Harber, 1997; 1998; 2001; 2002b). In our book on school management and effectiveness in developing countries we discussed further examples in Chile and Colombia (Harber and Davies, 1997).

Another instance of growing democracy and power-sharing is the whole questioning of single leadership. Do schools need a single headteacher at all? In Zurich Canton in Switzerland, schools, for example, have no headteachers. The basic unit of organisation is the classroom. Classroom teachers vote for a leader, a first among equals, to represent them on the school board, the employer. Teachers in Switzerland are the best paid in Europe (50 per cent better in real terms than in Britain). Switzerland spends 6 per cent of its gross domestic product on education – twice as much as Britain. The schools are small and so are the classes. Eleven-year-old Swiss children are among the most literate and numerate in Europe (Rafferty, 1998). The article in the *Times Educational Supplement* from which this information is drawn provoked a letter from an education academic at Leicester University in the following week's edition which pointed out that Switzerland was not the only country where headteachers do not exist:

> In the Reggio Emilia early years system in Northern Italy, schools have an administrator (clerical level) and an *atelierista* who is responsible for ensuring quality curriculum planning and implementation. In addition a pedagogista (a high quality trained teacher) is attached to a small group of schools, with a main responsibility for staff development and training decisions. Even those roles are not perceived by staff to be hierarchical, the staff taking full and joint responsibility for promoting the quality of education within their schools. I have never spoken to such committed teaching staff – with no-one to whom the 'buck' can be passed it is evident how responsible individuals feel. Other noteworthy features to which we aspire in this country were the parents' apparent satisfaction with and support for the schools and the staff, the high standards achieved by very young children and the very evident atmosphere of mutual respect and cooperation. But then, Reggio Emilia staffing is around 12 children to one adult!

> (Moyles, 1998)

In a chapter in a book *Educational Dilemmas*, Davies (1997) made a case for 'leaderless schools' or at least rotational leadership. This derived from concerns about the dangers of the new managerialism in education with apparently charismatic and manipulative heads leading an intensification of teachers' work. Models and metaphors of effective leadership are still patriarchal, militaristic and sporting in many parts of the world, with combative leadership styles matching competition between schools for results and reputations. Davies's argument was – and is – for federalism and mutual ownership, with a matrix model, a range of elected posts and multiple memberships of different groupings. 'Strong leadership' may indeed be necessary in times of crisis, but collegial styles better suit innovation, collaboration and the teamwork necessary in modern democracies (see also Torrington and Weightman, 1989). The case for leaderless schools predictably provoked a reaction (Fidler, 1997), with the argument that parents should not have to suffer the 'vagaries' of a collective of publicly funded teachers, that clear lines of accountability are needed, that it is difficult to improve a school with collegiate decision-making. It is argued that there appears to be a strong psychological need for a single leader, for someone who can mobilise for action. Yet we would still claim that acceding to this need can be undemocratic and even hazardous.

Grint, in his *The Arts of Leadership* (2000) is nicely cynical about 'the leader':

> Many of our problems stem not from what our leaders do but what we let them get away with. It is important to note that the power of leaders rests not in themselves, as possessions, but in their followers, as a network of relationships. Just as leadership is indeterminate, one of the ways that leaders persuade their followers to obey them or follow them is by suggesting that leaders can determine the future, that what is negotiable is actually non-negotiable. The dereliction of followers' responsibility is not simply something that can be laid at the feet of failed leaders. It fits too often on the shoulders of those who silently followed without resistance, of those who refused to speak out against their own leaders and whose inaction allowed the leaders to proclaim that, since none was against them, all must be for them . . .
>
> The trick of leadership – and the real invention – is to develop followers who privately resolve the problems leaders have caused or cannot resolve, but publicly deny their intervention. Thus leadership reverts to its talismatic origins: it performs a ritual that followers appear to require. Whether it actually works miracles is irrelevant, because, as long as followers believe they need leaders, leaders will be necessary . . . As the organisational jungle joke goes: when leaders look down from the top of the tree in the jungle, all they see is their organisation staffed by monkeys. When followers look up at their leaders from their position at the bottom, all they see is bums . . . It is followers who save leaders and therefore make them. (ibid., pp. 419–20)

While many leadership studies have focused on the 'successful leader', with its connotations of willing and captivated followers, this chapter argues against this approach as being highly dangerous historically – and, indeed, anti-educational.

BUT IS DEMOCRATIC LEADERSHIP UNIVERSALLY APPLICABLE?

The question of crisis versus stability leads on to the question of contingency and context to determine leadership. Let us imagine a range of existing diverse contexts, forms, purposes and clienteles of education, as follows:

- Distance education provided via written packs, television, radio, the Internet and some face-to-face contact.
- Home-based education where parents educate their children at home.
- Steiner Waldorf schools where teaching does not begin until age six and where there is an emphasis on nourishing the emotional and motivational need of the child and where art, drama and music have a central place in the curriculum.
- Green schools where the emphasis in all school-based activity is on ecological sustainability and seeing the world holistically and as interconnected.
- Schools in areas which have recently been affected by violent conflict and where priorities are conflict resolution skills, addressing grief and psychological/social stress, landmine awareness and health awareness.
- The education of refugee children.
- The education of street children who have to earn a living partly or wholly on the streets of big cities throughout the world.
- The education of nomadic children.
- A school with no running water, electricity, telephone or inside latrines and where the nearest town is two hours' drive away.
- A school with a large number of AIDS orphans and where teachers are dying of AIDS on a regular basis.

Is it possible to talk about educational leadership or democratic leadership in a generalised manner to cover all these common situations? Does it not matter what is being led? Moreover, each one of these examples has considerable diversity within it, depending on the context involved. Let us take a couple of examples and briefly suggest some implications for leadership.

How would educational leadership be exercised in the case of the education of street children? First, there would be a need to lead some research – who are the street children in the area concerned? How do they earn income? What are their work patterns? What dangers do they face? What might be their educational priorities be? Second, an educational leader in this situation would need to establish flexible forms of organisation and provision that suited the needs of street children and not the other way around. This might involve very flexible timetabling of provision at all times of the day and working out in the community/on the streets. Third, the educational leader would need to staff his or her organisation with colleagues who were prepared to work in this way and to organise staff development that enhanced these skills and this may involve some street children themselves. Fourth, the leader, and through him or her the staff, would need to have to operate on a client-led basis in terms of the perceived needs of the street children themselves – both in the way they operated and in what was provided. Health education, counselling and self-defence might be more important than geography or chemistry. The actual answers and practices stemming from these issues would nevertheless still vary between Rio de Janeiro, Lagos and Jakarta.

Another example might be based on an existing secondary school in Kosovo. After years of running the 'parallel system' under the rule from Milosevic, whereby Albanian schools took place in homes and shops, a principal returned to his original school in July 1999, after the end of the conflict, together with three other teachers. The door was locked. He recounted:

> We didn't know what we would find inside. The military had been here during the air strikes. A cleaner, a refugee from Croatia, was here, living in one of the rooms. We thought there might be bombs, the classrooms were also locked, we unlocked them with knives. We found signs of the military, their uniforms. There was not much physical damage, but materials had all been taken . . . In September we started the school. The biggest challenge was that we didn't know whether the staff were alive, or the pupils. There was some information that one of the 16-year-old students had been massacred. Many students had lost their parents, or did not know how to contact them. The private houses where the parallel schools had been had all been burned, all the documentation. We had to make a new register according to how the teachers had remembered the names . . .

What are the challenges for leadership here? Too numerous to count. The principal isolated some: the stress and trauma of students and staff; the family breakdowns that had occurred during the war and in the camps; many young people having been abroad, and not familiar with the situation in Kosovo; and the current education reform. Students had heard of changes and liberalisation of education, but without any clarification – 'they think they have the right to do anything'. They were producing revolutionary pamphlets! Finally, the principal was aware that the society also had to be transformed, but 'it was difficult to know how'. It is clear that leadership in this highly volatile and sensitive situation required a complex array of activities, none of which had to do with performance management.

It would seem that any literature on educational leadership that tried to establish lists of prescriptive characteristics, tasks or skills for the 'effective leader' would need to be very wary unless the specific context and goal for these was made very clear – for example 'secondary schools in England aiming at GCSE results' (and even then there may be rural/urban differences). There are, for example, still too many books that glibly claim to be 'international' in the title but which only deal with industrialised nations (an example would be Day et al. (2000) recently reviewed by one of the authors).

There are a number of dilemmas here. First, at one level we are arguing for contextuality, which implies a sort of relativism, that there are no universal prescriptions, that everything is context driven. On the other hand we are arguing for important internationally applicable goals for education and an implicit set of democratic principles, applicable everywhere, to underpin them. Second, on the one hand, we are arguing for a match between process and goal, that democratic goals require democratic processes; on the other hand, we might want to argue that if democratic processes are so efficient, they would be just as useful in a terrorist organisation which had authoritarian aims. A third dilemma is, of course, in the very definition of democracy itself. Our recent research with teacher educators in the Gambia (Davies, 2002; Schweisfurth, 2002) revealed a number of different definitions, often revolving round the intersection between Islam and western interpretations, between autonomy and respect for one's family, for one's organisation and for traditional gender hierarchies. Can one be relativist even within the concept of 'democracy'?

SCHOOLS AND LEADERSHIP THAT DO NO HARM

Perhaps the only universal principle is the one often quoted by the medical profession: 'to do no harm'. The examples given above provided myriad examples of the ways that schools can harm people – students and staff. Schools are of course also – often simultaneously – doing good. Our aim should be to lower the levels of pain. There was a joke going round in the film industry at the time of the making of the film *Raise the Titanic*. The costs of making the film escalated so much that the producer was heard to mutter 'It would have been cheaper to lower the Atlantic'. Rather than a focus on 'raising standards' – which always disadvantages a large number – we might want a focus on 'lowering distress'. This matches the contemporary call for education to be involved in the elimination of distress factors such as poverty and conflict.

Our argument would be that some form of democratic leadership is the best way to do no harm. Democracy involves finding out what people want and giving them a voice to air their joys and pains. Democracy involves giving people a change to eject leaders that cause them distress. Democracy involves giving people the knowledge to be able to make an informed choice about which leaders are likely to cause them the least distress and the most gain. The democratic school would be one where students and staff had the skills and knowledge to participate in deciding the leadership. The question is not 'what makes a good leader?' but 'what makes a good election for a leader?'

Similarly, democracy is about equity and about respect for others. It involves having the skills and knowledge to be able to challenge injustice. Again, the question is not 'what is effective leadership?' but 'what learning enables people to respect or conversely challenge those in power?' Admittedly, some of this learning might well be from the example of a leader: a principal of a Serb school in Brčko, Bosnia told one of the authors of his attempt to start the integration process between Serb and Bosnian schools after the conflict (Davies, 2001a). He started by organising a football match between his school and a neighbouring Bosnian school. Two parents (both war invalids) refused to allow their children to play; one was persuaded. It was a very successful occasion, but two Serb principals of other schools then objected, and tried to prevent his re-election as principal. However, he won, and eventually other principals came round to his position. The point of this narrative was that here was a principal who was prepared to take risks, to challenge the continuing mistrust and hostility in the region, and to act as a role model for that new spirit. Leadership for democracy and peace is not just about delegation and power-sharing, but about going out on a limb against the forces of authoritarianism.

Doing no harm, ironically, is not a passive approach but entails setting up situations of (positive) conflict. This could be a school council with teeth and with input into both curriculum planning and school discipline; competition not for academic achievement but for posts of responsibility (by head, staff and students); joint debates by students and staff over the vision of the school and its external role; classrooms which encouraged questioning and challenges to teachers and learners; and forays into injustice in school, in the local community or even in the national/ international community. This has obvious parallels with the notion of global citizenship. We have some published examples of headteachers who have 'led' schools in a democratic fashion (Trafford, 1997; Watts, 1989; Welgemoed, 1998), and all have been prepared to take risks and establish positive conflict to ensure maximum benefit.

Of course if new or previously traditional heads were to work in a democratic manner then they might need training – or at least much reflection – and this would have to involve not only the implications for practice but also the nature and philosophy of democracy. 'Being a leader, undertaking leadership and trying to hold on to educational leadership is highly political' (Gunter, 2001, p. 17). Leadership education for democracy needs to include considerations of structural issues such as gender as well as of school micropolitics (Davies, 1998). Yet, in England at least, headship training seems to exclude philosophical matters such as the culture and values of the school and concentrates on what can be learned quickly (Gunter, 2001, p. 90). Our experience from trying to examine 'effective' leadership in a range of international contexts is that, like democracy, it is a process, not an end-state. It cannot be learned quickly and for all time. And it can be learned only be setting up structures for challenging its very existence.

CONCLUSION

One cannot simply say that the good leader is one who has a 'strategic vision', if that vision is to bomb the hell out of another country. One cannot simply say the good leader is one who has 'high expectations' if those expectations are for uncritical but efficient avengers. Leadership must have a value base, with the links between that value base and daily school processes made transparent and coherent. Our reconciliation of contextuality and universality is twofold: first, that whatever the diverse context of educational provision, all institutions operate in a global arena beset by actual or potential tension, and hence need a goal at least not to add to this tension; and, second, that democratic processes (however messy and time-consuming) will be the only way to foster the active challenge to conflict escalation, to ensure sustainable learning for sustainable development.

REFERENCES

Behal, S. (2000) 'Exam stress prompts reform demand', *Times Educational Supplement*, 21 July.

Birkett, D. (2001) 'Future perfect', *Guardian Education*, 5 June.

Cosgrave, J. (2000) *Breakdown: The Facts About Stress in Teaching*, London: Routledge Falmer.

Davies, L. (1997) 'The case for leaderless schools', in K. Watson, C. Modgil and S. Modgil, (eds), *Educational Dilemmas: Debate and Diversity*, Vol. 3, London: Cassell.

Davies, L (1998) 'Democratic practice, gender and school management', in P. Drake and P. Owen, (eds), *Gender and Management Issues in Education*, Stoke-on-Trent: Trentham Books

Davies, L. (2001a) *Curriculum Harmonisation in Brĕko District, Bosnia-Herzegovina report to EC/CfBT.*

Davies, L. (2001b) 'Education, social identity and conflict', *Educational Practice and Theory*, **23**(1), 5–23.

Davies, L. (2002) 'The democratization of teacher education', in E. Thomas (ed), *Teacher Education: Dilemmas and Prospects: World Yearbook of Education*, London: Kogan Page.

Davies, L. and Kirkpatrick, G. (2000) *The EURIDEM Project: A Review of Pupil Democracy in Europe*, London: Children's Rights Alliance.

Day, C., Fernandez, A., Hauge, T. and Moller, J. (2000) *The Life and Work of Teachers: International Perspectives in Changing Times*, London: Falmer Press.

De Laine, M. (1998) 'State to help finance neo-Nazi private school', *Times Educational Supplement*, 6 November, 12.

Fidler, B. (1997) 'The case for school leadership', in K. Watson, C. Modgil and S. Modgil (eds), *Educational Dilemmas: Debate and Diversity*, Vol. 3, London: Cassell.

Fullan, M. (1991) *The New Meaning of Educational Change*, London: Cassell.

Ghouri, N. (1998) 'Battle to teach God's own law', *Times Educational Supplement*, 9 October, p. 10.

Grint, K. (2000) *The Arts of Leadership*, Oxford: Oxford University Press.

Gunter, H. (2001) *Leaders and Leadership in Education*, London: Paul Chapman Publishing.

Harber, C. (1989) *Politics in African Education*, London: Macmillan.

Harber, C. (1997) *Education, Democracy and Political Development in Africa*, Brighton: Sussex Academic Press.

Harber, C. (1998) *Voices for Democracy: A North–South Dialogue on Education for Sustainable Democracy*, Nottingham: Education Now in association with the British Council.

Harber, C. (2001) *State of Transition: Post-Apartheid Educational Reform in South Africa*, Oxford: Symposium Books.

Harber, C. (2002a) 'Schooling as violence: an exploratory overview', *Educational Review*, **541**(1), 7–16.

Harber, C. (2002b) 'Education, democracy and poverty reduction in Africa', *Comparative Education*, **38**(4). (forthcoming).

Harber, C. and Davies, L. (1997) *School Management and Effectiveness in Developing Countries*, London: Cassell.

Hill, A. (2001) 'Stressed students get ill to win good marks', *Observer*, 15 August, 8.

Moyles, J. (1998) 'Italians also manage without their heads', *Times Educational Supplement*, 3 July, 20.

Rafferty, F. (1998) 'Happy without a head', *Times Educational Supplement*, 26 June, 15.

Schweisfurth, M. (2002) 'Democracy and teacher education: negotiating changes to practice in the Gambia', *Comparative Education*, **38**(4), (forthcoming).

Sergiovanni, T. (2001) *Leadership: What's in it for Schools?* London: Routledge Falmer.

Sharma, Y. (2001) 'Primary pupils turn to stress pills', *Times Educational Supplement*, 13 July, 20.

Smith, W.F. and Andrews, R.L. (1989) *Instructional Leadership: How Principles Make a Difference*. Alexandria, UA: Association for Supervision and Curriculum Development.

Smithers, R. (2000) 'Exams regime harms pupils', *Guardian*, 4 August, 1.

Torrington, D. and Weightman, J. (1989) *The Reality of School Management*, Oxford: Blackwell.

Trafford, B. (1997) *Participation, Power-Sharing and School Improvement*, Nottingham: Educational Heretics Press.

Watts, J. (1989) 'Up to a point', in C. Harber and R. Meighan (eds), *The Democratic School*, Ticknall: Education Now.

Welgemoed, A. (1998) 'Democratising a school in South Africa', in C. Harber (ed.), *Voices for Democracy: A North–South Dialogue on Education for Sustainable Democracy*, Nottingham: Education Now, in association with the British Council.

FURTHER READING

Davies, L. (1997) 'The case for leaderless schools', in K. Watson, C. Modgil and S. Modgil (eds), *Educational Dilemmas: Debate and Diversity*, Vol. 3, London: Cassell.

Fidler B. (1997) 'The case for school leadership', in K. Watson, C. Modgil and S. Modgil (eds), *Educational Dilemmas: Debate and Diversity*, Vol. 3, London: Cassell.

Grint, K. (2000) *The Arts of Leadership*, Oxford: Oxford University Press.

Gunter, H. (2001) *Leaders and Leadership in Education*, London: Paul Chapman Publishing.

Harber, C. and Davies, L. (1997) *School Management and Effectiveness in Developing Countries*, London: Cassell.

Sergiovanni, T. (2001) *Leadership: What's in it for Schools?* London: Routledge Falmer.

*Section D: Perspectives on Leadership
in Practice*

10

LEADING HIGH-PERFORMING SCHOOLS

Mark Brundrett and Neil Burton

INTRODUCTION

The Beacon Schools scheme was devised by the UK's Department for Education and Employment as a project 'specifically designed to help raise standards in schools through the sharing and spread of good practice' (DfEE, 1999a). This chapter outlines the nature of the Beacon Schools scheme and examines and delineates some of the leadership implications of managing such schools. The analysis offered is based on an interest in the scheme that the authors have retained since its inception and draws on a series of published items. The first piece of research by the authors (Brundrett and Burton, 2001; Burton and Brundrett, 2000) was based on a quantitative survey of the initial 'cohort' of Beacon Schools within which the authors also requested if any such schools would wish to contribute to a series of 'case studies'. These case studies, written largely by the staff of the schools themselves, eventually developed into the text, *The Beacon Schools Experience: Case Studies in Excellence* (Brundrett and Burton, 2000) and a subsequent and similar process, which included new cohorts of schools involved in the scheme, enabled the construction of a second text, *The Beacon Schools Experience: Developing the Curriculum* (Burton and Brundrett, 2002).

A further 'grounded study' of a Beacon school sought to reveal some of the management practices and processes in one such school which may be associated with its success in gaining this accolade (Brundrett, 2002). One central contention of that latter piece of work was the suggestion that the increasingly ubiquitous management paradigm of 'collegiality', the strengths and inadequacies of which have been explored elsewhere (Brundrett, 1998), is neither a sufficient nor an accurate representation of effective models of school leadership. The latter part of the chapter offers an alternative conception of 'co-constructed' leadership which, at one and the same time, attempts to ensure equity and fairness in decision-making but also encompasses notions of legitimate 'authority' in school leaders.

THE BEACON SCHOOLS SCHEME

The strategic aim of the Beacon Schools scheme, noted above, was initially facilitated by the identification of 75 such schools, whose Beacon status commenced in September 1998, with a remit to operate in that capacity for three years. Beacon Schools were selected from among those institutions identified by the Office for Standards in Education (OFSTED) as the 'best performing' in their 1996/97 report (OFSTED, 1997). The scheme was subsequently extended in order to move towards a more even geographical distribution of such schools covering 'a wider range of social backgrounds' (DfEE, 1999a) and, by 1999, there were over 500 such institutions. On 22 March 1999, the Secretary of State for Education and Employment announced the 'Excellence in Cities' strategy aimed at improving inner-city schools. Under these proposals the Beacon initiative was expanded to 1,000 schools in 2002 with the intention that this number should include at least 250 secondary schools.

Beacon Schools receive additional funding in order to 'build partnerships to foster a two-way exchange of knowledge and ideas' (DfEE, 1999a) with other schools in their locality. Beacon Schools are thus encouraged to engage in a wide range of activities to disseminate their good practice including holding seminars with teachers from other schools, mentoring, work-shadowing, provision of in-service training, consultancy, links with initial teacher training institutions and support for newly qualified teachers (DfEE, 2001). It is particularly important to note that one central premise of the scheme is the notion that such development can only be based on the building of partnerships to foster a *two-way exchange* of knowledge and skills between professionals. The concept is not one whereby schools in the scheme seek to ensure that other institutions simply replicate practices from one school to another. It is, rather, one where Beacon Schools seek to share the ideas and systems that have worked for them, in their particular circumstances and environment, allowing partner institutions to decide for themselves whether the principles can be adapted to fit their own situation (Brundrett and Burton, 2000).

Equally, the scheme is not one that only targets help on schools in difficulty. The DfEE (1999b) point out that those who have identified weaknesses in their own school's performance may well wish to examine the work of the Beacon Schools in order to see if there is anything that they can learn from their success. Just as importantly, all schools may feel that they can learn more by developing supportive partnerships within which one, or more, Beacon Schools form an element. It has been found that the most common areas for partnership are literacy and leadership;

the most frequent methods of dissemination are consultation and lesson observation; each Beacon School has an average of nine partner schools; and around half of all Beacon Schools are engaged in Initial Teacher Training activities (DfES, 2002a; NFER, 2002).

The issue of the efficacy of different methods of dissemination has been the subject of a number of studies including early international comparative studies (Rudduck et al., 1976). There has, moreover, been a more recent resurgence of interest in the topic both in terms of disseminating research (see, for instance, Barnes and Clouder, 2000) in order to enhance school effectiveness and improvement strategies (Wikeley, 1998). Evaluation studies of dissemination practice in a cross-section of case study Beacon Schools emphasised the quality of relationships as being fundamental to the dissemination of good practice (Rudd, 2000). Furthermore, they point out that staff in Beacon Schools must know how to, and be able to, transfer the necessary skills and information across different school contexts and cultures (Rickinson and Rudd, 2001). A wide range of actual and potential benefits of the scheme for Beacon Schools themselves has been noted including a higher demand for places. Nonetheless the impact of some areas of Beacon activity may be particularly difficult to measure in terms of quantifiable success criteria since well-defined systems for evaluating the impact of Beacon activity are currently underdeveloped at both local and national levels. This has major implications for current and future practice if the flagship scheme is to encourage transformation in partner schools (Rickinson and Rudd, 2001).

SURVEY OF THE FIRST BEACON SCHOOLS

Research undertaken by the writers on the first 75 Beacon Schools had two central aims which were, first, to examine the management and other processes that were assisting in or detracting from the sharing of success which is at the heart of the initiative and, secondly, to assess to what extent schools were being successful in balancing the ongoing internal requirements of their schools with the provisions of the Beacon initiative. A questionnaire was sent to all 75 of the initial cohort of Beacon Schools within which the initial questions focused upon the school's general perceptions of the success of their year as a Beacon School. Overall the general impressions of the year from the headteachers or 'Beacon School' co-ordinators were very positive – the large majority of schools claimed that achieving the status led to further improvements and developments within the school. Indeed, over 80 per cent also believed that the year had been a worthwhile and positive experience, a significant vote of confidence in the initiative. Given that the success of a school year tends to be very dependent upon the progress of the pupils, it would appear that the prime function of these schools, to teach children, was not compromised by the initiative.

There was only slightly less support for statements suggesting that becoming a Beacon School enhanced the development of strong links with other schools. There was a similar positive response to the suggestion that it offered a means of publicly recognising the achievements of the school and the talents of the individuals and teams working there, culminating in a sense of pride for the whole school community. It would appear from these responses that recognition of achievement, at both institutional and individual level, were judged as significant motivational factors for the teaching staff (see also the work of MacGilchrist, Myers and Read, 1997; Sammons, Thomas and Mortimore, 1997). This would imply that the headteachers of Beacon Schools at least acknowledged the potential of the initiative to motivate and reward, through non-financial means, the work of those involved in the success of the school. The enhanced links with local schools similarly acknowledge the importance of peer recognition of achievement (Riches, 1997b, p. 93).

Most of the schools stated that they had been used extensively to support the development of other professionals, thus fulfilling one of their key roles as a Beacon School, to work with and help to develop the profession. The Beacon Schools' own rating of success in supporting other colleagues and institutions showed that, on the whole, they rated themselves as 'very successful' or 'successful' and there were few acknowledgements of particular themes not being taken up. Over 20 themes were reported and those with an emphasis on core skills, particularly literacy and numeracy, appeared to have been particularly successful, a fact which may reflect wider governmental initiatives on the development of basic skills. Some respondents reported that local education authorities had not supported the initiative fully. In contrast, however, nearly half of schools claimed an increased acknowledgement of their strengths within their own LEAs. Where conflict did appear to exist it was clear that one problem was that both the Beacon Schools and the LEAs concerned were offering support and professional development in the same areas.

In contrast to the suggestion made by Ghouri (1999) most of the respondents claimed that the requirements of Beacon Schools were not difficult to balance with their normal educational duties. Clearly the Beacon Schools project was a high-profile initiative which, like all such developments, has its supporters and its detractors. The resultant pressure being placed on the Beacon Schools to succeed from all quarters must be significant. The survey asked the respondents what contributed to this success. With each school offering different strengths, and operating within a different set of local circumstances, a wide range of reasons for success was given. A significant number of the respondents referred to the enthusiasm of the profession for the initiative as the key factor contributing towards such positive outcomes. Moreover it was clear that this enthusiasm applied to both the staff teaching within the Beacon School and the schools making use of the services offered.

Adequate preparation and liaison, both internally and externally, in the lead-up to becoming a Beacon School were regarded as essential, particularly by those who felt that they had received insufficient time for this. Successfully communicating the 'vision' of Beacon School status throughout the school, including constituents such as parents and the community as a whole, appeared essential for some, a feature explored by a number of commentators (Bailey and Johnson, 1997; Foreman, 1998; Weindling; 1997). This would appear to be an extension of the need for effective communication, important within the operation of any well-run school (see, for instance, Riches, 1997a).

As suggested in much of the literature on school effectiveness (see, for instance, Barber et al., 1995; Mortimore, 1998; Sammons, Hillman and Mortimore, 1995) the leadership of the head appeared to be the key driving force in Beacon Schools. In most responses there was the acknowledgement that the internal organisation of the school, as translated into management structures, was an essential element of the success. Schools staff need to be empowered to 'make things happen' and allow their talents to be realised. Using hindsight, the respondents were asked to suggest how they might have done things differently had they known then what they know now. This provided some useful pointers for aspiring Beacon Schools. There seemed to be two distinct ways in which Beacon status can be effectively developed. There were those schools that suggested a tighter focus involving fewer partner schools and the others who suggested one large-scale project involving a wider range of schools. In either scenario, the emphasis was on reducing the demands being made on the staff of the Beacon School, either by reducing the number of relationships that have to be managed or by reducing the breadth of support on offer. Both are consistent with good management practice – setting focused, achievable targets as a basis for future development, with clearly defined success criteria built in (Southworth, 1998, p. 81). The reduction in the number of partners encourages a deeper and more intense relationship offering the possibility of developing the relationship further in the long term. By focusing on a narrow range of strengths for a wider audience two options are possible. From that wider initial contact, closer relationships may be developed with a much smaller number of particularly interested partners, or the approach could be repeated to a different group of partners. Clearly, with the limited input, there is a degree of superficiality with this second approach but it does allow a key message to be spread far.

Respondents acknowledged the importance of managing the marketing of the Beacon initiative more effectively. This was expressed in a variety of ways, but each involved the communication with partner or potential partner schools. In particular the specificity of materials produced needed to be more focused in terms of content, expectations, to whom it was sent, the approach that it suggested, or in the wording that it used. The importance of 'treating the "customers" as professionals, who are able to offer expertise in their own right' was the way that one respondent expressed it (see also the work of Davies and Ellison, 1997).

THE CASE STUDIES

The case studies of the initial Beacon Schools (Brundrett and Burton, 2000) represented the diverse nature of the Beacon initiative. They were drawn from many of the divergent phases and types of school that make the patchwork of provision that has grown up in England and Wales. One was an infant school, two were primary schools, three were secondary schools and three were special schools. Of these, five were denominational schools and one a selective grammar school.

Most schools involved in the case studies had chosen a number of foci for the Beacon initiative. These foci included Accelerated Learning, ICT, Personal Social and Health Education, Sport, Performing Arts, Music, English, Mathematics, Music, Special Needs, Literacy and Numeracy. Unsurprisingly these topics tended to be drawn from perceived areas of expertise within the schools. Several respondents were keen to point out the indebtedness of Beacon projects to highly talented individuals or teams of individuals within their schools. There was a notable determination on the part of respondents. The writers betrayed little or no arrogance about their own achievements and seemed well aware that their methods and techniques might need adaptation to fit other situations or, indeed, might be inappropriate for others in different circumstances. Indeed, most respondents pointed out that that they had learned a great deal by taking part in the project and several were keen to point out that they felt that the institutions with which they worked provided mutually supportive partnerships.

Strategies employed in the development of effectiveness included joint In-Service Training days; the sharing of school documentation, proformas and equipment; 'masterclasses' conducted by teachers with especial expertise in given curriculum areas (Music); and classroom observation of effective teaching strategies. One of the schools had hosted a day-long 'Beacon School conference' and further such conferences were planned for the future. Visits to respective schools were considered of especial value

All respondents were asked to provide their overall reflections on the effects of the Beacon project within and between schools. The respondents were universally supportive of the initiative. One respondent in particular expressed concern about the stress felt by teachers who were striving to continue to enhance teaching and learning within their own institution while at the same time assisting another school. Overall, however, most respondents felt that the project had been of assistance in developing teaching and learning both within their own schools and in partner institutions. Indeed, one headteacher stated: 'As a profession, teachers are highly self-critical and in the view of the headteacher this initiative has made a significant step towards reinvigorating the quality of pedagogical exchange between practising classroom teachers.'

Overall the case studies revealed elements of the journey that a number of high-performing schools have undertaken in their attempts to provide the best learning environment possible for their pupils or students. Many of the features identified in the research on school effectiveness were embedded within the discourses that they offered. These features included strong leadership by the headteacher (see, for instance, Bell and Rhodes, 1996; MacBeath, 1998; Southworth, 1998); a commitment to a 'learning organisation' (see MacGilchrist, Myers and Read, 1997); and the importance of empowering staff, especially heads of departments (see Sammons, Thomas and Mortimore, 1997). The schools that contributed were striking examples of communities working together towards a common goal and by agreeing to be part of the Beacon scheme they had committed themselves to the sharing their experiences, knowledge and expertise with others.

The second group of case studies were focused on curriculum issues (Burton and Brundrett (2002), and a notable key theme running through the contributions was the focus on how individuals could become more effective learners. This was addressed in the learning context of both students and teachers, and in terms of both the content of their learning and their readiness to learn. It became increasingly apparent that many Beacon Schools had achieved their pre-eminence in learning and teaching by reflecting more closely on the relative merits of theories of learning and effectively applying these ideas to improve practice. The ability of schools focusing on the specific learning needs of particular groups of children (special schools) had enabled teachers to develop effective strategies to address specific challenges. The approaches that had been developed in these, often extreme, learning conditions had then been generalised for application in mainstream classes.

Significantly, schools, in developing learning in the classroom, had also begun to assess the ramification of these approaches to developing learning potential for staff development. These approaches, which proved to be so effective within the classroom, were being adapted and applied throughout the school in the pursuit of excellence as a truly 'learning organisation'. Gardner's work on multiple intelligences (Gardner, 1993) was clearly influential among some of the Beacon School practitioners, with at least one respondent noting that their whole project had been inspired by his work (Heightman, 2002, p. 24). Implication for learning must be considered as significant – both for pupils and students and the professional development of their teachers. Such a focus on 'individualised learning' was also apparent in excellent practice being developed in 'special schools' that was being disseminated to 'mainstream' colleagues (see, for instance, Simpson et al., 2002). In other case studies mainstream special schools demonstrated the leadership and courage of professional conviction to set challenging targets for their pupils (Dunkerton, 2002, p. 8) within the framework developed by central government agencies (DfEE, 1997).

The case studies also made clear that the use of advanced skills teachers (ASTs) within schools, to provide both an exemplar of good practice for others to observe and emulate and also to coach teaching staff as they progress towards mastery of new skills, was seen as a potent means of improving learning and teaching (Blades et al., 2002). Well-chosen presentations, raising awareness of pedagogical approaches, can therefore be developed into embedded practice through effective collaboration within the school. Once again this highlights the importance of the organisational structure of the school in the development of a learning culture. For learning to be most effective within the school, not only do the teachers need the skills to teach and support the learning of the children, they also need to be able to support the learning of colleagues. The development of a supporting learning culture offers 'ownership' of developments within the school to teachers, which might reasonably be expected to lead to increased motivation and reductions in the levels of uncontrollable stress.

Overall the case studies offered examples of how different schools had taken control of the learning experience and had enhanced student achievement as a result. In each case organisational culture which values both the learning of students and staff, could be seen as being one of the core foundations of the successful school.

MANAGING A SUCCESSFUL SCHOOL: TOWARDS A NOTION OF CO-CONSTRUCTED LEADERSHIP.

There is evidence that, in Britain, a collegial style of school leadership has become the 'official model of good practice' (Wallace, 1988). Indeed, much of the recent work on school improvement and effectiveness in Britain such as that of Hargreaves and Hopkins (1991; 1994), Hopkins, Ainscow and West (1994) and Gray et al. (1996) has either an open or tacit acceptance of collegial management styles as one of the keys to enhanced school development. A detailed exegesis of this model does, however, reveal that it contains within it a variety of inadequacies both as a functional description of good management practice and as a practical model for school leadership and governance (Brundrett, 1998). A case study of one Beacon School has led to the postulation that, at a time when accountability to external organisations is becoming increasingly important, collegial models may lead to conflicts between participation and accountability. Collegial models may, for instance, be difficult to sustain in view of the requirement that heads and principals remain accountable to the governing bodies which appoint them, and leaders may be sandwiched between these very different pressures (Bush, 1993, p. 12).

The headteacher in the study noted that: 'How can a school be 'collegial' when it is the Head who is in charge and who has to take responsibility for the decisions that are taken, especially to the Governors and to Ofsted?' (Brundrett, 2002). This accords with the notion that collegial models can make it difficult, particularly for external analysts, to establish who is responsible for organisational policy (Bush, 1995, p. 63) and there can even be a somewhat nightmarish scenario for the governance of the institution within which the locus of power seems, to the observer, to be forever 'receding' and 'the real decisions always seem to be taken somewhere else' (Noble and Pym, 1970, pp. 435–6). This is, however, only one of a nodal set of criticisms of the collegial model of management, perhaps the most cogent of which are presented in the ideological critique offered by Hargreaves and Dawe (1990) and Hargreaves (1994) who, while supporting the notion of genuine participatory and innovatory management of educational institutions, criticise what is seen as 'contrived collegiality'. Citing the work of Judith Warren Little (1990) Hargreaves posits that there are, in fact, different kinds of collegial relations in terms of their implications for teacher independence, and that the characteristics and virtues of some kinds of collegiality and collaboration are often falsely attributed to some other kinds (Hargreaves, 1994, p. 188). Within this view teacher empowerment, critical reflection and continuous improvement are claims made for collaboration and collegiality as a whole but are, in fact, attributable only to certain versions of it.

It is thus clear that collegiality places a methodological emphasis on what is shared in a manner which may exaggerate consensus based aspects of human relationships (Hargreaves, 1994, p. 190). It may be that indeed the ubiquitous use of the actual term 'collegiality', with its deeply embedded overtones of democratic decision-making, is actually inappropriate for the ways in which management does, and can, function, in successful schools under the current framework of governance. Nonetheless any wise school leader will wish to gain as much agreement and consensus around proposed changes as is possible. Thus the potential exists for a disequilibrium between the headteacher's accountability functions and the desire to operate in a quasi-democratic manner that will facilitate staff commitment to goals. The skilled headteacher in the successful school will counter-balance these potentially countervailing pressures by ensuring that issues are discussed fully and that strategic changes that are required by the Head do not appear as mere 'directives' which emerge without consultation.

One solution to this apparently dichotomous existence can be found in recent work on teaching learning that supports the efficacy of 'co-constructed' forms of learning, that integrate teacher or subject centred systems with pupil-centred approaches in order to create a third 'partnership' approach (Silcock, 1999; Brundrett and Silcock, 2002). This work argues that programmes devised by those who take recent cognitive developmental theory seriously (Adey and Shayer, 1994; Resnick, 1985; Resnick, Bill and Lesgold, 1992), are dedicated to co-constructivist techniques (Broadfoot, 2000) whereby twin perspectives, 'top down' *and* 'bottom up' (Biggs, 1992) spring both from pupils' experientially based attitudes and capabilities and the special features of subjects being taught. Crucial to this sort of teaching is peer interaction whereby pupils habitually challenge, support, comment, evaluate, debate each others' and standard views and a co-constructivist classroom is thus one where such talk is key. Adey and Shayer's (1994; 1996) and Resnick, Bill and Lesgold's (1992) evidence is that such talk works by developing critical states of mind (Piagetian formal operations; Vygotskian higher-order skills) and integrated forms of thinking (Broadfoot, 2000). All teachers co-operate, negotiate, reconcile views sympathetically, resolve differences, mediate between options, contest issues generously, present dialectical cases in ways making them vulnerable to argument, and generally act in a socially skilled manner. It follows that teachers in partnership with pupils will appreciate alternatives, experiment with radical positions, show a tolerance usually untested within mono-cultural settings, and use mediation and conflict-resolution as markers for their professional territory (Brundrett and Silcock, 2002, p. 91).

What is being posited here is that the skilled headteacher will function within the equivalent 'co-constructive' management style that integrates the apparently contradictory hierarchical management systems with collegial models. Just as the effective teacher will engender debate in order to reach curricular objectives, so the effective headteacher will create the climate for change by stimulating debate on new initiatives. The headteacher will tolerate competing views but will not abnegate responsibility for decision-making. Indeed it has been suggested that schools can be 'deliberative democracies' (Engelund, 2000, p. 307) within which pupils come to their rights, roles and responsibilities as members of communities (White, 1993). Pupils may not only experience democratic milieus and join in democratic decision-making, but find out at first hand how to be democrats and take full part in communal life. In fact such notions of 'democracy' in school organisation may be as inappropriate or impractical as collegial models, but what matters will not be so much the fact that schools are always hierarchically organised (Wilson, 2000), affecting the democratic quality of decisions made, as what pupils and staff learn from making such decisions (Brundrett and Silcock, 2002). This view of the classroom operating through co-constructed management can be extrapolated to the school as a whole wherein the deliberation is between headteacher and staff, staff and pupils.

Nonetheless this ability to initiate change, to engender discussion, to tolerate and encourage disputation, but finally to make decisions for which one is accountable, is undoubtedly the most severe challenge that faces any school leader. As the headteacher of the case study school commented: 'That's the hardest part of being a Head. There is formal training for the "big things" but no one really tells you how to relate to the staff' (Brundrett, 2002). One wonders how any system of training could instil the qualities required to take on the formidable panoply of skills required in a headteacher. The evidence of the quality of teaching and learning in Beacon Schools, and indeed the majority of schools in the UK, is that most headteachers, whether trained in the new 'national programmes' for school leadership such as NPQH or not, overcome the dichotomous objective of driving through change while at the same time ensuring a high degree of consensus and commitment by staff.

CONCLUSION

The Beacon Schools project provides reaffirmation of the importance of the salient features of school leadership and management identified in earlier school effectiveness and improvement studies. The scheme also provides encouraging initial indications that such features can be developed through the creation of mutually supportive partnerships between schools. The scheme is also one which offers an invaluable resource to researchers and practitioners alike since a searchable database of Beacon Schools' activities has been constructed which forms a data set that is of increasing interest to researchers in the field of leadership and management and in the wider fields of educational enquiry (DfES, 2002b).

It is, as yet, too early to tell whether the Beacon initiative will lead to sustained improvements in teaching and learning in partner institutions. Equally, it is for future studies to determine whether the notion of 'sharing success' will provide enhanced levels of achievement in schools throughout England in the way that the UK Department for Education and Skills expects.

Recent changes in the governance of schools have led to the increased desire for a technicist and rationalist systems of internal school organisation. The movement towards value-led management systems, which are often broadly characterised as being 'collegial' in form, is a welcome development since it holds out the potential for more inclusive and democratic systems of school leadership and management. The danger exists, however, that school leaders can become disempowered by such systems, thus leaving them open to accusations of irrationality with the concomitant danger of leaving schools to 'drift' at times when accountability and target setting form the dominant discourse of central government (Brundrett, 2002). Co-constructed systems of leadership hold out the possibility of empowering all the workers in the school organisation and offer a legitimation of the decision-making process. Through such co-construction the role of the headteacher/principal in leading the school is saved from the promiscuity of indefinite outcomes and inappropriately lengthy decision- making processes. It may be that the headteacher/principal is thus best described as being *primus inter pares* rather than the patrician ruler of school.

REFERENCES

Adey, P. and Shayer, M. (1994) *Really Raising Standards*, London: Routledge.

Adey, P. and Shayer, M. (1996) 'An exploration of long-term transfer effects following an extended intervention program in the high school science curriculum', in L. Smith (ed.), *Critical Readings in Piaget*, London: Routledge.

Bailey, A. and Johnson, G. (1997) 'How strategies develop in organisations', in M. Preedy, R. Glatter and R. Levačić (eds), *Educational Management: Strategy, Quality and Resources*, Buckingham: Open University Press, pp. 183–93.

Barber, M., Stoll, L., Mortimore, P. and Hillman, J. (1995) *Governing Bodies and Effective Schools*, London, DfEE.

Barnes, V. and Clouder, L. (2000) 'Dissemination as evidence? Deconstructing the processes of disseminating qualitative research', paper presented at the 'Qualitative Evidence-based Practice Conference', Coventry University, 15–17 May.

Bell, L. and Rhodes, C. (1996) *The Skills of Primary School Management*, London, Routledge.

Biggs, J.B. (1992) 'Returning to school: review and discussion', in A. Dimetriou, M. Shayer and A.E. Efklides (eds), *Neo-Piagetian Theories of Cognitive Development: Implications and Applications for Education*, London: Routledge.

Blades, B., Cade, J., Fletcher, M., Miles, F. and Taj, M. (2002) 'Using advanced skills teachers as change agents for effective teaching and learning', in N. Burton and M. Brundrett (eds), *The Beacon Schools Experience: Developing the Curriculum*, Dereham: Peter Francis, pp. 190–204.

Broadfoot, P. (2000) 'Liberating the learner through assessment', in J. Collins and D. Cook (eds), *Understanding Learning: Influences and Outcomes*, London: Paul Chapman Publishing/Open University Press.

Brundrett, M. (1998) 'What lies behind collegiality – legitimation or control?', *Educational Management and Administration*, **26**(3), 305–16.

Brundrett, M. (2002) 'Mission, faith and management: co-constructing leadership in a Beacon Lower School', *Education 3–13*, **30**(3), 42–7.

Brundrett, M. and Burton, N. (2000) *The Beacon Schools Experience: Case Studies in Excellence*, Dereham: Peter Francis.

Brundrett, M. and Burton, N. (2001) 'Sharing success: the development of the first

"Beacon Schools" in England', *International Studies in Educational Administration*, **29**(1), 19–28.

Brundrett, M. and Silcock, P. (2002) *Competence, Success and Excellence in Teaching*, London: Routledge Falmer.

Burton, N. and Brundrett, M. (2000) 'The first year of Beacon School status: maintaining excellence and sharing success', *School Leadership and Management*, **20**(4), 489–99.

Burton, N. and Brundrett, M. (2002) *The Beacon Schools Experience: Developing the Curriculum*, Dereham: Peter Francis.

Bush, T. (1993) *Exploring Collegiality: Theory, Process and Structure, E236 Managing Schools; Challenge and Response*, Buckingham: Open University Press.

Bush, T. (1995) *Theories of Educational Management*, London: Paul Chapman Publishing.

Davies, B. and Ellison, L. (1997) *Strategic Marketing for Schools*, London, Pitman.

Department for Education and Employment (DfEE) (1997) *Excellence for All*, London: HMSO.

Department for Education and Employment (DfEE) (1999a) http://www.standards.dfee.gov.uk/guidance/beaconschools, online.

Department for Education and Employment (DfEE) (1999b) http://www.standards.dfee.gov.uk/guidance/beaconschools/, online.

Department for Education and Employment (DfEE) (2001) *Individual Education Plans*.

Department for Education and Skills (DfES) (2002a) *Beacon Schools Site: NFER Evaluation – Interim Findings*, http://www.standards.dfee.gov.uk/beaconschools/general/447218

Department for Education and skills (DfES) (2002b) *Beacon Schools: Case Studies Index*, http://www.standards.dfee.gov.uk/beaconschools/?view=casestudiesindex

Dunkerton, J. (2002) 'Target setting and school improvement in a special school', in N. Burton and M. Brundrett (eds), *The Beacon Schools Experience: Developing the Curriculum*, Dereham: Peter Francis, pp. 8–21.

Engelund, G. (2000) 'Rethinking democracy and education: towards an education of deliberative citizens', *Journal of Curriculum Studies*, **32**(2), 305–13.

Foreman, K. (1998) 'Vision and mission', in D. Middlewood and J. Lumby (eds), *Strategic Management in Schools and Colleges*, London, Paul Chapman Publishing, pp. 18–31.

Gardner, H. (1993) *Frames of Mind*, 2nd edn, London: Harper Collins.

Ghouri, N. (1999) 'Beacon Schools battle to cope with success', *Times Educational Supplement*, 23 April, p. 16.

Gray, J., Reynolds, D., Fitz-Gibbon, C. and Jesson, D. (1996) *Merging Traditions: The Future of Research on School Effectiveness and School Improvement*, London: Cassell.

Hargreaves, A. (1994) *Changing Teachers, Changing Times: Teachers' Work and Culture in the Post-modern Age*, London: Cassell.

Hargreaves, A. and Dawe, R. (1990) 'Paths of professional development: contrived collegiality, collaborative culture, and the case of peer coaching', *Teaching and Teacher Education*, **6**(3), pp. 227–41.

Hargreaves, D.H. and Hopkins, D. (1991) *The Empowered School*, London: Cassell.

Hargreaves, D.H. and Hopkins, D. (eds) (1994) *Development Planning for School Improvement*, London: Cassell.

Heightman, S. (2002) 'Effective learning for students (and teachers!)', in N. Burton and M. Brundrett (eds), *The Beacon Schools Experience: Developing the Curriculum*, Dereham: Peter Francis, pp. 22–35.

Hopkins, D., Ainscow, M. and West, M. (1994) *School Improvement in an Era of Change*, London, Cassell.

Little, J.W. (1990) ''The persistence of privacy: autonomy and initiative in teachers' professional relations', *Teachers College Record*, **91**(4), pp. 509–36.

MacBeath, J. (ed.) (1998) *Effective School Leadership: Responding to Change*, London, Paul Chapman Publishing.

MacGilchrist, B., Myers, K. and Read, J. (1997) *The Intelligent School*, London, Paul Chapman Publishing.

Mortimore, P. (1998) *The Road to Improvement*, Lisse: Swets and Zeitlinger.

National Foundation for Educational Research (NFER) (2002) *Evaluation of the Beacon Schools Project*, http://www.nfer.ac.uk/research/down_pub.asp

Noble, T. and Pym, B. (1970) 'Collegial Authority and the Receding Locus of Power', *British Journal of Sociology*, **21**, 431–45.

Office for Standards in Education (OfSTED) (1997) http://www.Ofsted.gov.uk/pdf/i48/48536.pdf, online 23 November 1999.

Resnick, L.B. (1985) *Education and Learning to Think*, Pittsburgh, PA: Learning, Research and Development Centre, University of Pittsburgh.

Resnick, L.B., Bill, V. and Lesgold, S. (1992) 'Developing thinking abilites in Arithmetic class,' in A. Dimetriou, M. Shayer and A.E. Efklides (eds), *Neo-Piagetian Theories of Cognitive Development: Implications and Applications for Education*, London: Routledge.

Riches, C. (1997a) 'Communication in educational management', in M. Crawford, L. Kydd and C. Riches (eds), *Leadership and Teams in Educational Management*, Buckingham: Open university Press, pp. 163–78.

Riches, C. (1997b) 'Motivation in education', in M. Crawford, L. Kydd and C. Riches (eds), *Leadership and Teams in Educational Management*, Buckingham: Open University Press, pp. 88–102.

Rickinson, M. and Rudd, P. (2001) 'The success of Beacon partnerships', *Education Journal*, **57**, 30–2.

Rudd, P. (2000) *Evaluation of Pilot Beacon Schools*, Nottingham: Department for Education and Employment.

Rudduck, J., Kelly, P., Wrigley, J. and Sparrow, F. (1976) *The Dissemination of Curriculum Development*, Windsor: NFER.

Sammons, P., Hillman, J. and Mortimore, P. (1995) *Key Characteristics of Effective Schools: A Review of School Effectiveness Research*, report commissioned by the Office for Standards in Education, Institute of Education and Office for Standards in Education.

Sammons, P., Thomas, S. and Mortimore, P. (1997) *Forging Links: Effective Schools and Effective Departments*, London: Paul Chapman Publishing.

Silcock, P. (1999) *New Progressivism*, London: Falmer Press.

Simpson, I., Hutchinson, S., Griffiths, D., Bates, S. and Norris, D. (2002) 'SEN – effective inclusion', in N. Burton and M. Brundrett (eds), *The Beacon Schools Experience: Developing the Curriculum*, Dereham: Peter Francis, pp. 108–23.

Southworth, G. (1998) *Leading Improving Schools*, London: Falmer Press.

Wallace, M. (1988) 'Towards a collegiate approach to curriculum management in primary and middle schools', *School Organisation*, **8**(1), 25–34.

Weindling, D. (1997) 'Strategic planning in schools: some practical techniques', in M. Preedy, R. Glatter and R. Levačić (eds), *Educational Management: Strategy Quality and Resources*, Buckingham: Open University Press, pp. 218–33.

White, R. (1993) 'Autonomy as foundational', in H.J. Silverman (ed.), *Questioning Foundations*, New York: Routledge.

Wikeley, F. (1998) 'Dissemination of research as a tool for school improvement', *School Leadership and Management*, **18**(1), 59–73.

Wilson, J. (2000) *Key Issues in Education and Teaching*, London: Cassell.

FURTHER READING.

Brundrett, M. and Burton, N. (2000) *The Beacon Schools Experience: Case Studies in Excellence*, Dereham: Peter Francis.

Brundrett, M. and Burton, N. (2001) 'Sharing success: the development of the first "Beacon Schools" in England', *International Studies in Educational Administration*, **29**(1), 19–28.

Burton, N. and Brundrett, M. (2000) 'The first year of Beacon School status: maintaining excellence and sharing success', *School Leadership and Management*, **20**(4), 489–99.

Burton, N. and Brundrett, M. (2002) *The Beacon Schools Experience: Developing the Curriculum*, Dereham: Peter Francis.

Department for Education and Skills (DfES) (2002) *Standards Site: Welcome to the Beacon Schools*, http://www.standards.dfee.gov.uk/beaconschools/

National Foundation for Educational Research (NFER) (2002) *Evaluation of the Beacon Schools Project*, http://www.nfer.ac.uk/research/down_pub.asp

Rickinson, M. and Rudd, P. (2001) 'The success of Beacon partnerships', *Education Journal*, **57**, 30–2.

Rudd, P. (2000) *Evaluation of Pilot Beacon Schools*, Nottingham: DfEE.

11

LEADERSHIP IN FURTHER EDUCATION

Graham Peeke

INTRODUCTION

This chapter will focus upon leadership of further education (FE) colleges and begins by noting the leadership challenge for the colleges post-incorporation in 1993. This is followed by a brief consideration of what we know of college leadership from the literature. The chapter will then explore three key questions: what kind of FE institutions will we need leaders for in the future? What kinds of people will be needed to lead these institutions? What skills and qualities will these people need to be successful leaders? Three key issues will also be discussed: the tension between strategic leadership and the influence of external drivers, the tension between the core mission and the access mission of colleges, and the tension between leadership of institutions and leadership of learning.

CONTEXT

Clear definitions of what constitutes FE have always been fairly problematic. There is a blurring at the edges of the sector with regard to 16–19 education, which is delivered in both schools and colleges, and with regard to higher education because a substantial amount of this is delivered in further education colleges. With the creation of the learning and skills sector in April 2001, further education now finds itself to be a substantial sub-sector of a post-16 phase of education which includes school sixth forms, FE colleges, adult and community learning, and work-based training providers. To talk of leadership in further education is therefore to talk of leadership of the FE colleges. The issues and challenges of leadership may be similar across all organisations that constitute the new learning and skills sector, but insufficient is known about the wide

164

range of organisations within it so that such judgements cannot be made with any confidence.

Following the incorporation of colleges in 1993, the Further Education Funding Council (FEFC) virtually tutored college managers by correspondence in the management challenges of running an independent corporation. These challenges included strategic planning, estates, financial and human resource management, all functions which had previously been overseen by the local education authorities. The urgent need to focus upon such pressing matters was complicated for many college managers by having to cope with a major review of lecturer contracts, leading in many cases to difficult industrial disputes. This has been the standard explanation for the traditional focus of many college principals on matters relating to the running of their institution, rather than the leadership of learning. To paraphrase the above, it could be said that the challenges for principals post-incorporation were challenges of management not leadership.

An example of a focus on management rather than leadership is provided by college responses to the strategic planning process. As Lumby (1998) reports, the FEFC provided clear guidance on a framework for rational strategic planning. This led to the development of a body of expertise within colleges concerning the production of strategic plans, and 'led to the creation of a better structured, more consistent planning process' (Drodge and Cooper, 1997; p. 47), but not necessarily the development of strategic thinking within institutions. As Lumby (1998, p. 95) comments: 'evidence collected to date shows that the process of arriving at the plan, and the effectiveness of its implementation have not been entirely successful for many colleges'. From a management perspective, colleges became efficient at writing plans, but many lacked the strategic thinking that characterises effective leadership.

Given the focus in colleges upon management rather than leadership, it is not surprising that there is little literature on leadership in further education. The most comprehensive and recent review of the literature on this topic is that carried out by Sawbridge (2000). This work forms part of the Learning and Skills Development Agency's (LSDA) Raising Quality and Achievement (RQA) programme, an LSC funded initiative to improve quality and standards in FE. As Sawbridge (2001, p. 16) comments: 'There is little in the way of published research or evaluated practice to support effective leadership development in further education. Our understanding of what works in educational leadership is drawn largely from research in the schools sector.' While the main focus of the review was on the impact of leadership upon achievement, the review raises more questions about leadership in FE than information about how leadership is carried out.

Finding little in the literature that was specific to leadership in FE, except for a few case studies and personal accounts, Sawbridge draws on more general literature relating in particular to school leadership and the school effectiveness movement. The paucity of research into leadership is consistent with the relative lack of scholarly activity focused on FE. In reviewing the scope of research into FE, Hughes, Taylor and Tight (1996, p. 13), state: 'There has been relatively little critical analysis of policy or practice within further education, in the sense of trying to explain and understand these experiences from outside. There has been almost no theorisation or model building, making use of the wealth of available disciplinary frameworks from the social sciences.'

In examining the work on school leadership and effectiveness, Sawbridge raises a range of questions about the nature of leadership in FE and its possible impact upon student achievement, for example: what do we mean by leadership? Who are the leaders? Does leadership affect student outcomes? Sawbridge also outlines current approaches to leadership discussing, in particular, the transactional, instructional and transformational approaches.

Transactional leadership is usually associated with managerial, functional or action-based leadership, which focuses on the skills of leadership and its impact upon others. This leadership paradigm is frequently criticised for its mechanistic emphasis and tendency to reduce complex interactions to a set of skills to be acquired. Instructional leadership concentrates on the leadership of the curriculum and teaching and learning, and has close links with the school effectiveness movement. It emphasises the role of the leader in promoting learner outcomes but, although there appears to be a link between effective leadership and student achievement, it is not clear what constitutes this link. Transformational leadership concerns the leader's ability to transform the function of an organisation in order that staff and learners can function at a higher level. This approach tends to focus more on leadership behaviours and the ability of leaders to empower and motivate others and promote change. The approach has been criticised on the grounds that its preoccupation with continuous improvement ignores the important need to concentrate on the quality of teaching and learning. Sawbridge (2001, p. 15) concludes that 'Although there are exceptions, leadership in FE colleges in the UK largely conforms to a managerial or functional model'. This supports the proposition, suggested above, of a managerial approach developing in FE post-incorporation.

WHAT KIND OF FE INSTITUTIONS?

When considering leadership in FE it makes sense to think about what kind of institutions will need leading in the sector of the future. Like any educational establishment, FE colleges will be subject to curricular influences determined by the changing nature of society. Factors such as the development of a knowledge-based economy, high levels of consumption, globalisation and the international movement of populations all have major consequences for educational organisations.

In addition, the future is likely to bring significant changes in the systems for recognising and accrediting learning. As the Organisation for Economic Co-operation and Development (OECD, 2001, p. 69) comments: 'It is scarcely imaginable that significant progress can continue towards the knowledge-based, lifelong learning society without major changes in the systems for recognising and accrediting competence.' The OECD sees a future whereby monopolies over certification are broken, which may become viewed as a liberating factor for educational organisations as they come 'to focus more on learning and less on sorting and credentialing' (OECD, 2001, p. 69).

More immediately however, there are a number of key factors which will have an impact upon the nature of college organisation and structure. These are information and communication technology (ICT), the advent of the new post-16 learning and skills sector itself, and the inexorable pressure upon colleges to move more towards becoming learning organisations.

In terms of ICT, its increasing sophistication leads to important questions about the physical structure and existence of colleges, the role of teachers, and the role of colleges as social institutions and sites for the development of relationships between people. The creation of a wider post-16 sector and the emphasis on collaboration will also lead to the development of new post-16 organisational forms. Already, early in the life of the new sector, there have been a number of mergers between colleges and work-based training providers. It is expected that the overall number of work-based training providers will decline significantly as consolidation takes place. Closer links with employers through initiatives like the Centres for Vocational Excellence (CoVEs) and closer links between further and higher education, also suggest a new typology of organisations in the future. With regard to the development of colleges as learning organisations, the criticisms and imperatives that the OECD note for schools are likely to be equally valid for colleges. The OECD argues that too little has changed in the basic structural, organisational and behavioural characteristics of schools, and that they need to focus as much on knowledge creation as knowledge transmission. This would mean changes in the roles of teachers and the need to learn from a range of professionals rather than just teachers.

To capture the implications of a range of social, economic, political and technological factors upon schools the OECD have created six scenarios for the future of schooling designed to act as tools for reflection, rather than analytical predictions. Such tools help to clarify main directions and strategic options. This set of scenarios can be adapted for college purposes to create a set of possible scenarios for the future of colleges. Using this framework, these scenarios can be summarised as follows.

Scenario 1: More of the same

In this scenario the current bureaucratic structure of colleges remains much the same as at present. Problems of lecturer supply intensify, and although there is increased use of ICT, there is no radical change to the organisational structures of teaching and learning. The dominance of the teaching room with an individual teacher continues.

Scenario 2: Extension of the market model

Here, diversification of colleges and the emergence of new providers in the learning marketplace are key features of the scenario. This leads to greater experimentation with organisational forms and more specialisation within colleges. New types of partnerships between providers and other organisations will develop and colleges will face more international competition. Information and communication technology will be extensively and imaginatively exploited for learning and networking will flourish. The stability of colleges will be dependent upon the effectiveness of the market in meeting the needs of the economy and the community.

Scenario 3: Colleges as core social centres

Many diverse types of colleges will develop, but strong local links will be a feature of all. Colleges will be less bureaucratic and will combine teaching and learning with other community responsibilities. Information and communication technology will be strongly developed, and the functions of advice, guidance and support will be high profile. Colleges are more likely to be liberated from the excessive pressures of credentialism.

Scenario 4: Colleges as learning organisations

More specialisms would be catered for but all learners would experience a demanding mix of learning. Colleges will be flatter; team orientated organisations, with greater attention to management skills for all employees. Information and communication technology will be strongly developed as a tool for learning and communication. There will be many links with other knowledge industries and international networking will be common. Major increases in staffing levels are to be expected allowing greater innovation in teaching and learning, professional development, and research.

Scenario 5: Colleges as parts of learner networks

Learners will be involved in much individualised learning and learning through networks. Information and communication technology will be extensively exploited for learning and networking. Only a few colleges will remain, either to serve those excluded by the 'digital divide' or as part of community-based networks. New learning professionals will emerge, employed by major players such as media companies and software developers. There will be a decline in established curriculum structures and new forms of accrediting achievement.

Scenario 6: The 'melt down' scenario

This scenario is based on the presumption that the shortage of teachers becomes critical, leading to the development of diverse organisational arrangements. These could include the intensive use of ICT as an alternative to teachers, ICT companies actively involved in delivery, corporate and media interest in provision intensifying, and the expansion of semi-professional roles in facilitating learning. This scenario could lead to serious inequalities in provision; a strengthened centralised examination and accreditation system and established curriculum structures coming under intense pressure.

In summary, these scenarios suggest that whatever specific form the future takes, it is highly likely that the college leaders of the future will have to lead organisations characterised by

- flux and ambiguity
- greatly increased use of ICT for learning
- more specialisation of provision
- broader community responsibilities
- existence as part of a wider learning network
- emphasis on knowledge management in addition to knowledge creation.

A common feature of all the scenarios is the diversity of types of colleges and an increasing emphasis on specialisation. The CoVE initiative is an example of an attempt to create diversity of mission leading to the creation of more distinctive roles for colleges. The initiative is also a key device to promote the regeneration of technical and vocational education by systematically recognising and promoting high-level, specialist vocational provision in colleges. The developing emphasis on specialisation and distinctiveness is a source of tension for college leaders who have spent the years since incorporation concentrating on access and growth, factors which have been instrumental in encouraging breadth of provision rather than specialisation. As Kennedy (1997, p. 1) noted: 'Further education is everything that does not happen in schools or universities.' Greater clarity of core business will be a feature of colleges in the future.

The question of core business for general FE colleges is a complex one. Virtually all colleges will offer a substantial amount of provision at entry level and levels 1 and 2. For some this will constitute the vast majority of their provision and thus access is their core mission. For other colleges, the core mission is A-level provision, or general further education, once the access type of provision is acknowledged. The general FE colleges will need to further identify a core mission within their general technical/vocational provision. This is in order to develop a strong sense of priorities at institutional level which, is as apparent in the case of sixth form colleges and specialist schools, suggests greater success in achieving higher standards. The CoVE initiative should help in a similar way in the drive to raise standards and to position a college in relation to other providers.

The challenge for college leaders this presents, is to manage the tension between maintaining a broad emphasis on access and growth, and establishing a more specialised mission within the area of technical and vocational provision at higher levels of achievement. Breaking down potential barriers between the various aspects of the mission rather than creating them is a crucial task here. In essence, within the college this involves working with colleagues to secure their commitment to the revised mission. In order to balance an access mission with a specialised vocational one, and to move from a general to a more specialised mission, the mission needs to be agreed across the college. In addition, it needs to be evidenced in the actions of leaders and managers and to impact upon the day-to-day operation of the college.

Outside the college, there is a need to see clear local strategy emerge in partnership with the Local Learning and Skills Councils (LLSCs). Comprehensive provision across an area, rather than comprehensive provision in each college is the aim. This should result in energy and direction developing within colleges and should encourage new initiatives, with employers for example.

WHAT KINDS OF PEOPLE?

Detailed information on leaders in FE is difficult to find. An unpublished internal survey conducted on behalf of the DfES in 2001, found that the vast majority (68 per cent) of principals who responded to the survey, (78 per cent of the total in the FE colleges) were aged 51 and over. Of these, 36 per cent possessed a qualification in management, although the majority of these were gained at least six years previously. A high percentage of the respondents (45 per cent) had been employed as principals for six years or more. Seventy-nine per cent were senior post-holders in FE immediately prior to accepting a post as principal.

These figures can be compared with the results of a survey of almost 1,500 practising managers in a broad cross section of organisations conducted by the Institute of Management (Horne and Stedman-Jones, 2001). This survey found that 53 per cent of managers were over the age of 54, and that 57 per cent stated that they held a management qualification. In comparison, leaders in FE appear to be older and less academically qualified for the role than their counterparts in other parts of the public and private sectors.

Interesting figures available from the Institute of Management survey relate to gender and ethnicity. Twenty-five per cent of respondents to this survey were female, and 96 per cent of all respondents were white. No comparable official figures exist for FE. Research by Stott and Lawson (1997) showed that there were 81 women principals in the autumn of 1997, just over 17 per cent. However, this figure is likely to have increased substantially in recent years. No figures exist for women in senior management positions. In its *Update Report*, the Commission for Black Staff in Further Education (2001, p. 4) notes that it is commissioning work on the employment profile of Black staff in FE and that there are 'few Black staff in the sector'. It further notes: 'While there is data on staffing, there is little collation above college level and there is little evidence of analysis and action based on this data, or of systematic ethnic monitoring' (ibid., p. 27).

This brief statistical profile of FE leaders shows a picture of a group of people who are predominantly white, male and over 50. In addition, the majority has spent many years in the FE sector and, consequently, has little experience of the wider world of business and industry. It is clear that diversity is a key issue for the sector, currently leaders are drawn from a limited section of the population and rarely from outside the sector. This prevents FE from benefiting from a rich seam of both life experience and experience available in the wider public or private sectors. As important is the fact that both teaching, and leadership and management staff, rarely reflect the gender and ethnic profile of learners in the institutions in which they work.

In the context of consideration of the type of people who lead the sector, a key question is the way these leaders see themselves. A tension appears to exist between the role of leader as institutional leader or chief executive, and that of the role of leader as leader of learning. This becomes increasingly important as more emphasis is placed on leadership for achievement within the sector and the new common inspection framework awards grades for the impact of leadership and management upon student achievement. As OFSTED (2002, p. 54) comment, in relation to post-compulsory education: 'The Government has stressed that the new legislation places the individual learner as the central focus. The primary task of inspectors is, therefore, the direct observation of teaching and training sessions.'

Along with this goes an emphasis on the impact of leadership and management on the teaching and learning process. Post-incorporation leaders were encouraged to focus upon planning, organising and controlling, whereas today the emphasis has shifted to their impact upon achievement. In the broader sector of education and in North America in particular, there is increasing emphasis upon the features of leadership, which make a difference to learner outcomes. This shift in emphasis mirrors a wider debate in the field of leadership studies between transactional, skills-based approaches and transformational approaches which see leadership as a set of characteristics and behaviours which are evident in effective leadership practice.

As reported earlier, Sawbridge (2000) sees the dominant leadership paradigm in FE to be managerial or functional. However, if leadership is also about improving effectiveness, promoting excellence in teaching and learning, and the development of curriculum knowledge and expertise, then leadership practice based on an instructional leadership or transformational model is arguably more relevant. The impact of leadership upon learning also raises the notion of distributed leadership, for it is clear that others within the college than those with designated leadership roles, will have an impact upon teaching, learning and curriculum development. These are likely to be curriculum and course team leaders and individual teachers.

Research by Martinez (2000), demonstrates that many of the variables which have the greatest impact upon student achievement are those related to the structure of learning, curriculum choice, evaluation and monitoring of student progress and student support. Those closest to the learner experience, that is teachers and team leaders, are therefore likely to have a significant impact upon learner achievement. A key challenge for FE leaders is to acknowledge the leadership role of colleagues throughout the organisation, and to examine their own contribution to learner achievement.

Leaders who acknowledge the reality of shared leadership are likely to find it easier to tackle the demands of implementing multiple change. The concept of distributed leadership draws attention to the fact that each staff member can act as change agent. Colleagues throughout the college have considerable influence on how things work out in practice. The principal can articulate the importance of a focus on achievement, but it is down to course and curriculum leaders to translate this in practical terms and work with colleagues to turn it into reality.

WHAT SKILLS AND QUALITIES?

The starting place for an analysis of the skills and qualities needed by leaders in the FE sector is the set of national occupational standards published by FENTO (2001), for management in further education. The standards are presented in several parts including a statement of the values which underpin the practice of management, the generic knowledge and critical understanding needed of a manager, and the personal attributes describing why and how a manager operates. The core of the standards are the performance outcomes organised around four key areas: developing strategic practice, developing and sustaining learning and the learning environment, leading teams and individuals, and managing finance and resources. These key areas are further subdivided in the following manner:

A   Develop strategic practice
- A1 Develop a vision
- A2 Plan to achieve the vision
- A3 Manage change and continuous improvement

B   Develop and sustain learning and the learning environment
- B1 Develop and sustain services for learners
- B2 Manage quality in the delivery of services
- B3 Manage human resources to support the provision of services

C   Lead teams and individuals
- C1 Manage and develop self and own performance
- C2 Maintain and develop team and individual performance
- C3 Build and maintain productive working relationships

D   Manage finance and resources
- D1 Plan resource requirements
- D2 Manage finance
- D3 Manage physical resources

Sawbridge (2000, p. 26) argues that the standards 'reinforce the skills approach to leadership inherent in the managerial leadership model', thereby locating the model for the development of the standards within the dominant paradigm for leadership currently existing in the sector. Sawbridge (2000, p. 26) criticises the standards for reducing complex activities to 'a set of management activities performed to a predetermined criteria and again largely assuming a management by objectives approach'. However, he also acknowledges that there is strong emphasis within the standards on the development of personal attributes, which have the potential to reflect leadership behaviours as opposed to skills.

Despite concerns that attempts to identify performance outcomes or competences reduce leadership to a set of functions, frameworks of competences or capabilities are common across the developed economies of the first world. The University of Texas (2001) in its leadership programme for community colleges for example, groups leadership competencies around the twelve roles of visionary, task giver, motivator, figurehead, liaison, monitor, disseminator, spokesperson, entrepreneur, disturbance handler, resource allocator and negotiator. In Australia, Callan (2001) identifies nine core capabilities, with numerous sub-elements, as the main elements in a management and leadership capability framework for the vocational education and training sector. The capabilities are corporate vision and direction, strategic focus, achievement of outcomes, develop and manage resources, change leadership, interpersonal relationships, personal development and mastery, business and entrepreneurial skills, and develop and empower people.

Callan notes the emergence of transformational leadership as a new leadership paradigm and identifies the extent to which a leader can raise employees to a higher level of functioning, as a defining feature of the approach. He notes that the level of such leadership required from Australian leaders will continue to increase. Callan identifies the nine capabilities as crucial for the application of transformational leadership, thus avoiding the accusation that his list of capabilities merely provides a set of functions leaders need to display.

Respondents to the Institute of Management leadership survey (Horne and Stedman-Jones, 2001), identified the following key characteristics of leaders:

- inspiring
- strategic thinker
- forward-looking
- honest
- fair-minded
- courageous
- supportive
- knowledgeable.

The Institute of Management checked to see if respondents believed that these characteristics added up to any systematic model of leadership. They ascertained that they relate primarily to a relational model, which emphasises interpersonal and motivational skills, thus corresponding closely with the transformational paradigm.

A common element to all these frameworks is an emphasis upon strategic thinking. This emphasis raises the issue of the extent to which leaders in FE have responsibility for strategy. Frequent contact with principals through a range of development activities provided by the LSDA, suggests that a number of principals view their strategic capability as severely limited by constant external interference from government or the funding agencies. The establishment of the Learning and Skills Council (LSC) and its 47 local arms, with a remit for planning provision across the local area, casts further doubt over the degree of freedom colleges have to think strategically. Smith et al. (2001, p. 2) believe that the FE sector has 'fallen victim to a mechanistic view of strategy as planning through a filter of ever reducing degrees of freedom rather than a more holistic perspective incorporating strategic thinking, formulation and implementation.' The authors believe that a sole reliance on strategic planning as a vehicle to formulate strategy is both inappropriate and ineffective. Their research supports the view that 'within the FE sector a range of "logics" exist which serve to help principals, governors and SMTs (senior management teams) "make sense" of their environment and help prioritise the strategies which they consider valid and useful' (Smith, et al. 2001, p. 7).

The three sets of dominant logics they discern are:

1 *Stability maximising*: Principals of these colleges argue that in reality neither they nor their team are strategists but operators who are there to provide an education-based, community service as efficiently and effectively as they can within the constraints set by funders and other stakeholders.

2 *Market maximising*: The principals of these colleges have embraced the 'college as business' model, which accepts commercial realism and points to market orientation as the only viable option. Colloquially, Pritchard (2000, p. 150) reports this approach as one of 'find a market, get into it, suck it, satisfy it and move on'.

3 *Resource maximising*: Here the dominant strategic logic centres on the college as a set of educational resources and capabilities. There are educational needs, which need to be met, and these are congruent with the focus of the college. These colleges do not ignore the market but attempt to benefit from their capability rather than seek markets and learn how to exploit them.

If these logics reflect the dominant patterns of strategic thinking in colleges, it is clear that many principals and senior managers will not see their main role as strategists in the usual sense of the word, but as operations managers. In this role their key task is in ensuring that colleges make the most effective provision, given the resources available and the policy imperatives which impact upon their operations. This view is further reinforced by the role of local LSCs in planning. With the LLSCs' brief to plan provision across their area, it can be argued that the role of college principal is reduced to that of 'branch manager', ensuring the supply of educational courses and services within a framework determined at 'head office'. This planning brief is reinforced by the findings of OFSTED (2002, p. 53) that:

> The lack of strategic direction and co-ordination of 16–19 education and training has been a common feature of many of the areas inspected. The introduction of Local Learning and Skills Councils and new funding regimes will oblige providers to look more critically at the rationale behind what they offer and ensure that planning takes account of the needs of the area as a whole and avoids unnecessary duplication.

The need to plan college provision in collaboration with the LLSC does not detract from the need for strategic thinking within individual institutions. Colleges will continue to need to seek out new opportunities, to take some commercial risks and to form strategic alliances and partnerships. Principals will need to lead strategic change within their colleges and, as mentioned earlier in this chapter, manage change that leads to the redesign of their colleges as learning organisations. Challenges in terms of quality improvement, team operation and performance-based reward systems will all require principals to provide vision and direction through which they can lead change. These are not strategic planning challenges, but the challenges of implementing strategic change.

Recent debates about the nature of leadership within the FE sector have focused on the concept of emotional intelligence (Goleman, 1998). The LSDA's leadership development programme for principals has been based around a set of individual diagnostics measuring emotional intelligence, leadership styles and organisational climate. These instruments are developed and administered by the HayGroup, who run the programme in partnership with LSDA, and are based upon a similar model and set of diagnostics as those used in the leadership programme for serving head teachers, which is also run by Hay. About 350 principals have participated in these development programmes between 1999 and 2002, creating a common vocabulary within the sector about leadership styles and the application of emotional intelligence. As Callan (2001, p. 21) remarks:

> Managers who have high levels of emotional intelligence show a propensity to suspend judgement and to think before they act. They show trustworthiness and integrity, are comfortable with ambiguity, and are open to change. In addition, managers who are emotionally intelligent are empathetic. They demonstrate an ability to understand the emotional makeup of other people, and show skill in treating people according to their emotional reactions. In addition, they demonstrate expertise in building and retaining talent, and in providing service to clients and customers.

There are no studies exploring the impact of emotional intelligence upon college management. However, it does appear that a major capability required of today's leaders is a willingness to engage in personal development and acquire a sense of personal mastery of one's own weaknesses and strengths, as well as those of others.

The notion of emotional intelligence has been criticised for the lack of data about its impact on life achievement and organisational effectiveness. It is also possible to criticise any approach to leadership that relies on the identification of personal characteristics and behaviours, as rooted in a personological paradigm that asserts that human behaviour is a function of individual characteristics. This is opposed to the view that behaviour is a function of situation or interaction.

Sala (2002, p. 18) reports on the impact of the various leadership styles upon college success and the link between organisational climate and success. He comments:

> As suggested by previous research, managerial styles were found to be associated with various measures of institutional success. Managerial styles seem to most impact student retention rates and overall ratings for the management of the college. More specifically, the Authoritative style seems most important since it was significantly correlated with student retention rates, support for students, and college management ratings.

Sala goes on to add: 'Furthermore, these findings may confirm earlier research that suggested that presidents (*sic*) ought to utilise Authoritative and Coaching styles – which were found to be more characteristic of business leaders – rather than Affiliative, Democratic and Pace Setting managerial styles' (ibid., p. 18).

In terms of organisational climate, Sala found that 'Climate was positively related to student retention rate, student support, college management, academic achievement scores and classroom attendance rates' (ibid., p. 19). Overall, Sala (ibid., p. 21) concludes that:

> Presidents might consider the way they manage their colleges and the climates they subsequently create, and the impact that those styles and behaviours have on their faculty of staff. Education leaders cannot change the relative deprivation of their students; they cannot manipulate the unemployment rate of the areas that their colleges serve; they can however, change the style with which they lead their colleges and they can change the organisational climate that they create.

SOME CONSEQUENCES FOR LEADERSHIP DEVELOPMENT

What does the foregoing imply for the development of leaders in the FE colleges? With the development of new perspectives upon the role of leaders, it is clear that a debate needs to take place regarding the purpose of leadership. Is the leadership of learning, the development of personal mastery and the capacity to promote strategic change more important than the effective functional leadership tasks of monitoring finances and other resources? The proposed establishment of a national college for leadership and management for the learning and skills sector provides an opportunity for the college to become a focal point for leadership and, perhaps, to resolve questions of purpose and strategy for the development of leaders in the future.

The lack of diversity in the current cadre of college leaders needs to be addressed. Specific initiatives to encourage more leaders from Black and other ethnic backgrounds already exist on a small scale, but these need to be extended. In particular, there needs to be a focus on the development of middle managers to ensure that a supply of potential leaders from a broader ethnic background is generated. Widening the pool of candidates available for top posts in colleges also involves consideration of the viability of encouraging more applications from outside the colleges, either from the wider public sector or perhaps from the private. Simply broadening the range of candidates applying for top posts does not guarantee change. It is also important to look at the recruitment practices of governing bodies. It is likely that some governing bodies will recruit principals who reflect their dominant values and characteristics. While this may lead to relatively harmonious relationships between principals and governors, it is unlikely to lead to new perspectives, creative tension, or to challenge sector norms in terms of standards and innovative practice.

Leadership development activity should be subject to scrutiny. Before the structure and content of development programmes themselves are reviewed there is a need for a national strategy. As the DfES (2002, p. 5) comments: 'The college will build on the best of the existing programmes, to create a clear national strategic framework for managers and leaders. There will be a clear routeway for managers to access as their careers develop, including preparation for and induction to leadership.' Leadership development programmes should reflect new thinking on the nature of the leader's role. This includes a focus on the leader's role in promoting achievement, personal development and strategic change. In addition, there is a need for leadership development initiatives at curriculum team level, and for opportunities for cross public sector programmes of development.

Underpinning developments such as these is also a need for more research into leadership in FE. There is currently insufficient evidence as to what is effective in terms of leadership development. There is also insufficient basic information about leaders in FE – the gender and ethnic breakdown, career progression, turnover, wastage rates and lack of systematic career tracking of individuals. Finally, there is an urgent need for a clearer understanding of which leadership behaviours are successful in delivering high-quality FE.

CONCLUSION

This chapter began by highlighting the dearth of research into leadership in the FE colleges. It also pointed out that the majority of leadership practices fit into the managerial or functional approach to leadership. It is not enough for leaders simply to be good managers. If the colleges are to transform themselves to deliver the step changes in standards that government requires, then more radical change is necessary. We need leaders who can balance the tension between promoting access and growth at the same time as a more specialised vocational mission, who are willing to share leadership responsibilities across the college, and who can promote personal development and strategic change. This will necessitate the encouragement of a more diverse pool of leaders, more focused and strategic leadership development, and more research into what works.

REFERENCES

Callan, V.J. (2001) *What Are the Essential Capabilities for Those Who Manage Training Organisations?*, National Centre for Vocational Education Research/Australian National Training Authority. Leabrook, South Australia.

Commission for Black Staff in Further Education (2001) 'Tackling racism together', *Update Report,* May.

Department for Education and Skills (DfES) (2002) *Raising Standards Training and Development for Leaders and Managers*, consultation paper, February.

Drodge, S. and Cooper, N. (1997) 'The management of strategic planning in further education colleges', in K. Levačić and R. Glatter (eds), *Managing Change in Further Education*, FEDA Report, 1(7), 21–52.

Further Education National Training Organisation (FENTO) (2001) *National Occupational Standards for Management in Further Education*, London: FENTO.

Goleman, D. (1998) 'What makes a leader?', *Harvard Business Review*, November–December, 93–102.

Horne, M. and Stedman-Jones, D. (2001) *Leadership: The Challenges for All*, London: Institute of Management.

Hughes, C., Taylor, T. and Tight, M. (1996) 'The ever changing world of further education : a case for research', *Research in Post-Compulsory Education*, 1(1), 7–18.

Kennedy, H. (1997) *Learning Works: Widening Participation in Further Education*, FEFC, Coventry.

Lumby, J. (1998) 'Strategic planning in further education', in D. Middlewood and J. Lumby, *Strategic Management in Schools and Colleges*, London: Paul Chapman Publishing.

Martinez, P. (2000) *Raising Achievement: A Guide to Successful Strategies*, London: FEDA.

Organisation for Economic Co-operation and Development (OECD) (2001) *What Schools for the Future?* OECD.

Office for Standards in Education (OFSTED) (2002) *The Annual Report of Her Majesty's Chief Inspector of Schools*, London: The Stationery Office.

Pritchard, C. (2000) *Making Managers in Universities and Colleges*, Buckingham: SRHE and Open University Press.

Sala, F. (2002), 'Leadership in education: effective UK college principals', unpublished paper from HayGroup.

Sawbridge, S. (2000) 'Leadership for achievement in further education: a review of the literature', unpublished FEDA paper, September.

Sawbridge, S. (2001) 'Leadership in further education: a summary report from a review of the literature', in C. Horsfall (ed.), *Leadership Issues: Raising*

Achievement, London: LSDA.

Smith, C., Gidney, M., Barclay, N. and Rosenfeld, R. (2001) 'Dominant logics of strategy in FE colleges', paper for SCRELM special edition of *Research in Post Compulsory Education*, June.

Stott, C. and Lawson, L. (1997) 'Women at the top in further education', *FEDA Report*, **2**(2).

University of Texas (2001) 'Community College Leadership Program', *Block Guide*, Autumn.

FURTHER READING

Gorringe, and Toogood, P. (1994) 'Changing the culture of a college', *Coombe Lodge Report*, **24**(3), Bristol: The Staff College.

Hallinger, P. and Heck, R.H.C. (1998) 'Exploring the principal's contribution to school effectiveness: 1980–1995', *School Effectiveness and School Improvement*, **9**(2), 157–91.

Hooper, A. and Polter, J. (2000) *Intelligent Leadership – Creating a Passion for Change,* London: Random House.

Horsfall, C. (ed.) (2001) *Leadership Issues: Raising Achievement*, London: LSDA.

James, K. and Burgoyne, J. (2001) *Leadership Development: Best Practice Guide for Organisations*, London: Council for Excellence in Management and Leadership.

Marsh, D.T. (1992) *Leadership and its Functions in Further and Higher Education*, Mendip Paper MP035, Blagdon: The Staff College.

Peeke, G.C. (1994) *Mission and Change*, Buckingham: SRHE and Open University Press.

PIU (2001) *Strengthening Leadership in the Public Sector*, a research study by the Performance and Innovation Unit, Cabinet Office.

Somekh, B., Convery, A., Delaney, J., Fisher, R., Gray, J., Gunn, S., Henworth, A. and Powell, L. (1998) 'Improving college effectiveness: a scoping study', *FEDA Report*, **2**(12).

12

LEADERSHIP IN UK HIGHER EDUCATION

David Watson

INTRODUCTION

The question of whether universities and other institutions of higher education are 'led,' 'managed', 'administered' (or any combination of the three) is one fraught with ideological as well as practical significance. Careers have been built out of inventing and attempting to validate typologies which play across this continuum (McNay, 1995), as well as of exploring the implications for recruitment to and survival within senior positions (Middlehurst, 1993). The tone of much of the resulting literature oscillates wildly, between disappointed nostalgia and brittle triumphalism. The former normally issues into hard criticism of claimed phenomena like 'new managerialism' (Deem, 1998; Trowler, 1998a; 1998b). The latter normally degrades into homiletic 'tips for managers' in the mould of railway bookstand literature. An example is the much touted 'Warwick Way' (Warner and Palfreyman, 2001, pp. 167–204). Instances of attempts to marry 'research-based evidence' and 'practical strategies', such as Paul Ramsden's guide for department heads are rare and unashamedly provisional (Ramsden, 1998, p. 9).

A harsh empirical fact is that university leadership has changed less – in terms of both its operational context (as set for example by governance arrangements) and in performance – than commentators at either end of the spectrum would like to admit. This conclusion is underlined by two studies from the University of Leeds on university governance and university leadership by chief executives (Bargh, Scott and Smith, 1996; Bargh et al., 2000). To take a historical analogy, scholars of early modern Italy like to contrast the experience of Venice, with its centuries of steady, unadventurous bureaucratic rule by the doges, and the much more volatile and varied trajectories of the mainland city states (Pullan, 1974). You sense that the authors of these two books wanted UK higher education to look like Florence; instead, they discovered Venice.

In the first, *Governing Universities*, they try to find a new breed of lay governors challenging the 'donnish dominion' in the interests of institutional differentiation, market sensitivity and entrepreneurship. Instead, they find only a marginal and qualified impact of new types of governor upon what 'remain in many respects traditional and conservative organisations' (Bargh, Scott and Smith, 1996, p. 172).

The analogous hypotheses in their second study, *University Leadership*, centre on 'new forms of executive leadership . . . based on managerial expertise rather than collegial or charismatic authority', as well as 'a power shift in universities, with vice-chancellors becoming the dominant figures in defining their cultures and determining institutional missions and performance' (Bargh et al., 2000, p. 162). Neither proposition is significantly borne out by the evidence they find. Instead, as in the earlier work, the authors have to concede powerful lines of continuity within the internal arrangements of universities, regular deference to 'traditional' values and practices, and only limited organisational responses to considerable pressure from outside.

The evidence in this second volume is of three key types: historical, sociological, and quasi-ethnographic. Of the three types, the historical is by far the most powerful. The book contains subtle and sensitive accounts of the recent development of the UK system of higher education, the institutions which make it up, and of the office of vice-chancellor (or equivalent). Much of this is structured around a paradox: as public interest in higher education has waxed (with an increasing range of stakeholders demanding a broader set of outcomes), so the 'planning' tendency has waned. The result is a sector of quasi-autonomous institutions struggling to meet political, economic and social demands without any secure framework for collective response.

The sociological data centres on the formation, attributes and attitudes of the leadership group themselves, which shows radical lines of continuity over the half century in question. Changed expectations of university heads have not been matched by changed recruitment patterns, and the wall between the former binary sub-sectors remains high. United Kingdom data is then compared with the views of a sample of US presidents and European rectors. From an international perspective, external pressures on universities have converged, but the same is not true of the leadership roles charged with meeting them, which stubbornly maintain their national characteristics.

The ethnographic material attempts to test models of leadership in action by surveying and then shadowing vice-chancellors in action. Interview data from 10 institutions is supplemented by material derived from 'shadowing' three vice-chancellors over two to three weeks. Some of the resulting 'vignettes' are arresting. They certainly demonstrate the capacity of the subjects for profound multivalence: 'I delegate most things – and then interfere'; or 'the average dean doesn't spend enough time running his faculty. He's given too much of an opportunity to help run the university' (Bargh et al., 2000, p. 157). However, there is little warrant for any of the major hypothetical shifts: from transactional to transformative intentions, from collegial and charismatic leadership to managerial and entrepreneurial skill, and so on. More expository weight than is perhaps justified, given this very complex context, is placed on three case studies of work-shadowing. Nonetheless, these do have the virtue of bringing to life the essentially messy business of what the authors call 'a process of accretion and renewal rather than transformation and control' (ibid., p. 161).

The grand picture here is of university institutions renewing themselves in the changed context of a globalised, knowledge economy and of increasing social expectations of the positional good of participating in higher education. The cross-national comparative focus on the careers and expectations of the leadership group is of interest in policy terms. However, individual vice-chancellors can apparently take comfort from the fact that they are not alone in facing hugely conflicting demands and muddling through; just like the doges.

In these circumstances the question of how university leaders are made can be answered empirically quite simply: they reproduce themselves. A more difficult question is how they could (and possibly should) be made, together with its corollary of how they can be assisted to work more effectively once they have arrived.

The vice-chancellors' club (Universities United Kingdom [UUK]) is currently looking hard at this question, not least in response to something of a whispering campaign in government circles that higher education management is seriously off the pace of private sector practice. There has always been an asymmetry between university and business perceptions of how 'business-like' the former could or should be (Watson, 2000, pp. 37–8). The DfES has recently announced an initiative to organise 'business mentors' for university leaders (DfES, 2001), while the sort of thinking that suggests the flow of advice should be unidirectional is aided by such devastating public reports as Michael Shattock's on the expensive failure of Cambridge's new financial system (CAPSA).

> When I read in Dr Gordon Johnson's excellent introduction to Cornford's *Micrcosmographica Academica* that 'We are still, many say, governed "very badly" but that does not seem to affect the University's capacity to achieve academic distinction,' sentiments echoed with various emphases by many of those who came to see me, I am bound to ask whether Harvard or Stanford, two obvious international competitors, would tolerate the implicit suggestion that their governance and management should be permitted to be less effective because their universities are outstandingly successful academically. Even less would they support the notion that ineffectiveness in these areas might be some sort of concomitant of academic success as one or

two of my respondents have implied.

(Shattock, 2001, para. 1.3).

(Interestingly, the author cannot resist drawing in the 'Warwick Way' here as well [ibid., paras 2.22–26].)

Measured by its outcomes, the management and leadership of UK higher education has been outstandingly successful in several areas during two decades of remarkable, often officially inspired turbulence. 'Hits' have included contribution to economic growth, efficiency, student satisfaction and employability, democratisation and diversity, research quality, 'service', and international reputation. Perhaps most remarkably, this has all been achieved by working operating resource margins down to the bone. Meanwhile the 'misses' have often been reciprocals of these successes. Among the most notable have been mission convergence, a failure to tackle the class base of participation, and a reluctance to rationalise provision (at the subject and the institutional level) until *in extremis* (Watson, 2002).

Against this background it is useful to reflect on how top leadership within universities may be different: different from the other educational cases covered in this volume; and different from the commercial and industrial models that are prayed in aid. This is possibly the only way past the railway bookstand offerings of context-independent 'models' of leadership as well as the ideological traps alluded to above. Having considered what is peculiar about the higher education case, it is then possible to differentiate those leadership challenges which are new and those which are simply continuous. Together these forms of analysis then allow an assessment of what policy interventions might make a positive difference to the quality of leadership.

HIGHER EDUCATION EXCEPTIONALISM

There are at least three ways in which higher education institutions can claim to present special issues for their leaders.

The first arises from their own version of organisational 'flatness'. Power relationships within universities are paradoxical. A very high-profile individual leader, surrounded by a small functional team, heads an essentially flat organisation, which tolerates hierarchy for limited practical reasons only, and cannot accept superior authority in the most important parts of its professional life. In academia this has been a design principle since the beginning, as individuals and small teams have taken responsibility for both curriculum and academic standards.

Much ceremonial power is vested in the head of the higher education institution, and many heads have been able to convert such power into broad and deep moral suasion. The best of them have also been able to walk the line between protection of their operation (by garnering resources, deflecting external attack and acting as a lightning rod for unproductive controversy) and involvement (of all staff in understanding and 'owning' not only the institution's mission, but also a mature appreciation of its objective position).

As Burton Clark puts the point, somewhat more brutally, 'Universities are too bottom-heavy, too resistant from the bottom-up, for tycoons to dominate for very long' (Clark, 1998, p. 4). There are analogues within faculties, departments and (to a lesser extent) support departments. But at the end of the day 'flatness' rules: the reputation and standing of the institution rest with the lecturer marking examination papers, the Examination Board deciding degree classes, and the ethical commitments of the researcher.

The second feature of higher education (HE) 'exceptionalism' arises from a further role for their heads (alongside the trinity of 'leadership, management, and administration'): that of 'stewardship'. Universities are, in the words of the dean of Westminster, 'institutions' and not merely 'organisations' (RSA, 1998). This echoes Eric Ashby's (1958, p. 73) theory of 'split personality' within universities: 'Men with tidy minds are bound to ask whether universities could not be run more efficiently if their efforts were co-ordinated and planned from above. The short answer is that a university is a society, not a public service or an industry.' However, universities are now increasingly expected to behave as 'organisations' while simultaneously holding on to both structures and values associated with 'institutions'. The strain is showing.

Thirdly, and in the same vein, universities and colleges have to live with being formally and informally in both the public and private sectors. Although proudly independent from the state and guaranteed 'autonomy' by either their charters or the legislative conditions of their incorporation, they nonetheless rely on the public sector as a hugely dominant purchaser: of student places, of research and consultancy, and of other services.

There are external and internal dimensions to this situation, each shrouded in ambiguity. Externally, many bodies (such as Regional Development Agencies [RDA]) typecast them as belonging to the 'public sector', neatly forgetting the many private companies which also rely for survival on government contracts. Internally there are the conflicting drives for staff to be entrepreneurial and go-getting while always maintaining the best values of public service. Leaders of institutions can play such ambiguity to strategic advantage. They should never forget, however, that they are leading perhaps the classic examples of 'social businesses' (as well as the dean's 'institutions' or the late Lord Ashby's 'societies'). According to Richard Pinto, such 'social businesses' are ' organizations which set out to deliver a service to the community by operating in a business-like fashion' (Pinto, 1996, p. 1).

CONTINUITY AND CHANGE

Much of higher education's exceptionalism is historically based. State-supported mass higher education has, however, brought about some new problems.

The first of these challenges is political. In the UK in the past five years, New Labour has made it clear that it has serious, policy-related ambitions for higher education, as indeed it does for the education service as a whole (Watson and Bowden, 2001). Tony Blair's possibly most famous quotation from his first term was the declaration of the three priorities of 'education, education, education' (Seldon, 2001, p. 405). In introducing his second Parliament he declared unambiguously that 'in the second term, we want to get money into secondary schools and universities' (CIHE, 2001, p. 4).

These ambitions are chiefly of two types: as a significant contributor to the new 'knowledge economy'; and as an engine room of democratisation and social inclusion (Blunkett, 2000). This has created twin poles of expectation. Our universities must be globally competitive, at the forefront of wealth creation in the so-called 'new economy' and, hence, 'excellent'. They must also be accessible and socially progressive and, hence, 'equal'. In this way they are an archetype of current social and economic policy. Great Britain must be modern, lean and efficient, but simultaneously goals like full employment and the ending of child poverty are to be achieved (Toynbee and Walker, 2001, pp. 7–8).

Like most recent governments, New Labour has sought to use funding levers to bring about their goals. A new term in Whitehall is 'something for something'. Thus, new resources for higher education invariably come with strings attached, institutions cannot afford to forgo 'special initiatives', and, as a result, working in higher education is more and more like working in the National Health Service.

There is a principle at work here, which can be validated all over the world. Basically, as governments and the state become more interested in higher education, so they expect more from it. Inside the system, institutional leaders feel ambivalent about these priorities: they welcome the interest (they would welcome the implied investment even more), but they worry about the situation when 'official' priorities might clash with their own.

Inside the academy 'excellence' is most regularly related to research. Some of the most extreme tensions within the system centre on the status, role and funding of research. There is now widespread acknowledgement across the system that carefully focused research is a legitimate part of the mission of all higher education institutions (HEIs); that – to put the point in reverse – there is no such thing as a 'teaching only' university. The implications of this rejection weigh heavily on the internal value-system of a modern university. They up the stakes for collaboration (as not all institutions can maintain the infrastructure they need). They reinforce traditional models of the academic career. In a 'mass' system they also arouse concerns about value for money (there is, for example, growing resentment in the USA about tuition increases funding research).

Meanwhile, it is clear that the core business of the university is now even less of a monopoly than it ever was.

There have been two influential theoretical interventions on this theme. The first is the now canonic analysis by Michael Gibbons and his collaborators. They see an inexorable and irreversible shift from 'mode 1' thinking (pure, disciplinary, homogeneous, expert-led, supply-driven, hierarchical, peer-reviewed and almost exclusively university-based) to 'mode 2' (applied, problem-centred, transdisciplinary, heterogeneous, hybrid, demand-driven, entrepreneurial, network-embedded etc.) (Gibbons et al., 1994).

The second, more contested, thesis is Ron Barnett's account of 'the death of the university' in the face of 'supercomplexity.' The key text, *Realizing the University* starts with a ringing call for a clean break with the past; 'the death is *required*' (emphasis in original), and yet we are constantly reminded that 'the old lives on within the new' (Barnett, 1999, p. 11). How, for example, does the array of new 'values' for the age of supercomplexity really differ from those we have been traditionally committed to (at least in theory)?

> What is required is the capacity to tame supercomplexity, to inject a value structure into it even as all value structures are put into the dock. The university has to hold on to the value system that helped to generate supercomplexity – of openness, courage, tolerance and so on – even as supercomplexity puts these same values under the microscope. Supercomplexity deprives us of a value anchorage for answering such challenges. The value background that spawned supercomplexity, on the other hand, can help us to just that. The values implicit in rational critical dialogue helped to generate supercomplexity and they can help to keep supercomplexity in its place . . . The ladder of the university's value background has to be kept in place, not kicked away.
>
> (ibid., p. 83)

Close your eyes, and we are back in the world of Barnett's earlier influential works, *The Idea of Higher Education* (Barnett, 1990) and *The Limits of Competence* (Barnett, 1994).

At the other end of the scale, 'inclusion' brings equally intensive challenges to leadership. The most recent surge of expansion in higher education has made huge differences in the internal population of universities in terms of gender, age, ethnicity, and even disability, but only the tiniest inroads on working-class participation. Social class is proving difficult for the sector to tackle at a fundamental level. It is well known that the participation rates in higher education by social class go down dramatically from 72 per cent of the children of professional classes to just 13 per cent of children of unskilled workers. The figures show the participation of these groups has grown, but has not significantly improved proportionately within the growth of the sector as a whole. This is a much more profound problem than that of recruiting well-qualified students from poorer areas. Tackling it, together with maintaining (and ideally improving) retention, is now urgent. Certainly, there has been progress in widening participation as a result of special initiatives, partnerships, flexible entry and targeted financial support for students. However the sector is still in a situation where supply has met demand for the middle classes and those well qualified, and where a much smaller impression has been made on social groups IIIm, IV and V (HEFCE, 2001).

In effect UK higher education is at a fork in the road. Either the sector will contribute to further social polarisation, or it will make a major contribution to overcoming it. In other words, higher education is deeply implicated in the solutions to the wider problems of a society increasingly separated by divergences in skills, in access to information and to work itself. A recent discussion paper for the No. 10 Downing Street, Performance and Innovation Unit, has shown the divisive effects of higher education both as a strong safeguard against downward mobility for 'dull middle class children' and as an increasingly critical positional good (the more people have it the less valuable it may be, but simultaneously the penalties for not having it increase) (PIU, 2001, para. 25). Genuinely widening participation might be hard to tackle, but it is a core leadership question for higher education.

So, too, is the vexed question of organisation within and differentiation across the sector.

Much of the dramatic expansion in student numbers between the late 1980s and early 1990s was driven by officially sponsored competition: competition between different parts of the sector, and between individual institutions. As numbers levelled out under the last years of the Conservative government, and as much more targeted expansion has been renewed under New Labour, official rhetoric has shifted from competition to collaboration, and funding councils have been directed to encourage and reward such behaviour.

Cynics will instantly say that the shift to collaboration is defensive, and largely driven by resource constraints. This issue has to be tackled head on, and it has to be admitted that it contains more than a germ of truth. Any objective economic appraisal would probably indicate that the UK has too many, and too many too small, HEIs for all to be able to prosper. The management across the sector of operational surpluses down to wafer-thin levels without widespread institutional failure has been an heroic achievement. Unfortunately, it has also been accompanied by a number of less desirable features, such as risk aversion, mission uncertainty and the underpricing of research. Meanwhile, in its eagerness to achieve policy-related returns for increased investment in higher education, the government may have made collaboration harder rather than easier to achieve.

But it would be wrong to regard either economic necessity or official policy as the exclusive engines of change in this direction. It is also necessary to take account of such influences as the increasing role of partnerships in research and development, the 'joined-up' training agenda required by key clients of higher education such as the National Health Service, and the new national and regional patterns of responsibility for social and economic policy.

In doing so, it is important to remember some key facts about the history of the sector. For example, as Peter Scott pointed out in his study of *The Meanings of Mass Higher Education*, three-quarters of UK universities have been created since 1945 (Scott, 1995, pp. 44–9). Nor should the role of mergers, acquisitions, alliances and status shifts in the development of nearly every institution that is now a member of UUK be forgotten.

Similarly, it would be wrong to assume that mergers and acquisitions are either the inevitable, or indeed the only, outcome of collaboration and co-operation. There is plenty of advanced industrial experience of 'partial' or 'mixed' alliances, whereby corporations agree on the areas in which they will collaborate and those in which they will continue to compete. In this respect they operate like some of the larger US systems (like the University of California) which have different elements – almost equivalent to separate UK-style institutions – operating within them.

This exposition has been predominantly about challenges to the sector and its leadership at the national level. Equally important pressures (some with similar sources) impact at both the international and the local (especially regional) level. On the one hand, there is the need to balance an ethical and an entrepreneurial approach to the global market. There are many opportunities to improve an institution's bottom line through international ventures. There is also the priceless historical reputation of the British system in helping other nations and societies to develop their own higher education. On the other hand, all the dilemmas of 'excellence' versus 'inclusion' play across regional relationships and agendas, together with the tensions of competition, collaboration and complementarity.

At the time of writing, UK higher education is going through one of its most turbulent phases since the mid-1980s, and the conditions which brought about the National Committee of Inquiry into Higher Education (the Dearing Committee). This turbulence has several sources: a perception of rapidly increasing financial strain; a documented breakdown in the market mechanisms of 'supply and demand'; the government pressures to deliver on a universal (and felt to be contradictory) agenda of both 'excellence' and 'inclusion'; panic over the outcome of the 2001 Research Assessment Exercise (RAE); a review (that has become a 'consultation' – always a sure sign that the sponsors do not know what to do) on student support in England, which seems to have motivated a lot of potential applicants to 'wait and see'; a significant downturn in the numbers of full fee-paying international students as a result of reluctance to trust intercontinental air transport after 11 September 2001; and renewed rumblings within the research-rich Russell Group of institutions (apparently with official encouragement) about a break-away from the rest of the sector (if the price is right). In such circumstances the need for principled, brave and effective leadership in UK HE has probably never been higher. How can such leadership be assured?

WHAT IS TO BE DONE?

Interventions in policy and practice need to separate two phases; that of preparing the next generation of university and college leaders, and that of supporting them when they have arrived. This difference between 'getting there' and 'being there' has bedevilled much of the discussion about (and many of the plans for) professional formation of university leaders, not least in the equal opportunities arena.

Activities centred on succession planning, on growing capacity and on improving diversity within the top management group are being undertaken in the UK at both the institutional and the sectoral level. Accredited training has been provided by Higher Education Staff Development Agency (HESDA), the sector's national training organisation in the form of a 'Top Management Programme' (a sector-specific and marginally cheaper form of the Cabinet Office Programme with the same name). Partly under the aegis of a Higher Education Funding Council for England (HEFCE) selective initiative (the 'Good Management Programme') a number of institutions have developed their own versions (HEFCE/HESDA, 2002). These programmes join a longer established set of initiatives directed at overcoming gender discrimination in particular ('Room at the Top' – also from HESDA was specially directed at senior women managers, partly at the instigation of the informal 'Glass Ceiling' group). It remains to be seen whether such efforts successfully diversify the population of university leaders, or whether they frustrate participants led to believe that achievement within them will assure promotion. The 'background' analysis at the beginning of this chapter suggests that there is still a long way to go.

Meanwhile UUK and the Standing Committee of Principals (SCOP) of colleges of higher education are attempting to codify, systematise and increase the amount of peer support that is available to those already in leadership positions (UUK, 2002). Discussions within these groups suggest that what chief executives in particular want is highly focused, quick reaction, support on those difficult issues which have a habit of sweeping across the sector (new legislation on disability or health and safety, for example, along with a dramatic rise in student complaints, or a rash of demonstrations on animal houses). They also welcome networked systems of informal 'coaching' and 'mentoring' by more experienced peers on a confidential basis. What goes down least well is banal and generalised 'good practice' guides, which frequently labour to state the obvious. Vice-chancellors are, however, instant and voracious readers of 'bad practice' stories (such as the CAPSA saga above) on the time-honoured principle of 'there but for the grace of God go I'.

A PERSONAL CODA

This last section is essentially personal reflections, based on personal experience as well as the analysis above. These reflections are offered in the form of 10 'adages'. These are of lesser status than formal (falsifiable) propositions, but ideally more forceful than anecdotal observation. Rather in the spirit of 'grounded theory', I hope they will prove useful in appropriate circumstances.

First, *higher education leadership has to be more than usually respectful of the processes of production*. The 'flatness' of academic authority, as well as the consensual base of academic governance, mandates this. That said, secondly, it *must not simply give way to misplaced nostalgia or 'fifth amendment'-style claims about academic freedom*. It must always be free to challenge, to guide, and to set out alternative directions of strategic development.

Simultaneously (third), it needs to *adopt a fully professional approach to support functions* (finance, personnel, estates, marketing and development, information systems, etc.). If higher education is to punch its weight in the knowledge economy, and to provide modern working conditions for its staff, it cannot afford even benign amateurism in these areas. Teamwork is also of the essence here, across both the academic and support functions.

Fourth, in terms of both personal and professional relationships, there is the necessity of *maintaining dignity and good humour in what is a professionally argumentative community*. The stakes here are heightened by a law of academic life: that academic confidence grows the further the speaker is from his or her true field of expertise. In other words, 'at home' scholars will handle ambiguity, provisionality and incremental insight with deftness and humility. 'At large', and dealing with difficult aspects of their working environment, they will know exactly what needs to be done, and who else should do it. As a consequence, the institutional leader will need to be thick-skinned about some issues (especially the receipt of insults masquerading as forthrightness – although never giving way to the temptation to reply in kind) and thin-skinned (or hypersensitive) about others (especially the early identification of bullying). Relentless courtesy

– even under provocation – is a vital asset (see Watson, 1994).

As a result, the fifth adage is to *be clear about when to be humble and when to be assertive.* It has long been understood that the most effective academic leadership is by stealth. However, Thomas Hughes probably erred too much on the side of humility in his encomium for Dr Arnold at the end of *Tom Brown's Schooldays.*

> And that's the way that all of the Doctor's reforms have been carried out when he has been left to himself – quietly and naturally, putting a good thing in the place of a bad, and letting the bad die out; no wavering and no hurry – the best thing that could be done for the time being, and patience for the rest.
>
> (Hughes, 1856, pp. 302–3)

Eric Ashby got the balance much better in his description of the Principal 'feeding in' ideas and devoting 'a large proportion of his time, and the bulk of his reserves of moral stamina' ensuring their survival and success when adopted by others (Ashby, 1958, p. 72).

A route through this minefield can be found (sixth) by the leader's *taking responsibility – internally as well as externally – for the narrative glue which holds the institution together.* The modern term is 'sense-making' (Taylor, 1999). This is one feature of successful large private companies which is probably transferable. It does not imply a vainglorious cult of personality; it does mean the ability to express what colleagues across the institution, at their best, are striving for.

Effective university and college leaders need to be *self-reflective*, especially about their personal motives and their techniques of self-presentation. The history of the sector is littered with examples of high-profile leaders who have proved either highly functional or seriously dysfunctional. Some, almost tragically, became caricatures of their former, better selves (in other words, the promise showed in 'getting there' seeped away during the course of 'being there'). In this very tricky area, the first adage (about maintaining respect for the intellectual capital of the institution) is probably the best guide.

Meanwhile, perhaps the most valuable task a university leader can perform is to *help colleagues to understand their institution's actual and potential place within the scheme of things.* This is not just about safe-guarding the bottom line. Strategic scoping and decision-making may result in forgoing some apparent immediate institutional advantages or exposing some institutional weaknesses. This will be especially true in the fraught arena of collaboration and alliances. In these circumstances 'leading' the choice of options, and 'managing' the consequences can come together in a very profound way.

Penultimately, and perhaps most obviously, the effective leader has to *be prepared to act, and to act decisively* in certain circumstances. Respect for the operation must not mean reluctance to put right what is wrong and to defend what is right.

Much of this can sound disturbingly like a counsel of perfection. Another strand in the rather thin literature on HE management outlined at the beginning of this chapter is the 'advice book' contributions of superannuated leaders. Many of these could be reduced to 'do what I say rather than what I did' (American former Presidents are especially susceptible to this syndrome, although there are also some classic British instances; see for example, Knight, 1990; Sloman, 1964).

Emotional intelligence in the face of the 'wicked issues' which bedevil university communities is the essential requirement, although it can be hard to apply in specific circumstances (Watson, 2000, pp. 80–7). The final adage is in this spirit. Top academic and institutional leadership is about values, and it is about setting *the balance between continuity and change*: between understanding and safe-guarding those elements which contribute to the real strength of the academic community (including those ripe for refreshment and renewal) and those where innovation, change and reinvention are the conditions of survival and prosperity. Being a doge will not be enough.

NOTE

Earlier versions of some of this material appeared in *Studies in Higher Education*, in lectures given to the Social Market Foundation and the University of Kent at Canterbury, and in workshops for the HESDA Top Management Programme and University of Strathcylde 'Leaders for Tomorrow' Programme in early 2002.

REFERENCES

Ashby, E. (1958) *Technology and the Academics: An Essay on Universities and the Scientific Revolution*, London: Macmillan.

Bargh, C., Bocock, J., Scott, P. and Smith, D. (2000) *University Leadership: The Role of the Chief Executive*, Buckingham: SRHE and Open University Press.

Bargh, C., Scott, P. and Smith, D. (1996) *Governing Universities: Changing the Culture?* Buckingham: SRHE and Open University Press.

Barnett, R. (1990) *The Idea of Higher Education*, Buckingham: SRHE and Open University Press.

Barnett, R. (1994) *The Limits of Competence: Knowledge, Higher Education and Society*, Buckingham: SRHE and Open University Press.

Barnett, R. (1999) *Realizing the University in an Age of Supercomplexity*, Buckingham: SRHE and Open University Press.

Blunkett, D. (2000) *Modernising Higher Education: Facing the Global Challenge*, speech at the University of Greenwich, 15 February, London: DfEE.

Clark, B.B. (1998) *Creating Entrepreneurial Universities: Organizational Pathways of Transformation*, Oxford: Pergamon.

Council for Industry and Higher Education (CIHE) (2001) *The Funding of UK Higher Education*, London: CIHE.

Deem, R. (1998) 'New managerialism in higher education: the management of performances and cultures in universities', *International Studies in the Sociology of Education*, **8**(1), 47–70.

Department for Education and Skills (DfES) (2001) 'Business mentors for vice-chancellors', press release, 16 December.

Gibbons, M., Limoges, C., Nowotny, H., Schwarzman, S., Scott, P. and Trow, M. (1994) *The New Production of Knowledge: The Dynamics of Science and Research in Contemporary Societies*, London: Sage Publications.

Higher Education Funding Council for England (HEFCE) (2001) *Supply and Demand in Higher Education*, Consultation October 01/62, Bristol: HEFCE.

Higher Education Funding Council for England (HEFCE) and Higher Education Staff Development Agency (HESDA) (2002) *Senior Management Development: Eight Case Studies*, Sheffield: HESDA.

Hughes, T. (1856) *Tom Brown's Schooldays*, London: Hazel, Watson & Viney.

Knight, D.M. (1990) *Street of Dreams: The Nature and Legacy of the 1960s*, Durham and London: Duke University Press.

McNay, I. (1995) 'From the collegial academy to the corporate enterprise: the changing cultures of universities', in T. Schuller (ed.), *The Changing University?* Buckingham: SRHE and Open University Press.

Middlehurst, R. (1993) *Leading Academics*, Buckingham: SRHE and Open University Press.

Performance and Innovation Unit (PIU) (2001) *Social Mobility: A Discussion Paper*, London: PIU.

Pinto, R. (1996) *Social Business*, London: Newchurch.

Pullan, B. (1974) *The Significance of Venice*, Manchester: Manchester University Press.

Ramsden, P. (1998) *Learning to Lead in Higher Education*, London and New York: Routledge.

Royal Society for the Encouragement of Arts, Manufacture and Commerce (RSA) (1998) *Is There a Crisis in Leadership? RSA Journal*, **548b**(3), pp. 74–80.

Scott, P. (1995) *The Meanings of Mass Higher Education*, Buckingham: SRHE and Open University Press.

Seldon, A. (ed.) (2001) *The Blair Effect: the Blair Government, 1997–2001*, London: Little Brown.

Shattock, M. (2001) *University of Cambridge: Review of University Management and Governance Issues Arising out of the CAPSA Project*, http://www.admin.cam.uk/reporter/2001-02/weekly/5861/5.html

Sloman, A.E. (1964) *A University in the Making*, London: BBC.

Taylor, P.P. (1999) *Making Sense of Academic Life: Academics, Universities and Change*, Buckingham: SRHE and Open University Press.

Toynbee, P. and Walker, D. (2001) *Did Things Get Better? An Audit of Labour's Successes and Failures*, London: Penguin Books.

Trowler, P.R. (1998a) *Academics Responding to Change: New Higher Education Frameworks and Academic Cultures*, Buckingham: SRHE and Open University Press.

Trowler, P.R. (1998b) *Education Policy: A Policy Sociology Approach*, Eastbourne: Gildredge Press.

Universities UK (UUK) (2002) 'Developing a strategic framework for leadership and management development in higher education', unpublished discussion paper, 28 January.

Warner, D. and Palfreyman, D. (eds) (2001) *The State of UK Higher Education: Managing Change and Diversity*, Buckingham: SRHE and Open University Press.

Watson, D. (1994) 'Living with ambiguity: some dilemmas of academic leadership', in J. Bocock and D. Watson (eds), *Managing the University Curriculum: Making Common Cause*, Buckingham: SRHE and Open University Press.

Watson, D. (2000) *Managing Strategy*, Buckingham: Open University Press.

Watson, D. (2002) 'Can we all do it all? Tensions in the mission and structure of UK higher education', *Higher Education Quarterly*, **56**(2), 143–55, April.

Watson, D. and Bowden, R. (2001) *Can We Be Equal and Excellent Too? The New Labour Stewardship of UK Higher Education, 1997–2001*, University of Brighton Education Research Centre: Occasional Paper.

FURTHER READING

Boccock, J. and Watson, D. (1994) *Managing the University Curriculum*, Buckingham: Society for Research into Higher Education and Open University Press.

Bolton, A. (2000) *Managing the Academic Unit*, Buckingham: Society for Research into Higher Education and Open University Press.

Bourner, T., Katz, T. and Watson, D. (2000) *New Directions in Professional Higher Education*, Buckingham: Society for Research into Higher Education and Open University Press.

Deem, R. (2000) ' "New Managerialism" and the Management of UK universities', end of award report of the findings of an economic and social research council funded project October 1998–November 2000, Lancaster University.

Farnham, D. (1999) *Managing Academic Staff in Changing University Systems*, Buckingham: Society for Research into Higher Education and Open University Press.

Middlehurst, R. (1993) *Leading Academics*, Buckingham: Society for Research into Higher Education and Open University Press.

Prichard, C. (2000) *Making Managers in Universities and Colleges*, Buckingham: Society for Research into Higher Education and Open University Press.

Schuller, T. (Ed.), *The Changing University?* Buckingham: Society for Research into Higher Education and Open University Press.

Warner, D. and Crosthwaite, E. (eds) (1995) *Human Resource Management in Higher and Further Education*, Buckingham: Society for Research into Higher Education and Open University Press.

Warner, D. and Palfreyman, D. (eds) (2001) *Higher Education Management*, Buckingham: Society for Research into Higher Education and Open University Press.

Watson, D. (2000) *Managing Strategy*, Buckingham: Open University Press.

INDEX